The Maze of History

Komal Hok, O'odham Teachings,
and an Earth-Based Sense of Time

THE MAZE
OF HISTORY

DAVID MARTÍNEZ

University of New Mexico Press
Albuquerque

Printed in the United States of America

ISBN 978-0-8263-6912-3 (cloth)
ISBN 978-0-8263-6913-0 (paper)
ISBN 978-0-8263-6914-7 (ePub)

Library of Congress Cataloging-in-Publication data is on file with the Library of Congress.

Founded in 1889, the University of New Mexico sits on the traditional homelands of the Pueblo of Sandia. The original peoples of New Mexico—Pueblo, Navajo, and Apache—since time immemorial have deep connections to the land and have made significant contributions to the broader community statewide. We honor the land itself and those who remain stewards of this land throughout the generations and also acknowledge our committed relationship to Indigenous peoples. We gratefully recognize our history.

Cover illustration by Thomas Breeze Marcus

Designed by Isaac Morris

Composed in Adobe Caslon Pro, Barge, Iowan Old Style, and TT Autonomous Mono

Dedicated to Sharon Suzuki-Martinez.

More than a brilliant poet, Sharon has been my muse since the day
we met at a Joy Harjo poetry reading in Tucson, Arizona, when
we were both still struggling grad students.

What a wonderful journey it's been!

Contents

Introduction

Finding My Way to the Top of a Crooked Path

I must begin by asking the reader's indulgence with a confession. I did not grow up on the reservation, nor did my mother teach me our language. On the contrary, my mother raised me in Pomona, California, as a descendent of the Relocation Generation that was a part of the Termination Era of federal Indian policy during the 1950s and 1960s. After graduating from Haskell Indian School, my mother, Marilyn Martinez (née Lewis) migrated to Los Angeles, where she lived in the Bunker Hill neighborhood. Before she met my dad, Martin Martinez, and had me in the summer of 1963, she lived a single life that in her words meant that she "had it made." In addition to a small apartment, she worked for Max Factor. Among her friends was an Apache woman, Yvonne Williams, who spotted a call for auditions for a movie about Indians living in Los Angeles. Because my mom went with her friend, who did not want to go to the audition alone, she got a small role in Kent Mackenzie's *The Exiles* (1961).

I did not learn of my mother's silver screen experience until 2010, near the end of her life. My mom stayed with my wife, Sharon, and I at our apartment in Tempe, Arizona, and she mentioned Mackenzie's movie in passing, which prompted Sharon to search for the film. I was at Arizona State University teaching my classes for the American Indian Studies program when this occurred. After learning about her appearance in the film from Sharon, I purchased copies and watched the film, which had fortunately been restored and rereleased in 2008, with my mother. Her scenes are brief, but after she passed away they became a shrine to her memory. Moreover, her role in a historically important film in American Indian cinema symbolizes the Indigenous exiled life. My mom was an O'dham* raised on the reservation who went to the Presbyterian churches in Gila Crossing, Sacaton,

---

* O'dham is singular, O'odham is plural.

and Casa Blanca, was educated in boarding schools in Tucson, Arizona, and Lawrence, Kansas, and moved to Los Angeles under the provisions of the Indian Relocation Act (1956), yet she remained connected to her himdag. She remembered our language fluently and recalled much of what her elders told her about "being Pima."

Throughout my childhood, Gila Crossing Village in the Gila River Indian Community, was virtually my backyard. My mom and I returned "home" countless times, sometimes with my dad. Gila Crossing, moreover, was where my grandfather, Simon Lewis, served as minister of the Gila Crossing First Presbyterian Church; it was also where he lived with my grandmother Margaret (née Childs) in a tiny two-bedroom house. An equally important destination was Ajo, where my mother's only sister Sianna lived with her husband Leonard Charley, who worked at the Phelps Dodge mine. Ajo was where my great-grandmother, Martha Garcia, a Hia-Ced O'dham, grew up and married a white man, Tom Childs Jr., one of the founders of the copper mine where my uncle worked. Pomona, Gila Crossing, and Ajo marked the boundaries of my world as an O'dham. As for the boundaries that my dad brought into my life, they were largely limited to a handful of places in Los Angeles, San Bernadino, and Riverside counties, which is where his four siblings lived. His mother, Sixta Martínez (née Fierro Flores), lived in Corona, where my parents and I lived until I started elementary school. We lived in the shanty next door to my grandmother's house. There was a chicken coop in the back full of chickens. On the other side of my grandmother's house, next to the railroad tracks, lived an elderly man, Cornelius, who I called "Mr. Clean" because of his bald head. I thought he was my "next door grandfather" when I was little, but mom told me that he and my dad's mom were "only friends." My paternal grandfather, José Martínez, died a few years before I was born. Corona was naturally another important place in my personal geography, along with Chino, which was where my dad's older brother, Tommy, lived. My dad was a Korean War veteran, Army Ranger, ex-con (he did nine months in Leavenworth), and a lifelong factory worker. He tried and failed to start his own business selling used furniture in Pomona only to wind up spending the latter part of his life until he passed away in 1998 selling used items at the Phoenix Swap Meet. West Phoenix is where my parents moved in 1989. It was an easy drive down to Maricopa Village, where my Uncle Bevan, one of my mom's brothers, and his family often went to church. A few miles to the south was Gila Crossing. My mom worked at Wild Horse Pass Casino.

In case I am beginning to test my reader's patience, I should explain that the reason that I am providing an overview of my background is because kinship is essential to understanding my identity, particularly as an Indigenous person. This identity informs the chapters on O'odham philosophy that follow below. Kinship shapes a person's understanding of who they are, not only ethnically, but also their responsibilities within their family and community. Knowing one's relatives provides one's sense of self a source of grounding and stability. This is true even when someone grows up amidst an otherwise unstable family of origin. Thus, I know that I am an O'dham and Mexican person because of how my parents raised me, keeping me connected with my extended family and the places they lived.

One's relation to the land, another kinship tie, is equally important to establishing identity. Because of my O'odham family, places like Gila Crossing, which is Akimel O'odham, and Ajo, which is Hia-Ced O'odham, initiated my awareness of our jeved, our ancestral homelands. Because of my Mexican family, I knew that my dad grew up in Big Spring, Texas—which I have seen only twice—before they moved (the better word is migrated) to Downey, California, when my dad was still in elementary school. This was during the Great Depression. I remember seeing my dad's hometown only once. Otherwise, the center of my dad's world was Pomona, where we moved in 1971 when I was in third grade. Accordingly, my identity is a weave of O'odham oral tradition, reservation life, the barrio, Mexican American history, and 1970s and '80s California living, which was anything but glamorous. We were poor and socially marginalized.

In addition to Sianna, my mom had three brothers: Avery, Bevan (mentioned earlier), and Steve. All but Steve, the youngest, was raised in the Akimel O'odham neok, our language. However, none of their children, meaning my cousins and me, were taught the language. When I asked my mom why she did not teach me to speak O'odham, she said matter-of-factly, "Who were you going to speak to?" Supposedly my mom and her parents did not count as people I could have spoken with in our language. I was also not raised with Spanish, which was my father's first language. When I asked my dad why he did not teach me Spanish, he said sarcastically, "I would have felt stupid being the only one talking Spanish to you around the house!" My dad hid a lot behind his temper. Nonetheless, I was accepted and loved by both sides of my family. As I grew older, I learned that language deficiency, especially in the O'odham community, was commonplace. Yet to call what I experienced "normal" would misrepresent the hardships and injustices that my family, our communities, and our ancestors endured that made language loss the so-called norm.

In one respect, the book in hand honors my ancestors, or shohshon, by consciously resisting the fate, namely assimilation, that was assigned to them by our colonizers, the Americans, or mimilghan. As someone who identifies instinctively as an O'dham, my point of view as a teacher and scholar has always been in these terms. At the same time, I am always aware that the Americans in 1846 invaded and aggressively seized control of my Mexican ancestors' lands. This calamity not only led to the 1848 Treaty of Guadalupe Hidalgo, in which the Mexican Republic ceded half of its territory to the United States, but also to the 1854 Gadsden Purchase, which added lands below the Gila River to New Mexico Territory, which became Arizona Territory in 1863. Consequently, the O'odham jeved were divided by an international boundary that hehemajkam* (common people) on both sides did not ask for or want. What took many years to understand was that the two sides of my family, the two sides of my being, experienced colonization differently. Moreover, growing up I knew little of O'odham history due to jujkam, the Spanish-speaking Europeans, criollos, mestizos, and indios who migrated into the O'odham jeved. A part of my life's journey has been learning this history.

With respect to language deficiencies, it was commonplace, albeit unfortunate, that my generation of Akimel O'odham did not learn our language, although we were never shamed for it. On the other hand, for many years, into adulthood, I regularly encountered shaming, bullying, and sometimes pity for not speaking Spanish fluently. I took Spanish in college, learned to read it quite well, but remained reticent about engaging others in conversation. I am still this way, even as a senior scholar and teacher, complete

---

*   hehemajkam is plural, hemajkam is singular.

with twenty-five years as a professor. Such are the social and political forces that continue to influence how my identity is formed. Having said all of that, the book in hand is not about contemplating my belly button. While I have never failed to acknowledge my dual ethnicity, as noted earlier, I have naturally gravitated toward my O'odham heritage when it came to defining myself as a college-educated writer and thinker. As such, I have been less driven by ideology, theory, or social movements as an academic—though I am cognizant of these factors—and more influenced by the kinship ties I have maintained to my O'odham and Mexican families and communities.

A word now about methodology. When most people think about American Indian studies—alternately referred to as Native American and Indigenous studies—they tend to think of the social sciences, especially anthropology, as defining the American Indian studies discourse. This is despite the fact that from its inception in 1969 as a discrete academic field, American Indian studies has been interdisciplinary. Since 1969 American Indian studies programs have provided an American Indian–centered curriculum that is sorely lacking from American colleges and universities in all other fields of study. Hence one still sees classes on American Indian histories, literature, languages, and communities. All other fields have diversified over the past fifty-six years, but there is still a need for American Indian studies. An important development that emerged from the American Indian studies curriculum was the focus on federal Indian law and policy and the injustices inflicted on American Indians under the auspices of the Indian Bureau. This development likely led to a more social science focus in American Indian studies, be it reforming federal Indian law, tribal economic reform, initiatives in Indian education (such as tribally controlled colleges), language revitalization programs, and health and human services (especially aimed at addressing historical trauma). What does not come up typically is philosophy, which is my doctoral field. Suffice it to say, even taking into consideration that I also have a degree in American Indian studies, my work was cut out for me. There were any number of ways to make philosophy, as a discipline firmly lodged in the Western intellectual tradition, relevant to the American Indian experience. So what did I do? In order to answer this, I must beg for my reader's further patience as I recount another (brief) anecdote.

When I was struggling to figure out my research agenda as a youngish assistant professor in American Indian studies during the early 2000s, I remember thinking a lot about Vine Deloria Jr.'s scathing criticisms of anthropology in *Custer Died for Your Sins* (1969) in addition to Charles Eastman's disparaging reference to Bureau of American Ethnology reports as a "pile of bones."[1] Consequently, as someone trained in a philosophy doctoral program, which analyzes texts and ideas, I interpreted this as meaning I should conscientiously refrain from extracting anything from Indigenous people without good reason, and definitely not without their consent. What I wound up doing, which I continue doing today—and which is on abundant display in the chapters below—is delving into published books, articles, reports, and archives for the purpose of liberating Indigenous voices from their westernized confines. I never read ethnographic papers for what anthropologists thought, except as points of contention, but for what Indigenous elders and knowledge keepers had to teach. In my first peer-reviewed paper, titled "The Soul of the Indian: Lakota Philosophy and the Vision Quest," I stated the purpose of my critical discourse on the Nicholas Black Elk narratives:

> I want to emphasize at the outset that, as the subtitle indicates, this is a work of philosophy. As such, my treatment of the vision quest, or hanbleceya, will differ substantially from the disciplines that typically define American Indian studies, such as anthropology, history, political science, and literary criticism. I especially want to stress that this is not an exercise in ethnography. Instead of accumulating data from physical observations or extrapolating conclusions from field interviews, I have analyzed the vision quest for its philosophical content, based on material already published, in which I highlight resources "written by" Lakotas, including works actually composed by Lakota writers and works in which a Lakota played a major collaborative role.[2]

This is a method that I applied to subsequent papers, including papers on O'odham culture and history that are now a part of the present volume.

Thus, the book that the reader now holds in her/his/their hands is a synthesis of papers I have written throughout my twenty-five years in

American Indian studies. Recently I began a meaningful joint appointment with the School of Transborder Studies, which was motivated by the work I am doing on behalf of the Hia-Ced O'odham. As I edited and revised my previous work into the current discourse, I had the important realization that my book was possible only because of the teachings of Komal Hok, also called Thin Leather, a mahkai (medicine maker) and ne'etham (traditional singer). As an elder and sage, Komal Hok collaborated with archaeologist Jesse Walter Fewkes, anthropologist Frank Russell, and amateur folklorist J. William Lloyd, in which he availed his knowledge of the Akimel O'odham origin narrative and other teachings. In *Aw-aw-tam Indian Nights* (1911), Thin Leather was given authorial credit in an otherwise collaborative project. In the other two, "Casa Grande, Arizona" (1906–1907) and *The Pima Indians* (1908), he was accorded recognition as a much-valued informant. While by no means the only historic O'dham who possessed an expansive knowledge of the Akimel O'odham himdag, which is our way of doing things, Komal Hok and his contributions to significant works in O'odham studies gave his name a stature that went unmatched until George Webb and Anna Moore Shaw distinguished themselves, respectively, with *A Pima Remembers* (1959) and *A Pima Past* (1974).

As for my humble contributions to O'odham studies, my inaugural effort consisted of writing a 2003 paper, "When the Gila River Ran Dry: Jesus, Elder Brother, and the Fate of the Pima Indians," about the Reverend Charles H. Cook, who was assigned to the Gila River reservation as missionary under the auspices of the Board of Indian Commissioners, which assisted the Office of Indian Affairs in "civilizing" its "wards" in the reservation system. My purpose was to understand how Presbyterianism became the dominant religion, in which churches (cheopi) supplanted rain houses (va'akikaj). Given the timeframe of Cook's mission, 1870–1917, the emergence of the Presbyterian Church (Mihsh kih), specifically at Sacaton and Gila Crossing, occurred concurrently with the Akimel O'odham water crisis. The Piipaash, or Maricopa, who shared the reservation with us, were also impacted by developments in the Gila and Salt River valleys. This environmental and humanitarian calamity was instigated by settler appropriation of river water at Adamsville and Florence, leaving the reservation with an exhausted supply.[3] The effect of Cook's missionization, as a federally mandated intervention into O'odham society, is symbolic of the cultural shifts that developed during this era, when the O'odham himdag grew to embrace the churches that community members built with their own hands. Thin Leather was among these early converts. As of this writing, the paper on "Pima Christianity," as I called it, remained unpublished until its inclusion here. Indirectly it formed the basis of my thinking about O'odham history, as illustrated by the personal references that begin this introduction.

Because my work in O'odham studies had to wait for other projects to germinate, most importantly my first two books, it would not be until 2010 when my first major work on O'odham history appeared. "Pulling Down the Clouds: The O'odham Intellectual Tradition During the 'Time of Famine,'" which the *American Indian Quarterly* published, was set within the first two decades of the twentieth century, when O'odham had been suffering famine (bihugig) for more than a generation. Komal Hok's knowledge, as it was related in works by Russell, Fewkes, and Lloyd, was not a mere tool for non-Indigenous researchers to validate their theories, but the product of a uniquely O'dham intellect and imagination. As portrayed in my paper, Thin Leather, Komal Hok, asserted his authority as knowledge bearer. Which is not to say that one sees Thin Leather speak truth to power, but rather that his status as revered elder shines through the discourses on salvage anthropology and archaeology. Consequently Thin Leather reaches across the generations, from a time when Indigenous people were presumed to be vanishing, to readers like me, who are a part of a generation defined by the Red Power movement, Indian nationalism, and decolonization.

In 2018, J. Brett Hill invited me to write an afterword for *From Huhugam to Hohokam: Heritage and Archaeology in the American Southwest.* "Whither the Huhugam? Decolonizing the Discourse on O'odham Cultural History" is a reflection, in contradistinction to the archaeological record, on the Akimel O'odham account of the rise and collapse of the ge'egdaj kikih,[*] the big houses, such as Casa Grande, which were constructed by the "Hohokam." For American archaeologists, "Hohokam" developed into a distinct historical stage in human habitation of the Gila and Salt River valleys, which terminated with the collapse of "Classical Hohokam" civilization at the end

---

[*]   ge'egdaj kikih is plural, ge'e kih is singular.

of the fifteenth century. For the O'odham, huhugam** who constructed the big houses and canal system are ancestral O'odham, whose descendants adapted their riverine culture, their himdag, to a life without big houses. They originated instead the olas kih, a small domed house. Nonetheless, they still managed their canals and fields. Toward that end, Komal Hok's account of the army (son:tal) of I'itoi, or Elder brother, is less of a historic event and more of an allegory of the environmental upheaval that razed the big houses, which compelled O'odham to rethink their relationship to their jeved. After the big houses fell, O'odham eventually reclaimed their ancestral homelands, their jeved, from the Gila and Salt Rivers to the Gulf of California, and eastward to the Santa Cruz and San Pedro Rivers, then southward into Pima Bajo jeved. Everywhere hahashañ (saguaros) grew was O'odham jeved, even far into what is today Sonora, Mexico. As Komal Hok recounts in Russell's *The Pima Indians*:

> While [I'itoi's] war raged along the Gila some of the inhabitants of the Salt River pueblos sought safety in flight toward the Colorado. They descended that stream to the Gulf of California, the east coast of which they followed for some distance, then turned eastward and finally northeastward, where they settled, and their descendants are the Rio Grande pueblo tribes of to-day.[4]

When Italian Jesuit priest Father Eusebio Kino appeared near the end of the seventeenth century, an untold amount of time had passed since the era of the big houses. What Kino encountered were O'odham villages where olas kikih (round houses) predominated, and only ruins remained of the huhugam. In my afterword, O'odham himdag signifies our teachings about respecting what I'itoi (Elder brother, also called Siuuhu) taught the hehemajkam about how to live in the jeved that Jeved mahkai (Earth medicine maker) created from the muhadag (the mud) from their chest, and which I'itoi helped to recreate after a great flood (wi'inthag). Himdag, more specifically, is a network of respect relations based on kinship ties, which were shaped into the jeved by I'itoi, compelling hehemajkam to endure hardships that

---

**   huhugam is plural, huhug is singular.

generated the knowledge they needed to sustain themselves. Consequently every aspect of the jeved is part of the O'odham narrative of how they came to be here. For example, a mountain, be it Muhadag do'ag (Greasy mountain), Waw giwulk (Narrow cliff), or Chuk do'ag (Black mountain), is not just a mountain but a living being with a story that explains its relationship with the people. I'itoi ki, Elder brother's maze-like home, exists in each of these places. O'odham teachings, thus, are more than natural history recounting the creation of ecological phenomena. They also explain the interrelatedness of the O'odham jeved and all that dwells within these homelands in a balanced relationship between humans, nonhumans, and spirits. Indeed, the O'odham concept of illness is informed by this intrinsic connection between people and place, such that the concept of illness (mumkithag) is divided between those that are endemic to the O'odham jeved and those that are not.

"Earth Medicine Man Makes This Place: A Prolegomenon to an Akimel O'odham Environmental Ethics," which appeared in a 2019 issue of *Natural Communions Journal*, regards the O'odham origin narrative as a form of philosophical thinking, which expresses ideas about the land (jeved) as an integral part of the kinship (wehm kihgag) that binds O'odham to their respective villages as well as the landmarks that define the places in which these villages (kikiham) exist as O'odham homes (kihthag). In order to explain these concepts, an important part of this discourse examines the ways in which O'odham philosophy as story (ha'ichu ahgithadag) is a categorically different type of discourse than what typically defines the western philosophical tradition.[5] Unlike the western philosophical tradition, in which Socrates, Kant, Nietzsche, and Sartre sought to liberate morality from the social and religious conventions of their times and societies, my discourse on O'odham environmental ethics is about the relevance of the O'odham himdag to the contemporary lives of the O'odham hehemajkam, whose jeved is colonized by forces beyond their control.

Complementing "Earth Medicine Man Makes This Place," "Elder Brother Dwells Here: How the Man-in-the-Maze, I'itoi Ki, Became a Symbol of the O'odham Himdag," which I wrote for the 2020 Southwest Symposium Archaeological Conference, focuses on I'itoi ki as an example of O'odham symbolic thinking. While certainly not the only symbol or pattern that O'odham basket weavers put into their designs, the man in the maze nevertheless emerged as a universal symbol of the O'odham way of being. O'odham basket weaving, moreover, is integral to the emergence of this symbol due to being the medium through which the symbol spread across O'odham communities. At the same time, while the symbol encapsulates the oral tradition about I'itoi ki, the man-in-the-maze design as a discrete basket pattern did not appear until the early twentieth century. Significantly, the only published example of the story about I'itoi ki is in Anna Moore Shaw's *Pima Indian Legends* (1969), titled "The Maze, or Se-eh-ha's House." As an Akimel O'dham, Moore locates I'itoi ki solely within South Mountain, near Phoenix, Arizona. According to O'odham oral tradition, as recounted by Komal Hok, I'itoi ki is also in Baboquivari and Sierra Pinacate. All three mountain peaks (dodoag) are the presumed source of the legend that Shaw tells, while the man-in-the-maze symbol is an innovation of the O'odham imagination. Given that I'itoi ki appeared at a time when O'odham across southern Arizona—and into Sonora, Mexico—were living under duress, when they had little sovereignty over their lives, the I'itoi ki symbol is also a symbol of O'odham resiliency. It evokes the story of I'itoi, in which the sisivani* that ruled over the big houses, tried to kill I'itoi—something that Thin Leather recounts at great length—only to return to cleanse the land and restore the himdag.

During the summer of 2021, I wrote an invited paper for the Desert Humanities Initiative, which is a part of Arizona State University's Institute for Humanities Research, that appeared a year later in a one-time journal dedicated to the saguaro cactus. Contributors portrayed this Sonoran Desert denizen as an environmental, historical, literary, and cultural symbol of the land in which we live. My essay was about the significance of the haashañ** to the O'odham. Similar to my earlier works on O'odham culture and history, my discourse was based on O'odham oral tradition, which recounted stories in which O'odham metamorphosed into hahashañ that explained why they are regarded as ancestors (shohshon) who mark the natural boundaries of the O'odham jeved (homelands). The haashañ is also a gift whose power is contained in its fruit (bahithaj), which is transformed into a ceremonial

---

*   sisivani is plural, sivani is singular.
**   haashañ is singular, hahashañ is plural.

wine (nawait) that beckons the rain (juhk). The haashañ in a sense embodies the O'odham sense of time and space. It is as much a symbol of our himdag as I'itoi ki.

Finally, in 2023, I wrote another invited paper for a recently published anthology of papers on trends in environmental philosophy titled *Environmental Reflections on the Anthropocene: Nature Transformed*, edited by Gabriel Ricci. My contribution, "When Coyote Stole Rabbit's Heart: O'odham Himdag, Environmental Sovereignty, and the End of the American Empire" is prompted by the question, What becomes of an ethical theory when that theory is not based on the western philosophical or religious tradition? From an indigenous perspective, namely O'odham, I argue for an ethic based on oral tradition, which resists being abstracted into theory—and therefore universalizable—but instead must remain in narrative form as told and retold by O'odham ne'etham, such as Komal Hok. By virtue of Indigenous radical doubt, if you will, western ethical theories are cast asunder as products of the colonizing empires that have oppressed Indigenous ways of knowing. Instead, the O'odham himdag reclaims its relationship to the O'odham jeved against the American annexation of this land through conquest. Ultimately, rehabilitation of O'odham land depends on a resurgence of O'odham language, culture, and sovereignty. This is a relationship, our himdag, that goes back to the time when Bán (Coyote) stole Rabbit's (Tohbi) heart (ihbthag).

Before explaining how the present volume is organized, I would be remiss if I did not say something about the one work not included here, but which is nonetheless guiding the work in hand. In 1993 I completed a master's degree in American Indian Studies at the University of Arizona. My thesis, titled *The Epiphany of the Earth: An O'odham Environmental Ethic*, elevated the concept of himdag into a philosophical idea. In other words, rather than being limited to a shared value that ethnographers can observe in O'odham social and ceremonial behavior, himdag expresses an understanding of the lived world, the O'odham jeved, as a living being, which requires a respectful response from people (hehemajkam) who live *here*. For lack of a better term, himdag evokes the O'odham world view. Though, this world view is uniquely O'odham, as opposed to being a universal concept. As explained in my thesis, the root of himdag is "him," which means "to walk." Affixing -*dag* (or -*thag*), signifies rootedness, as in being indigenous to here, this jeved. Himdag, then, as a word for O'odham culture, means a way of being that is endemic to *here*. Why *here* is the O'odham jeved is explained through O'odham teachings, namely the origin narrative, in which Jeved mahkai (Earth medicine maker) shaped the earth from the madag (grease or fat) from their body. From this earth, the first people were made. I'itoi, Elder brother, who lived among hehemajkam, would teach them their himdag. Consequently, the O'odham himdag is the accumulative knowledge of the jeved (the lands) based on innumerable generations living with what Earth medicine maker gave them as their *home*. Of course, this meant making mistakes and enduring upheavals, learning difficult lessons, which includes "big houses" like Casa Grande, in which the land needed to be cleansed of corruption. In the end, the big houses gave way to the olas kikih, the small domed houses that defined O'odham habitation when the colonizers arrived.

As for my argument, I contrasted himdag with Immanuel Kant's "categorical imperative," or "moral law," as developed in *The Critique of Practical Reason* (1788). I did so in response to the historic disregard for the Indigenous intellect among European thinkers, be they philosophers, spiritual leaders, or statesmen. Typically the Indigenous mind was relegated to being either "depraved" because they lacked any knowledge of the Christian god, or else "primitive" due to underdevelopment in evolutionary biological terms. Consequently it was commonplace among European scholars—not to mention their American counterparts—to assume that Indigenous people were incapable of rational thought, let alone higher-order thinking like science and philosophy. Without feeling obliged to explain myself as an Indigenous scholar and intellectual, I wrote my thesis making the contrary assumption. Hence I engage in an O'odham critique of Kant's *Critique* without hesitation.

Essential to Kant's analysis of moral reasoning is the preposition that what connects Man to God as his creation is the mind. Man is notoriously flawed and in need of moral guidance. Indeed, he is fallen. But he is also capable of redemption. However, in order to be truly moral, one has to comprehend why being moral is an intrinsic good. Man is made in the image of God, which implies that there is *something* that can transcend Man's baser instincts and connect him to the supreme good. This something is Man's inherent capacity for reasoning and understanding. Thus, when making moral choices, one's ability to choose an action—even when alternatives are possible—on the basis of its *suitability as a universal law* is feasible insofar as universalization exists as a precept in the human mind. If Kant's thesis is correct or valid then, for example, *doing unto others as one would have them do unto one* is sensible, or practical. With this Kantian analysis in mind, I demonstrated two facets of O'odham moral reasoning: first, that O'odham exhibited moral awareness through their kinship relations, their himdag; second, that the grounding of the moral law is not the Christian god but the earth, the jeved. While I have not revised and included my thesis as a separate chapter in this volume, I have integrated it into the book as a whole.

Naturally, in order for my papers and master's thesis to become a monograph, as opposed to an edited anthology, I needed to organize and revise these disparate publications into a coherent discourse. What I have created through this process is a book on O'odham philosophy of history, which of course is an earth-based philosophy. Nevertheless, this is not a linear and time-centered discourse that postulates a destiny or purpose, be it the apocalyptic history of Augustine or the dialectical systems of Hegel and Marx. As an Indigenous mode of philosophizing, the O'odham concept of history is grounded in the jeved, meaning that O'odham origin narratives, which are the basis of O'odham oral histories (which are themselves village-based), which in turn form the foundation on which an O'odham concept of history is developed, not into theory, but what I call a philosophical narrative.

As such, the origin narratives that Thin Leather recounted for Russell and Lloyd may differ from ones other O'odham storytellers told to other researchers. Some of these are cited throughout the present volume. These differing teachings stem from the cultural and historical diversity that exists between Akimel O'odham, Tohono O'odham, Hia-Ced O'odham, and Wa:k O'odham (Sobaipuri). Not referenced as much, for practical reasons, are O'odham that jujkam called "Pima Bajo," which are Òob O'odham, Ó O'odham, and Taramil O'odham. Because my focus is on Komal Hok's legacy, these distant parts of the O'odham jeved appear only fleetingly. At the same time, these narratives share common threads, such as Jeved mahkai (Earth medicine maker) creating the earth from the muhadag, the grease, from their chest, which formed into a flattened disc, on which the first plant, the shegoi (creosote bush) was planted. O'odham storytellers also share teachings about Coyote, Elder brother, the first people, and the rise and fall of the big houses.[6]

Historical events, on the other hand, are significant if they impact a given village and are recorded on a calendar stick, or ooshikbina, for that village. O'odham therefore often do not reference people or events that Americans regard as important, such as their Civil War or Arizona's statehood. This is why I am reluctant to use the term "world view" to describe O'odham perspectives on history.

Indeed, the O'odham jeved is not even in America. Nor, for that matter, in Mexico. America is another country, one that drove the Mexicans (jujkam*) away, south of a border (for which the O'odham do not have a word). Now the mimilgahn** (Americans) claim control of the land. Nonetheless, they are mimilgahn, not O'odham. But they are also not enemies (o'obga***) like the Ndee (Apaches) and Yavapai. Nor for that matter are they enemies like the Quechan and Cocopah, who long ago began fighting their relatives, the Piipaash, whom Akimel O'odham call O'obab, and jujkam called Maricopas.[7] Sometimes the Piipaash called on their Akimel O'odham friends to help them fight their ancient rivals, so they did. Similarly, the Americans (mimilgahn) asked the Akimel O'odham, who they called "Pimos" and "Pimas" because they learned these names from jujkam, asked them to fight as well. Most often against o'obga, in which many battles and fatalities are recorded on calendar sticks. As for the mimilgahn, although they desperately needed their O'odham friends, who sometimes wore their uniforms as "scouts" under the provisions of the 1866 Army Reorganization Act, they did not always remember the debt they owed to O'odham for their sacrifices, let alone the land they took from them.

As more Americans settled their newly colonized territory (the 1862 Homestead Act brought thousands of migrants), they constructed their railway lines and built their farms, ranches, and towns. They also mined the mountains. And most significantly, they appropriated and wasted more and more river water, which eventually led to a water crisis that would take generations to resolve. During the height of the crisis, the 1870s to the 1910s, the O'odham and Piipaash barely eked out a living. This too is recorded on

---

*   jujkam is plural, juhkam is singular.

**   mimilgahn is plural, milgahn is singular.

***   o'obga is plural, obga is singular.

calendar sticks. Some thrived under the auspices of the Bureau of Plant Industry, which was developing a new strain of "Pima cotton" in Sacaton. However, O'odham farms in general were no longer sustaining the community but rather providing surplus crops for the general produce market. One cannot eat cotton and alfalfa, to put it succinctly. Consequently, the success that some O'odham and Piipaash farmers enjoyed was not shared by all. Many people starved. During this time of famine, Cook missionized the O'odham, Thin Leather worked with Russell, and O'odham basket weavers spread the man-in-the-maze symbol. It was a time of upheaval but also of resilience.[8]

At this point it may seem pretentious to begin talking about an O'odham philosophy of history, considering that these historical highlights document a steady decline in O'odham political and cultural sovereignty. Moreover, the effects of colonization were instigated by forces beyond O'odham control, including the Spanish mission system, American westward expansion, or the recurring periods of obga attacks and the spread of disease. From Father Eusebio Kino's first mission, Nuestra Señora de los Dolores de Cósari, founded in 1687 along the San Miguel River in Sonora, Mexico, to Arizona statehood in 1912, the ancestral boundaries of the O'odham jeved steadily shrunk, divided into reservations, reduced to ejidos, and overtaken by nation-states, local governments, and private land owners. All of which is in addition to the language, cultural, and political divisions that colonization created between O'odham on both sides of the border.[9] Nonetheless, what I am arguing here is that it is precisely because of the colonization of the O'odham jeved that an O'odham philosophy of history is necessary. O'odham need a way to think about what has become of their jeved. More to the point, an O'odham discourse on "history" stands as a corrective to the colonizer's reasons, policies, and post hoc justifications for occupying O'odham land. Thus, the question driving this discourse is, What is the meaning of history when a people is not a proponent but a victim of empire building, colonization, assimilation, and progress? In the case of O'odham, one can observe the world and its events as did the calendar-stick keepers, in which case history must be expressed in the plural as histories and viewed as a community of voices.

Before proceeding, I should acknowledge that the art of the oo-shikbina—"upon this stick you cut"—has been lost. As far as this O'dham author knows, while the oral histories that calendar sticks embodied are still remembered, the custom of maintaining these uniquely O'odham chronicles is not today an active part of the culture. Therefore my proposition of basing an O'odham philosophy on ooshikbina requires some explanation. This discourse, insofar as it claims to be driven by an Indigenous intellect, embarks on a critical analysis of the contexts—or con-*texts*, as I might have written during the height of Deconstruction—in which these ooshikbina appear, which are resources created by non-Indigenous researchers working in fields defined by the Euro-American intellectual tradition, such as anthropology. Consequently, whereas customarily a calendar-stick keeper would teach an apprentice to maintain the ooshikbina for their village, their kihhim, I have inherited these oral histories through the pages of two books and a paper. My purpose is not to simply accept that O'odham history is now locked in the colonized pages of those who recorded my ancestors' voices but rather to liberate these O'odham voices in the pages of my discourse. In other words, my intention is to deploy the methodology that I initiated when I published my first paper on the Lakota hanbleceya.

What follows in the next seven chapters is at one level a synthesis of the papers I have published over the years, along with unpublished work, on O'odham culture and history; at another level I am propounding an O'odham notion of history that sees events that occur across the O'odham jeved as an extension of O'odham origin narratives. In one sense, such a concept of history only makes sense for O'odham, be they Akimel O'odham, Tohono O'odham, Hia-Ced O'odham, or Sobaipuri O'odham, not to mention the O'odham of Mexico. In other words, just as our teachings, our oral traditions, are meant only for us, so too is this reflection on O'odham histories. "Stories," George Webb explains in the preface to *A Pima Remembers*, "were handed down from generation to generation, but today there are only a few of us who know them, and we do not make a practice of telling them."[10] At another level, what I am asserting is an O'odham perspective on history which is of value to non-O'odham and non-Indigenous readers who may be pondering how "Western history," from the Age of Discovery to the high-tech age in which we live today, is understood by an Indigenous mind. Examples abound of course in the historical archives, beginning with the Nahua (or Aztec) codices that recounted Hernán Cortez and the Spanish invasion of Tenochtitlán. Other

Indigenous peoples up and down the Western Hemisphere remembered and retold their experiences with multiple waves of occupiers. In addition to oral histories, Indigenous people initiated an array of media to preserve and honor their histories. From petroglyphs to quipu to winter counts and birchbark scrolls, Indigenous histories were written and recounted in an equally diverse array of Indigenous languages. O'odham calendar sticks are a part of this nonliterate—meaning non-alphabetic—phenomenon among Indigenous peoples. Suffice it say, as we proceed into the first chapter, such place-based and non-western values and ideas about history continue to inform and influence Indigenous thinking even under the duress of colonization. Enter the generation that raised Komal Hok into an O'odham sage and storyteller, who did not need to know how to read or write, let alone speak, English in order to bequeath to his descendants an origin narrative that has influenced O'odham thinking into the current era. I am one of these descendants.

A Note on How I Write in the O'odham Neok

O'odham and those well-acquainted with O'odham studies have likely noticed my idiosyncratic way of notating O'odham words and names. More to the point, they have observed my predilection for the Dean and Lucille Saxton system, which, in collaboration with Susie Enos, is published in their still-useful *Tohono O'odham/Pima to English, English to Tohono O'odham/Pima Dictionary*. My preference, however, is neither ideological or political but rather circumstantial—the Saxton and Enos dictionary appeared when I was a college undergrad, so immediately influenced how I wrote in O'odham. At the same time, I am acutely aware of the standardized orthographies that have emerged today at Tohono O'odham Nation and the Salt River Pima-Maricopa Indian Community. Preferred spellings, such as Huhugam (as opposed to Hohokam) or O'otham (as opposed to O'odham)—some even use a double capitalized O'O—are details that I respect. I rarely presume to correct another O'dham's way of writing our language. So my way of writing O'odham is admittedly subjective yet reflects how I am interpreting the origin narrative and its teachings.

As for my writerly habits, I am most influenced by O'odham speakers I have known throughout my life and career, beginning with my mother and my extended Akimel and Hia-Ced O'odham family. In the case of my family, they never thought of O'odham as something written. My mom would say, "Don't ask me how to spell it!" whenever I asked her how to say something in our language. However, because I became a scholar, the work of Ofelia Zepeda, my thesis director at the University of Arizona, and Don Bahr, who I got to know when he was at Arizona State University, also had an influence on my thinking. In fact, it was because of these two that I became aware of the issues and differing opinions about writing in O'odham. Having said all of that, my transcription of O'odham names, for example, Jeved mahkai as "Earth medicine maker," and my seeming aversion to capitalization still need to be explained.

When my capable and perceptive editor copyedited my text, she asked me about my translation of I'itoi, "I understand that you generally prefer to keep O'odham terms lowercase, but I wanted to ask how English translations of O'odham names should be styled. For example, should the English translation of 'I'itoi' be styled as a generic noun (elder brother) or a proper noun (Elder Brother)?" My response was, "My idiosyncratic way of spelling O'odham will likely irk some. However, O'odham does not abide by the rules of English syntax, so neither should its English spelling counterpart. O'odham names, if you will, are nonbinary, neither proper nouns or generic nouns. They are both."

As an example of how my idiosyncracies will irk some, when this book went through peer review, one of my readers said in her report, which was otherwise quite laudatory, that she noticed that I tended to not capitalize the letter j in jeved when writing about the O'odham jeved. She preferred to write it as "O'odham Jeved." I understand the preference, having used it in some of my publications, which have now been revised into the present volume. More than signifying a proper name, capitalization is a way of elevating words into concepts, ideas, and cultural values, which have names that should be acknowledged and definitions that should be an integral part of any serious discourse. So O'odham Jeved (capital J) denotes an O'odham territory, even nation, that defies the colonial boundaries of the United States and Mexico and their respective states. Similarly, Jeved mahkai is often written as Jeved Mahkai and translated more frequently as "Earth Medicine Man" and "Earth Doctor." (I should note for my reader that there are alternate spellings for all the terms used here.) So, why do I write O'odham jeved and Jeved mahkai? Am I not diminishing the significance of the O'odham neok as a way of asserting O'odham agency in an otherwise colonized world?

As I explained to Michael Millman, my acquisitions editor at the University of New Mexico Press, "as I continue to learn more about my O'odham neok, my O'odham language, and its cultural values, or himdag, the way I write O'odham has grown and changed." Consequently, regarding capitalization, "O'odham do not reify abstractions as frequently as English speakers. . . . In the case of jeved, which means earth, soil, or dirt, the singular and plural are the same, namely jeved." Accordingly, "my use of O'odham jeved is a reference to the O'odham lands, plural, which make up the O'odham jeved, or O'odham homelands, which Jeved mahkai, Earth medicine maker, made from him/herself." Jeved, first and foremost, is the earth beneath one's feet, which is experienced in the subjective perspective of the individual, their family and village. As a descriptive term, O'odham jeved, singular and plural, evokes the narrative quality that the term acquired when Jeved mahkai made the jeved, which Thin Leather recounted and left to us more than a century ago. Thus, my reason for using capitalization sparingly is to preserve the narrative and evocative quality of O'odham neok. As with other Indigenous languages, O'odham is at its most compelling when expressed in song. Thus the worlds that are made in origin narratives are typically sung into existence. Capitalization, to the contrary, has a way of freezing words in time. However, when I write a name, say "I'itoi" (Elder brother) as a phrase, to my ear it evokes the beginning of a story.

With this note in mind, what I have created in this book is one O'dham's perspective on O'odham storytelling. My comments on language, writing, and history are not meant to be didactic, let alone a criticism of what my predecessors have done. Rather, *The Maze of History* is my ooshikbina, my calendar stick containing seven notches, seven inscriptions—meaning my seven chapters—which recount my thoughts, observations, reflections, and arguments on O'odham experiences on the O'odham jeved. With that, I hope the reader will join me and let me show you what I mean.

Pulling Down the Clouds

*Komal Hok, Jose Lewis Brennan, and the Origin of
O'odham Literature*

The Society of American Indians's (SAI) 1913 list of active members includes only five "Pimas" (Akimel O'odham), named: Mrs. Jessie C. Morago, Lewis D. Nelson, Mary W. Nelson, John Plake, and Olie Walker. All were residents of Sacaton, Arizona.[1] Throughout the eight volumes of the SAI's journal, spanning the years 1913–1920, not a single O'dham contributor was published, though occasionally one of the O'odham communities was mentioned in an article, usually within the context of problems with the Indian Bureau. For example, Carlos Montezuma (Yavapai) in his article "Light on the Indian Situation" dramatically recalled his 1868 abduction by a "Pima raiding-party."[2] As the era of American colonization began in the aftermath of its 1846–1848 war with Mexico, which led to the 1854 Gadsden Purchase, O'odham were holding as tenaciously as they could to their jeved. In 1859, because of their friendly relation with the mimilgahn, which included protecting settlers from obga attacks, Akimel O'odham—and their Piipaash neighbors—were accorded the first reservation in Arizona Territory.[3] It was an epoch that historian Jennifer Bess saw as defined by Chief Antonio Azul's leadership.

> During [Azul's] tenure, the 1870s brought resource deprivation that resulted in extreme hardship, including water shortages that left fields barren for decades to come and, by the mid-twentieth century, led outside observers to conclude that Akimel O'odham farmers had become "as rusty as their farm tools." But even in times of famine, the Akimel O'odham eschewed presenting

themselves as victims and instead continued to strive to live up to their responsibilities as world-builders, emphasizing their agency and their rightful role in America's economic network.[4]

When Bess summarized the O'odham reservation experience in *Where the Red-Winged Blackbirds Sing*, she equated "world-building" with the O'odham himdag. What this meant is that, although O'odham were powerless to change federal Indian policy, they nonetheless resisted having their minds wiped clean of their values, beliefs, and teachings. It was during these times that an O'dham thinker emerged as a resource, a deep well of knowledge, who left a legacy that continues to influence O'odham studies into the present era. He is remembered as Komal Hok, which the mimilgahn (Americans) translated as "Thin Leather" and "Thin Buckskin." According to Jesse Walter Fewkes, Komal Hok was "popularly called Higgins," a name that appears in "A Fictitious Ruin in Gila Valley, Arizona" (1907), analyzed below, then again in Lloyd's *Aw-aw-tam Indian Nights* (1911), in which his first name "William" is added.[5]

In a footnote to the introduction of Donald M. Bahr's 1994 book on ancestral O'odham history, *The Short, Swift Time of Gods on Earth*, he states, "Thin Leather's mythology . . . was taken down independently three times, first by Frank Russell (published in condensed form in 1908), then by J. W. Lloyd (published in a more oral, more Indian English in 1911), and finally by [Jesse Walter] Fewkes (excerpts published in 1912)."[6] Noteworthy is the observation that the fieldwork for these anthropology projects was conducted prior to 1910, during which time *The Pima Indians* by Frank Russell and "Casa Grande, Arizona" by Jesse Walter Fewkes appeared in print, followed closely by *Aw-aw-tam Indian Nights* by J. William Lloyd. More specifically, Russell and Fewkes published with the Bureau of American Ethnology (BAE) in 1904–1905 and in 1906–1907, respectively; whereas Lloyd published his work independently with the Lloyd Group of Westfield, New Jersey, in 1911. Also significant is that while Thin Leather is listed as an informant in the BAE reports, he is given more prominent credit in *Aw-aw-tam Indian Nights*, whose title page describes the book as "being the Myths and Legends of the Pimas of Arizona as received by J. William Lloyd from Comalk-Hawk-Kih (Thin Buckskin) thru the interpretation of Edward Hubert Wood." Wood, it should be noted, was Komal Hok's nephew.

As indicated earlier by the references to the Society of American Indians, the appearance of "educated Indians," meaning Indigenous men and women educated in the English-based curriculum of Indian boarding schools, were few and far between. Nonetheless, their numbers were growing, and distinguished people of letters ascended into the Progressive-Era Indian rights movement. Among these were prominent leaders of the SAI Arthur C. Parker (Seneca), Charles A. Eastman (Dakota), Carlos Montezuma (Yavapai), Zitkala-Sa (Lakota), and Laura Cornelius Kellogg (Oneida). Some, like Eastman and Zitkala-Sa, published anthologies of "Indian stories," which, because they were fluent in their Indigenous languages, they translated and edited themselves. Eastman published *Red Hunters and the Animal People* (1904) and *Old Indian Days* (1907), while Zitkala-Sa published *Old Indian Legends* (1901), which was complemented in 1921 with *American Indian Stories*. Publishers typically presented these oral traditions as children's literature. Consequently there are no scholarly footnotes or interpretive essays and, most unfortunately, no original in the Indigenous languages.[7] Nevertheless, Indigenous writers and thinkers were exhibiting an agency that would not be exceeded until the Red Power movement and the Native American renaissance that characterized Indigenous literature during the 1960s-1980s.[8] However, the point being made here is that Komal Hok's work with Russell, Fewkes, and Lloyd appeared during a progressive period in American society when Indigenous persons—with the right credentials marking them as civilized—began acquiring a voice in the world of published authors. Particularly in *Aw-aw-tam Indian Nights*, Komal Hok became a part of this marginal but not insignificant Indigenous community. But Thin Leather, as noted earlier, emerged without any O'odham peers. Komal Hok, probably without realizing it, invented O'odham literature. Consequently, Komal Hok was the Akimel O'odham's first intellectual.

Before proceeding, it is necessary to stop and consider whether or not it is appropriate to call Thin Leather an "intellectual." Unlike Eastman and Parker, Thin Leather was not a writer. Nor did he possess an education. Komal Hok's contributions are based on allowing others to translate his O'odham words, as well as edit and present his stories and teachings.[9] Calling Komal Hok an intellectual sounds naïve. However, by whose standard ought one to assess Thin Leather's intellectual value? In 2014 I reflected on the phenomenon of the "intellectual" among Indigenous communities in settler-colonial America, which was my way of identifying an adaptation that Indigenous people were making to their colonization. What I wrote then was with thinkers like Samson Occom, Eastman, and Vine Deloria Jr. in mind. Nonetheless, including Komal Hok is justified and necessary. Academic standards need not apply.

> The Indigenous intellectual is seen as forging his or her identity outside the confines of academia, thriving instead along the margins of tribal society, where one may be acknowledged as a relative and tribal member yet communicate effectively in a non-Indigenous language, in which one has to take all of the risk and responsibility for representing one's tribe to an audience completely alien to the world in which one grew up. Maintaining this connection to one's peoplehood without giving in to the dominant society's preconceptions of Indians is one of the more challenging obstacles to getting one's Indigenous perspective acknowledged by others.[10]

Komal Hok took a greater risk than he likely knew at the time when he shared his knowledge with the mimilgahn. Thin Leather was an O'dham from Ge'e Kih (Sacaton), who communicated effectively in English through translators, who were his relatives, to unknown and alien audiences. Lingering in the pages of the white man's books, it would take generations for Komal Hok to be elevated from the annals of anthropology and into the status of a shohshon, an ancestor. As such, Komal Hok has joined his place among the huhugam, the revered ancestors who learned our himdag from Siuuhuu, our Elder brother.

If then, one is to evaluate the work of an Indigenous intellectual, it should be less in terms of how it matches with their mainstream counterparts in academia and more with how effectively that work retains the language and values of one's ancestral community. As such, one is an Indigenous intellectual only if one is an Indigenous person in the first place, which means being born into one's community's traditions and teachings, such that these form the basis of one's relationship with their homeland, language, kinship, and sacred history. Even taking the effects of colonization into account—complete with significant language and land loss—one can still privilege one's ties to one's people, history, and culture; however, the latter may manifest themselves under settler-colonial conditions. All Indigenous people bear the scars of their ancestors' colonization.

Beginning with Samson Occom, the eighteenth-century Pequot minister, there have been numerous individuals in Indigenous communities who learned to thrive within the white man's world. Komal Hok was one of these. The author of this text is another. There is no shame in surviving. For us both, the sources of our himdag are nonliterate. Philosophical and religious ideas and insights are expressed primarily through narrative, be it story, song, speech, or ritual action. Consequently, Thin Leather is an intellectual because he possessed an abundant knowledge of the O'odham himdag, not because he met the definition of intellectual that defined the work of the men who appropriated his knowledge, such as Russell, Fewkes, and Lloyd. If anyone wanted to know about the Akimel O'odham, they needed to seek out someone like Komal Hok. Fewkes and Russell could not find anyone like this in the anthropology department at Harvard University.[11] Otherwise, by milgahn scholarly standards in which the certification conferred by an academic degree is presumed, one cannot say that an O'odham intellectual tradition appeared until 1978, when Tohono O'odham Alice Paul earned her doctorate at the University of Arizona with her dissertation "Development of a Classroom Based Procedure for Assessing Aspects of Intellectual Functioning for First Grade Children."[12] George Webb and Anna Moore Shaw, whose works are analyzed below, did not count, as neither was college educated. From an O'odham perspective, of course, they are highly respected writers and thinkers.

Thin Leather—obverse to Alice Paul—remained solely within an O'odham oral tradition, never writing down his thoughts, although he communicated through O'odham translators who were capable of reading and writing in English, namely Jose Lewis Brennan and Edward Hubert Wood. In light of this, Thin Leather is an intellectual insofar as this coincides with chegitokam, the O'odham word for "thinker." Lloyd stated that Thin Leather was a "see-nee-yaw-kum, or professional traditionalist, who knew all the ancient stories."[13] Intellectual, of course, is a term of convenience. As used here, the term encompasses the nuances of Komal Hok's life as a mahkai, a storyteller, a singer, and a weaver. Because he did not write, research, or lecture, as did Fewkes and Russell, he is not an intellectual in the same way as the American anthropologists who wrote about the O'odham.[14] In this way Thin Leather is similar to Owl Ear, also called Chukud Naak, another of Russell's informants in *The Pima Indians*, who is described as "an old man [an elder, kelimai]" who lived in Salt River village and was "the first from whom a calendar record was obtained."[15] In this capacity, Owl Ear served as a historian, keeping the annals of locally important events notched on a long wooden staff, an ooshikbina.

Calendar sticks, as Paul Ezell describes them, are "mnemonic devices with each notch representing a year, 'the owner being expected to remember the events of that year.'"[16] Much of what Owl Ear recounted for Russell consisted of the strife that plagued the region due to the Americans seizing control of O'odham land, consequently putting O'odham into conflict with their ancestral enemies. On December 28, 1872, for example, at the "Tanks," an area within the Superstition Mountains, Akimel O'odham fought against Ndee (Apache) warriors. The O'odham that fought did so alongside American soldiers stationed at Fort McDowell. Owl Ear remembered this as "a sight long to be remembered."[17] Anna Moore Shaw, in *A Pima Past* (1974), refers to Owl Ear's historical recollections as evidence that he "had a gift for telling stories as well as a good memory. Some of the events recorded on his stick also appear in history books, [such as Russell's *The Pima Indians*]." At the same time, Shaw observed, "the Pimas often attached significance to happenings the white man thought unimportant. They just had different ways of seeing things."[18] When an O'dham slew a rival, for example, it required the victorious warrior to return home for a sixteen-day purification ceremony, complete with an honoring dance. For what was important, more so than the act of killing an enemy, was restoring the balance, the himdag, that was disrupted by obga attacks.[19] When the Americans killed their enemies, they were most concerned about protecting their control over their territory, making the "frontier" safe for milgahn settlement, and expanding their empire. In other words, mimilgahn fought for profit.

Concurrent with the work of Owl Ear and Komal Hok, a very different O'odham world appears in the 1913 volume of *The Quarterly Journal of the Society of American Indians*. In these pages Tohono O'odham student José Ignacio had an excerpt from his essay quoted in an article featuring other

Indian boarding school students. The excerpts were taken from submissions to the SAI's contest for the best Indian student essay on education. Ignacio was credited with stating:

> It is in accordance with the motto "Step out," that we are getting our education, because it is on this point where many of the returned students failed. He has not gained sufficient strength to stand the hard knocks of the habits and customs of his people. He must have a better education to make a center rush on the old Indian ways and make a touchdown. It is clear he must have an education and one necessary to produce results, for the Indian's greatest aid in the future must be himself."[20]

It is unclear if this is the same José Ignacio who went on to become chairman of the Papago Tribal Council (1937–1940).[21] What is known from the contest information is that the student whose essay was published in full as the "Honor Essay" was by James Smith (Warm Spring), who wrote "Education and Progress for the Indian."[22] With respect then to the O'odham intellectual tradition, of which Owl Ear and Komal Hok are a part, it would not be until after World War II when one sees the appearance of any writers of consequence, namely George Webb (1893–?) and Anna Moore Shaw (1898–1976). Both preceded Alice Paul, but neither obtained a college degree, let alone became a part of academia, which are differences that are significant to appreciating Paul's historic distinction. Webb and Shaw, on the contrary, were a part of the American Indian intellectual tradition that anticipated what Vine Deloria Jr. called "the Indian protest movement," which took place during the years 1964–1974, complete with the establishment of American Indian/Native American studies academic departments.[23]

It is precisely because he emerged as an O'dham chegitokam without speaking or writing English, nor ever attending school, let alone college, that Komal Hok provides a compelling example of Indigenizing the intellectual life. Thin Leather's endeavors as an O'dham knowledge keeper, though shaped beyond his control by the academic process, retain their impact because of his connection to the O'odham himdag. My work as one of Thin Leather's descendants is to recover, honor, and revitalize his voice, recognizing it as foundational to O'odham research and scholarship. Komal Hok's distant yet familiar stories bespeak a people suffering from the effects of losing our akimel, the Gila River, which precipitated cultural decline over a seventy-year period, as O'odham ceremonies, most importantly the wiigiida[24] (the cactus-harvest ceremony), which beckons the summer monsoons, withered in a waterless desert. "People must unite in desiring rain. If it rains their lands shall be as a garden, and they will not be as poor as they have been."[25] Because O'odham did not control their own land, which was now under Indian Bureau management, and were discouraged from turning to their mamahkai* for spiritual guidance, as they were expected to be Christian, the Akimel hehemajkam still desired rain. Only now they had to pray for rain in church rather than gather for the wiigiida. There is no record of what Komal Hol thought about this.

The water crisis was referenced twice in a 1914 issue of *The Quarterly Journal of the Society of American Indians*. John M. Oskison (Cherokee) briefly recounts his visit to the "Pima Reservation" in "Acquiring a Standard of Value," in which he provides a firsthand survey of living conditions in central and southern Arizona. What is appalling in Oskison's observations is the condescending way that he degrades O'odham grievances as pettiness, even though he is the one that admits that he knows little about either O'odham irrigation or the pertinent water laws.

> I have been down, within a few weeks, to the Pima Reservation, in Arizona, and I saw there a gradation of opportunity that seemed to me exceedingly interesting. The first group of Pimas that I went to lived [sic] near Mesa, in a section which is highly developed and all under irrigation. I found it difficult with my lack of knowledge of the irrigation technique, to follow their talks. They had a series of grievances about their water supply, and it all hinged on certain degrees of service. They were A, B and C users under certain contracts with a certain water users'

---

*   mamahkai is plural, mahkai is singular.

association. They got so many acre-feet, and got the water on the land at a certain time. From there I went over to Sacaton, and there found a different set of grievances. The men at Sacaton wanted to talk. They seemed at Sacaton to understand less definitely what they wanted. From Sacaton I went to Black Water, and *at Black Water it was a whole lot of petty details, like a bunch of children complaining that their teacher favored somebody else*; there was internal dissensions based on what seemed immaterial things [my emphasis].[26]

In spite of the 1908 Winters Doctrine, which guaranteed water rights to reservations, the Akimel O'odham nonetheless endured a critical water shortage that threatened lives and their agricultural economy. Clearly Oskison did not understand, let alone appreciate, the legal nuances of the complaints, as they were contingent on a complicated analysis of reserved water rights. Obviously Oskison was not the representation that the O'odham needed.[27]

In "Shall the Pimas Be Robbed of Water?" a more sympathetic and informed essay presented evidence that a famine persists, even amidst an allegedly progressive era in American society. Likely written by Arthur C. Parker, who edited the volume, the status report on the "Pimas" was published between a lengthy editorial condemning the Indian Bureau titled "Hon Cato Sells, Commissioner of Indian Affairs" and a summary of "Local Meetings or Conferences":

The Pima Indians [Akimel O'odham] need water if they are to continue to live. The Pimas need the water that nature provided. That water has been appropriated by the white settlers. To offset the injustice the Pimas were sold wells of poisonous water [full of alkaline] whose chemical deposits spoil the land for agriculture. The Pimas did not want those wells. But the Pimas must pay for them. For centuries the Pimas have used the waters of the Gila River, but now they are deprived of it and given instead well water pumped by electricity at such great cost that its use, even if free from alkali, is prohibitive. The Pima Indians wish to live; they do not wish to become paupers and beggars. *The United*

States has no right to slaughter the Pimas industrially. The guardian Government has no right to sell the birthright of the Pimas. Yet it has failed to protect them. The Pimas appeal to the Nation, they appeal to Congress, they appeal to you, reader. Help the Pimas; help right; forbid injustice! You have the opportunity of writing your Congressman [sic] in support of the bill introduced by Hon Carl Hayden (HR 17016), providing for the construction of the San Carlos Irrigation project. This bill provides for furnishing the Pima Reservation with water free of construction charges, which shall be judicially determined if entitled by reason of prior appropriation by the Pimas. The Indian Rights Association indorses the bill [my emphasis].[28]

The "industrial slaughter" of which this article speaks is a pre–World War II figure of speech signifying what today is called "genocide." It was under these circumstances that Frank Russell published his 1908 Bureau of American Ethnology (BAE) report *The Pima Indians*, to which Thin Leather contributed. Russell, to his credit, was cognizant of the severe conditions in the Gila River community.

During this bihugig, Russell recorded calendar sticks from Gila Crossing and Salt River villages. In 1872 and 1873, "the Pimas had had little water to irrigate their fields and were beginning to suffer from actual want when the settlers on the Salt River invited them to come to that valley."[29] The settlers in this instance were not milgahn (American) but Onk Akimel O'odham, who took pity on their Gila River relatives. From 1898 to 1899 at Blackwater Village, "there was no crop this year," to which Russell added in a footnote:

The water of the Gila had been so far utilized by white settlers above the reservation, for the most part more than a hundred miles above, that there was none left for the Pimas. It is difficult to obtain accurate information at this time of the number who perished either directly or indirectly by starvation. During this and the following year five persons are known to have died from this cause, and it is probable that there were others. Most of the Pimas will not beg, however desperate their need may be, so that not all cases were reported.[30]

In 1903, not long after Russell completed his 1901–1902 field research, two Carlisle Indian School graduates tried to create a constitution for the Gila River reservation. "A Pima Constitution," which Russell edited, appeared in *The Journal of American Folklore*, where readers learned of Solon Jones, the interpreter for the Pima Agency at Sacaton who first suggested the idea for a constitution, and Earl A. Whitman, the disciplinarian at Sacaton School who took on the job of writing their ideas down on paper. Unfortunately, there is little about Jones in the archival record. However, in a congressional hearing dated April 23, 1912, E. B. Linnen, inspector for the Secretary of the Interior, and Walter Lowrie Fisher entered a letter from the previous secretary, Richard Achilles Ballinger, that stated: "Solon Jones, an educated Pima Indian, who was carried on the pay rolls as 'forest guard,' but who really did some office work, measured wood, did errands for Supt Alexander, did his bidding, and performed crooked acts without question."[31] In a subsequent hearing dated 1913, Ballinger read into the record:

> The sworn testimony of Solon Jones shows that he was selling cattle, beef, and wood to Supt JB Alexander, at Sacaton Agency, in his own name and in the names of 8 or 10 other Indians whose names he furnished at the request of Supt Alexander, who knew that the cattle, beef, and wood which was being delivered in the names of these various persons belonged to Solon Jones.[32]

Whitman, on the other hand, attended Carlisle from 1898 to 1900. School records list his unnamed father as "deceased." In a survey dated January 20, 1912, Whitman stated that upon graduating in 1900 he did not pursue his education any further. At present he was a "grading foreman" for the US Bureau of Reclamation, implying experience as a skilled laborer. At the same time, Whitman did not claim a home anywhere, explaining, "I am not trying to make a home to call it mine because it looks like . . . our land is going to be allotted."[33]

According to Russell, the motivation for constructing a constitution were the hard times the community was enduring.

> In recent years those living about the agency on the Gila have been deprived of water for irrigating their farms by the white

settlers who have taken out ditches from the river above them. The stream which formerly furnished far more water than they could use is now a white stretch of blistering sand the greater part of the year. This has resulted in the impoverishment of the Indians; a few have died of starvation, and many others, owing to lessened powers of resistance, have succumbed to disease.[34]

Out of this strife a new era was born in which a younger generation sought to lead "the Santan community," which "had become displeased with the miserly character of its old chief,"[35] in a new direction. Jones and Whitman attempted to address the water crisis with ancestral O'odham water management practices passed down to their generation by the huhugam who built the original canal system.

In October 1901, the Gila River community acquired "a more extensive system of canals."[36] In light of this, the Santan community selected a new chief and collaborated on the composition of a constitution, which was submitted to the Indian superintendent at the Pima Agency in Sacaton, as well as O'odham elders, for approval. The proposed governing document was "'modelled after that of the United States.'"[37] Superintendent Elwood Hadley stated on August 15, 1901:

> In my last report, I expatiated on the starving and helpless condition of the Indians under my charge and the necessity for the building of a storage reservoir by the Government. Practically the same conditions exist now, and the experience of the past year has confirmed me in my opinion and emphasized the need for the reservoir.[38]

Russell noted that both the Indian agent and the community acceded their approval "with scarcely a dissenting voice."[39] But would the Office of Indian Affairs listen and approve of this initiative at self-governance? In 1901 the Bureau was under the leadership of Indian Commissioner William A Jones, who served during the William McKinley administration (1897–1904).

The constitution, in spite of its proclaimed model, consisted of a set of bylaws governing the duties of key tribal positions, such as Head Chief,

Assistant Chiefs, Minute Men, and the Council, as well as the management of community resources, such as the canal system, water usage, roads, livestock, fields, ditches, and dams. O'odham customs and values, meaning the himdag, informed the Pima constitution, connecting it to O'odham oral tradition about the huhugam who built Casa Grande, which they called Sivan vahki.[40] Fewkes observed in his 1908 excavation report of the Casa Grande Ruins near Florence, Arizona:

> The present Pima say that they now organize to construct irrigation ditches in a way somewhat similar to that of the ancients [huhugam]. As all clans [villages] enjoy the advantage of the water thus obtained, every clan has its representatives in constructing the canals, and failure to work involves loss of water right, although a clan may be represented by members of other clans. The amount of labor necessary in construction of new ditches is settled in council, in which all clans interested take part.[41]

Although the constitution was immediately met with opposition—instigated, according to Russell, by fines for violating land and cattle bylaws, which the violators did not want to pay—the document itself, contrary to the times in which it was composed, may be described as a statement of inherent sovereignty. The Akimel O'odham knew that they were more competent than the Indian Bureau at managing their water and irrigation needs. At the same time, lest the claim for inherent sovereignty sound naïve, there was nothing in the Pima constitution that asserted political independence from the United States. In this way Jones and Whitman's constitution anticipated the 1934 tribal constitutions that were generated from the Indian Reorganization Act.

Although Akimel O'odham were suffering, as were all Indigenous nations, from the consequences of settler communities soaking up resources and the heavy hand of the Indian Bureau oppressing their political freedoms, they still maintained their aboriginal right of occupancy that came with inhabiting an area recognized by the federal government as exclusively O'odham land. Nonetheless, beginning in 1850, the inaugural year of the

American period,[42] the Akimel O'odham went from being "friends" to destitution within a generation.

Because they were regarded as friendly toward white immigrants, O'odham were recognized as a vital source of provisions, not to mention protection from the Apaches. Thus, because the amity between the two communities, O'odham sided with American soldiers on sorties into Obga, Ndee territory. Juan Thomas, a calendar-stick keeper from Blackwater Village, recalled for 1856–1857:

> The Pimas and Maricopas [Akimel O'odham and O'obab] joined the white soldiers in a campaign against the Apaches under White Hat. Two Pimas were killed and two wounded, but no Apaches were injured. While the Pimas were on their way home still another of their party was killed. The Pimas burned their dead. Later they killed several Apaches who were raising corn on Salt River.[43]

Upon building a stage-line between El Paso, Texas, and Fort Yuma, Arizona, which brought in droves of immigrants, especially soldiers, Akimel O'odham did not see an adequate return for the land use that Americans were taking for granted, be it in terms of compensation, humanitarian aid, or water rights. Ezell points out that what the O'odham observed instead was that American migrants brought in a much larger quantity of trade goods than did the Mexicans who preceded them. Equally significant, mimilgahn were conspicuously wealthier than their jujkam counterparts. The Americans were also aware of this fact, which influenced O'odham-American relations. US government employees typically reacted to O'odham entreaties with the stony indifference of a powerful and headstrong nation. Be they Indian agents, soldiers, or traders, all mimilgahn came across to O'odham as greedy and insensitive. "However well or poorly perceived or understood by the Indians," Ezell noted, "federal regulations influenced their attitudes toward government personnel from the beginning of their contacts."[44]

Emblematic of Indian-white relations was John Walker, newly appointed Indian Agent assigned to Sacaton Village. Along with Lieutenant Alfred Chapman, who was assigned to Fort Buchanan, and (either) Juan Antonio

Llunas or Antonio Azul, depending on the storyteller, Walker promised "Pimas" a supply of "plows, spades, shovels, axes, and every article necessary for their comfort." O'odham leaders soon learned to their frustration that the promised items were not forthcoming. In response O'odham offered to purchase the much-needed implements. Lt. Chapman explained in turn that he was prohibited from selling them government property. The O'odham doubled their offer. Chapman repeated his explanation. Exasperated, an O'odham headman declared to Chapman's face: "I believe your people are a nation of liars, and you are a liar individually; you came with your agent and you heard what he said—you sanctioned it. . . . I trust you no more." Adding insult to injury was news that the obga (Apaches) were provided plows and shovels, and other tools, even though they did not want these things in the first place.[45] Unlike the O'odham, Apaches did not consider themselves as a farming people. None of this mattered to the mimilgahn, who thought they could remake all Indians in their image.

After the American Civil War conditions in Akimel O'odham villages became dire. A fresh wave of settlers motivated by economic opportunity moved in, which brought about "the depletion of the Pimas' Gila River water." During the 1870s "settlers had located above the Pima reservation, opened large canals, and were wasting water rather than returning it to the Gila."[46] For decades ensued a time of famine (bihugig). Akimel O'odham saw themselves transition against their will from independent farmers competing with their white counterparts to becoming underpaid wage laborers and welfare recipients. Russell, as noted earlier, documented the travails of this precipitous economic decline, which included episodes of "alcoholism, increased killing as Indians quarreled more, and increased intercommunity strife."[47] Komal Hok grew up during this epoch. The ooshikbina as a historical record began in the 1830s. Komal Hok, who did not know his age, was likely born during the 1820s. So as an adult he witnessed much of what was recalled by the calendar-stick keepers.

When Jones and Whitman wrote their constitution, Akimel O'odham had already undertaken drastic steps at adapting to—the better word may be surviving—their life-threatening circumstances. In addition to giving up their farms for wage labor in the newly founded city of Phoenix and its environs such as Mesa and Chandler, many Akimel O'odham converted to

Christianity during the 1890s, Presbyterianism in particular, and opened schools run by white teachers, such as the Cook School in Sacaton. The Cook School opened in 1871 and became a boarding school for O'odham children in 1881. By 1902 there were day schools at Gila Crossing and Salt River, as well as in Blackwater, Lehi, Maricopa, and Casa Blanca. Several O'odham parents even sent their children as far away as the Carlisle Indian Industrial School in Pennsylvania, where seventy-one "Pima" students attended during its nearly forty years of operation.[48] Seventeen others, including members of Antonio Azul's family, went to the Hampton Normal & Agricultural Institute in Virginia.[49] In *The Pima Indians*, Russell quoted a version of the Akimel O'odham origin narrative written by a boarding school graduate, which was a startling example of the decline in cultural fluency among O'odham youth. "It [the alternate origin narrative] illustrates the confusion existing in the minds of the younger generation; to some extent, also, the order of words in the Pima [O'odham neok] sentence, as well as the difficulties that must speedily beset the ethnological investigator as soon as the older people have gone."[50]

Lest we blame the victims, what Russell documented was ethnocide. As Russell and Komal Hok's contemporaries witnessed the desolation of the reservation system, which was exacerbated by the boarding school system, an outcry emerged that has lasted generations. Since the 1880s, when Susette La Flesche (Omaha) demanded "citizenship" for Indians as a way of redressing the humanitarian crisis in the reservation system, Indian rights advocates have called for an end to America's corrupt and abusive federal Indian policy. In 1881 Helen Hunt Jackson contributed substantially to the Indian rights movement with *A Century of Dishonor*. During Thin Leather's era, the Society of American Indians also sought citizenship rights for all Indians, something that the 1887 General Allotment Act failed miserably at providing (the statute was more adept at expropriating Indian land than at protecting Indian property rights). In the first volume of *The Quarterly Journal of the Society of American Indians*, the SAI published its political platform, which included a statement about Indian education:

> That we respectfully urge that school facilities be speedily
> provided for the thousands of Indian children without such

advantage; that all Indian schools be standardized, so far as practicable to conform to the courses of study provided in the various states in which they are situated. That teachers intrusted [sic] with the development of Indian children be carefully examined and selected with the view of putting the schools in the hands of those of exceptional ability and fitness, and that facilities and encouragement for more advanced training be provided.[51]

Considering this statement, it is worth reminding ourselves that, as documented in the introductory paragraph of the current chapter, there were Akimel O'odham members of the SAI. In addition, there were O'odham young people, like Ignacio, who earned recognition for their progressive thinking about education. We also should not forget Jones and Whitman, the authors of the Pima constitution. Whatever justifiable concerns Russell had with the deleterious effects of boarding school education on the O'odham mind, it was clear that O'odham wanted to play an active role in their own future.

The Indian Bureau was the source of most Indian grievances, including the ones that Oskison failed to understand, and there were those like Carlos Montezuma who were adamant that the only solution to the so-called Indian Problem was to abolish the bureau altogether. Then, perhaps, Indians could obtain the education that they deserve, which was no more or less than what their white counterparts enjoyed.

The Indian boys and girls are schooled on the reservations near their Indian homes. By promotion they go into non-reservation Indian boarding-schools. To go higher, they enter Carlisle, Haskell or other government Indian boarding-schools, and when these same boys and girls finish the eighth grade, they are carefully sent back to their homes on the reservations. That end [sic] his or her school chapter, and what has been the outcome of such method of Indian schooling? Back, back in everything, of course.[52]

In Russell's opinion, the "subject-matter of [Jones and Whitman's] constitution" exhibited significant faults. For example, "the arrangement is not good, the phraseology is bad, in places condensation would improve, and in others there are omissions."[53] Nevertheless Russell argued that the men who crafted the constitution were "worthy of *our* respect" (my emphasis).[54] Russell's collective "our," it should be noted, was premised on the assumption that other scholarly persons like himself were included. To Russell, Jones, and Whitman, in addition to the Akimel O'odham who voted to approve their constitution, deserve praise for the "progress" they showed at civilizing themselves.

> At the time of [Jones and Whitman's] birth their people [the Akimel O'odham] had not a single house more pretentious than the willow ki, shaped like a beehive and scarcely high enough to enable its occupants to stand upright. They have grown up with almost purely aboriginal surroundings, their homes separated by several miles of absolutely uninhabitable desert from the nearest white habitations.[55]

When Russell penned these words, he likely bore in mind his 1901–1902 observations of "Pima villages," in which he saw scant "progress" in "Pima architecture" beyond the olas kih. Peter Nabakov, in *Native American Architecture* (1989), described the O'dham home as a "brush and mud-covered structure" that "was slightly excavated and banked with earth, [complete] with a domed adobe-plastered roof . . . often accompanied by a ramada."[56] Russell, for his part, condescendingly referred to the olas kih as looking like "an overturned washbasin."[57] Regarding Pueblo-style architecture as further up the evolutionary ladder, Russell pointed out that the "first Piman adobe house was built by the head chief, Antonio Azul, twenty-two years ago, and since that time the people have made very commendable progress. Some villages—such as, for example, at Blackwater—now contain few dwellings that are not of adobe. However, there are others, such as Skâ'kâîk [Skakaik, or Many Snakes], that retain the old-time ki."[58] Despite working with the Akimel O'odham during his field research, Russell failed to appreciate the sophisticated way in which the olas kih was perfectly adapted to its environment. As an extension of the O'odham mind, the olas kih exhibited a deep knowledge of the plants and trees, which availed themselves as durable building material. George Webb described the "olas-ki" in *A Pima Remembers* (1959):

> The *olas-ki,* or round house, [was] made of mesquite posts, willow and arrow weeds. This type of house is no longer used. It was enclosed all around, with a little dirt and straw on top to keep the rain out. The only opening was a small hole about two feet wide and four feet high which was used as a door. This door was always to the east. To get in, one had to get down on hands and knees.[59]

As an expression of himdag, the olas kih was a demonstration of humility, as opposed to being a shrine to one's ego. People gathered within its humble space to share food, stories, and rest. If Russell had thought of why the Akimel O'odham did not want ge'edaj kikih (big houses), as recounted in their origin narrative, he might have realized that what the O'odham lacked in material wealth and status symbols they more than made up for in the teachings of their himdag, which is a connection to the jeved that remained beyond the mimilgahn's grasp.

Before proceeding, I will include a word about Many Snakes, or Skakaik, and its place in Akimel O'odham history. Unexpectedly, in a congressional hearing about the San Carlos Irrigation Project, which was proposed as a solution to the Gila River water crisis, testimony on Skakaik was documented.

> *Snaketown Canal.* On the south side of the river opposite the Bapchil [Bapchule] is the present point of diversion of the Snaketown Canal, called in Pima, Skakaik ("many snakes"). Like the Stotonic fields across the river, this district is one of the ancient rancherias of the Pimas, and the history of the early irrigation in this region has already been given under the title of "Previous cultivation." At the time of this survey the area cultivated under this ditch was 354 acres. The area of previous cultivation has already been discussed under that heading. The

Meskimons survey of 1904 showed an area of 3,499.1 acres, representing past and present cultivation in this district.[60]

Snaketown eventually rose into the annals of "Hohokam" archaeology when Emil W. Haury shared his findings in *The Hohokam: Desert Farmers and Craftsmen, Excavations at Snaketown, 1964–1965*. Commenting on "The Old Village of Snaketown," Haury purportedly referenced local oral history with respect to the name:

> When in the late 1870s, a dozen or so Pima [Akimel O'odham] families established a new site on the old one because of the availability of tillable land on the lower terrace, they observed the higher reptile population here than elsewhere and called their new home "Skoaquick," the Place of the Snakes, or "Skâ' kâĭk, Many Rattlesnakes, as given by [Frank] Russell.[61]

A plenitude of rodents was also observed by O'odham who erected their olas kih and farmed this area. Toha chuuvĭ, the Antelope jackrabbit, was also in abundance at Snaketown.[62] To an O'dham this evokes the story of when Snake got its fangs, which is part of the origin narrative. In *The Pima Indians*, Komal Hok recounted this teaching:

> For a time after the creation of the four tribes of men and the animals they were confined in a great house together. Rattlesnake was there, and was known as Ma'ik Sol'atc, Soft Child. The people liked to hear him rattle, and little rest or peace could he obtain because of their continual prodding and scratching. Unable to endure it longer, he went at last to Elder Brother to ask help of him. Elder Brother took pity upon him and pulled a hair from his own lip to cut in short pieces to serve as teeth for Soft Child. "Now," said he, "if anyone bothers you again, bite him." In the evening Ta-api, Rabbit, came to Soft Child as he sat at the door and scratched him as he had so often done before. Soft Child raised his head and bit his tormentor as Elder Brother had instructed him to do. Feeling the bite, Rabbit scratched Soft

Child again, and again was bitten; then he ran about telling that Soft Child was angry and had bitten him twice. Again he went to him and again he was bitten twice. During the night his body swelled and the fever came upon him. All through the dark hours he suffered and throughout the next day; often he called to those around him to prepare a place that might give him rest.[63]

The story of Soft Child and Rabbit is relevant to Haury's references to Snaketown because Haury could not comprehend the connection with the huhugam. According to Marilyn Martinez, her father Simon Lewis explained to her that Skakaik referred to more than a bed of rattlesnakes but also to the huhugam who dwelled here generations before the historic village. In other words, skakaik expressed awareness that this place belongs to huhugam, such that the skakaik are protecting this place from meddlers.

The Pima Indians was originally published in the *Twenty-Sixth Annual Report of the Bureau of American Ethnology, 1904–1905*, then republished as a book in 1908. Frank Russell (1868–1903) based his report on fieldwork conducted from November 1901 to June 1902. From his base in Sacaton Village, Russell accessed the places and informants that make up the content of this historically important work. Significantly, Russell noted "the aid of five native interpreters"—José Lewis, Melissa Jones, Jacob L. Roberts, Carl Smart, and Thomas Allison[64]—who assisted him with recording the knowledge of "ten Pima men and women, selected because of their intelligence and special aptitude in certain lines."[65] In a lengthy footnote, Russell provided the names of his informants, complete with brief biographical descriptions. Using the now long obsolete American Phonetic Alphabet[66] for O'odham names, Russell recognized Kâ'mâl tkâk (Komal Hok), or Thin Leather; Sala Hina, also known as Sarah Fish, or Hina; Sika'tcu, Dry; Antonio Azul; Ki'satc, Cheese; William Blackwater; Ha'hali, Juan Thomas; Tco'kût Nak, Owl Ear; Benjamin Thompson; and Kâemâ-â (Coy-e-mau), Rattlesnake Head.[67] At the top of Russell's list was the most respected elder in the group:

Kâ'mâl tkâk [Komal Hok], Thin Leather, an old man, is said to be the most popular of the few remaining narrators of myths and speeches, or "speakers." He is an intimate friend of the head chief,

Antonio Azul, and has always occupied a prominent place in the councils of the tribe. In his prime he exceeded 6 feet in stature and was strong and sturdy of frame. Indeed, his hand grasp is yet vigorous enough to make his silent and friendly greeting somewhat formidable. Intelligent, patient, dignified, his influence must have been helpful to those youths who formerly came to him for instruction. From him was obtained the cosmogonical myth of the tribe, many speeches, songs, and much general information. He also made a model of a loom and a few other specimens for the collection of material pertaining to the Pimas.[68]

Thin Leather's status as one "of the few remaining narrators of myths and speeches" may unfortunately be attributed to the cultural decline caused during the time of famine. Under an Indian Bureau that disregarded Indigenous knowledge and practice as primitive and obsolete, O'odham were subjected to milgahn political and economic forces on their lands, water, and society, pushing them away from their himdag. Russell perceived Thin Leather's knowledge as endangered when he ruefully referred to young people "who *formerly* came to him for instruction." Was it Thin Leather who put this forlorn notion in Russell's mind? Did he bemoan the lack of an apprentice? Granted, salvage anthropology was premised on the preconception of Indigenous people as "vanishing," but it is also possible that Komal Hok saw in his own way a decline in the number of young people practicing O'odham customs and instead taking up the ways of the whites little by little.

J. William Lloyd (1857–1940) recounted the time he was introduced to Thin Leather by Edward H. Wood, Thin Leather's grand-nephew. "We found the old man," Lloyd recalled, "plowing for corn in his field. The strong, friendly grasp he gave my hand was all that could be desired." Then, in a courteous regard for Komal Hok's status, Lloyd said of the revered figure: "Tall, lean, dignified, with a harsh, yet musical voice; keen, intelligent black eyes and an impressive manner, *he was plainly a gentleman and a scholar, even if he could neither read nor write, nor speak a sentence of English*" (my emphasis).[69] Thin Leather defied the expectation in American learned society that "a gentleman and a scholar" ought to embody a professorial image, not to mention be a white male. Still, if one wants to give Lloyd the benefit of the doubt, his remarks about Thin Leather may have been his humble attempt at disabusing his readers of presuming that "Indians" on the reservation were ignorant and destitute. Many of them were still wealthy in their ancestral culture and language. Thin Leather's character, moreover, was beyond reproach. Komal Hok, to be sure, was not the only O'dham "gentleman and scholar" dwelling in the villages along the Gila River. As noted earlier, Thin Leather was one of several informants Russell consulted.

Russell's observations of Mavith Kavdom, Lion Shield, more commonly known as Antonio Azul (ca. 1817–1909) are pertinent. Azul "was the head chief of the tribe, and from [whom] much information concerning war customs and recent history was obtained."[70] The Reverend Charles H. Cook, who began missionizing the Gila River villages in 1870, recalled in a letter dated March 29, 1893, that the Akimel O'odham ughchu (headman) was "probably about seventy-five years of age" at the time of their encounter. At that time, Azul recounted an expedition against o'obga,* Ndee, in which O'odham scouts sortied under the command of "General [sic?] AJ Alexander."[71] At the same time, Azul was well known for being a strong advocate for Akimel O'odham rights, especially to their land and water. He always expected something in return for pledging his community's alliance with the mimilgahn. Anna Moore Shaw stated many years later, while commenting on a photograph of the aged head chief: "Chief Antonio Azul was my wihkol—a distant relative on my mother's side. . . . I remember him as a very old wise man . . . but I have been told that in his youth he was a fiery and handsome example of Pima manhood."[72] Azul's influence over the Gila River is important context for understanding the world in which Komal Hok grew and aged, for Azul symbolizes Akimel O'odham resistance to the abuses heaped upon the hehemajkam struggling to endure the reservation system. Every time Komal Hok shared his knowledge with other O'odham, he was a part of the same resistance that Azul led as headman.

Because Komal Hok did not know English, the kind of resistance his work embodies requires a trustworthy translator. Jose Lewis Brennan (d. 1916), a Tohono O'dham who was noted as one of Russell's five translators in Sacaton, is especially notable in this regard. About Brennan, Russell informed his reader:

---

*   O'obga is plural, obga is singular.

The principal interpreter, who was employed by the month during the entire period of the writer's stay, was José Lewis [Brennan], a Papago [Tohono O'dham] who had lived from childhood among the Pimas. He had once been engaged by the Bureau of American Ethnology to write a vocabulary of his own language and to supply other information, so that he was acquainted with the phonetic alphabet and other approved methods of procedure. He was engaged in linguistic work the greater part of the time.[73]

Donald M. Bahr added an appraisal of Brennan's contribution as a linguist, observing that the "oldest known Pima-English text of ritual oratory was written by a Papago, Jose* Lewis Brennan, in 1897. It is a salt oration."[74] In regard to Brennan's work with Russell, Bahr further observes: "Brennan transcribed and translated the richest collection of Piman oratory ever made. In published form it runs for 50 pages and comprises ten different texts. Brennan also did the 56 pages of songs in the same volume."[75] Bahr then commends Brennan's impressive skills: "It is to Brennan's lasting credit that working simply with pencil and paper *he transformed Thin Leather's wholly oral product into the medium of writing.*[76] Extraordinary patience and good will must have existed between the two men, plus translating genius on Brennan's part" (my emphasis).[77] Tohono O'dham linguist and poet Ofelia Zepeda said of her intellectual ancestor: "Perhaps the earliest Piman [O'odham] person to write extensively in his native language was the Papago [Tohono O'odham], Jose Lewis (also known as Jose Lewis Brennan), who, among a variety of noteworthy accomplishments, set down in writing the bulk of the Pima textual material in Frank Russell's *The Pima Indians.* . . . This impressive work remains an extremely important source of linguistic and ethnographic data."[78]

One can argue cogently that Brennan and Komal Hok are the origin of O'odham literature, such that the present discourse would not exist if not for the work of these two O'odham. Adding urgency to Zepeda's assessment of Brennan's legacy is Bernard L. Fontana's observation sixty years earlier (1959) that "with the exception of the field notes of W. G. McGee [sic] for

---

*　　Historical records alternate between José and Jose. What is not known is Brennan's preferred spelling.

1894–1895 . . . few anthropologists wrote about the Papago Indians in detail until the 20th century."[79] Consequently it has taken generations for the O'odham intellectual tradition, in which Komal Hok sits at the pinnacle, to emerge as a discrete part of O'odham history.

In the decades since Fontana made his observation, much has transpired in terms of expanding his original bibliography. In 1959 one had to rely mostly on Frances Densmore and Ruth M. Underhill for Tohono O'odham ethnographies, such as *Papago Music* (1929) and *The Autobiography of a Papago Woman* (1936). Akimel O'odham studies as of 1959 were even more modest. Instead, "Hohokam" archaeology, which was largely centered in the Gila and Salt River valleys, overshadowed studies of historic and contemporary Akimel O'odham culture. Significantly, George Webb published *A Pima Remembers* in 1959, one of the University of Arizona Press's first publications. Since 1959, O'odham studies has grown. With respect to Akimel O'odham, Bahr contributed the most, publishing *Piman Shamanism and Staying Sickness (Ká:cim Múmkidag)* (1975), *Pima and Papago Ritual Oratory: A Study of Three Texts* (1975), and *Rainhouse and Ocean: Speeches for the Papago Year* (1979), among other works. Bahr's work necessarily overlapped with Underhill's work, as well as embraced the ongoing work in Hohokam archaeology. As for Thin Leather, he appears in *The Short, Swift Time of Gods on Earth: The Hohokam Chronicles*. As expected, Brennan's translations are a driving force in Bahr's body of works.

Russell's allusions to Komal Hok throughout *The Pima Indians* create a fragmented but fascinating picture, complemented by photographs,[80] of the revered storyteller. Thin Leather (born ca. 1827) was approximately seventy-five at the time of Russell's field work and became an adult well before the 1859 reservation, making him a part of a generation that knew the O'odham jeved prior to the time of famine.[81] The two photos show an elderly man from the chest up wearing a jacket and shirt of the era, complete with a neckerchief tied around the collar. White-haired with a flew flecks of black, Komal Hok's face is sagacious, alert, and pensive, as if pondering the strange ethnographic practice in which he has been asked to partake. Indirectly it becomes apparent that Thin Leather may have been more than a storyteller, but also a mahkai or medicine maker.

> Among the most important of the sacred objects in the paraphernalia of the medicine-men were the â'mîna, or medicine sticks [prayersticks]. They were usually of arrowwood; always bound

together with cotton twine of native spinning, either with or without feathers attached to each separate stick. There are six â'mîna bundles in the collection. One was made by Kâ'mâl tkâk [Komal Hok], to be used exclusively in the exorcism [healing] of the Tcu'nyîm, a spirit of disease. The bundle contains four groups of sticks: Two pairs, a bundle of 4, and one of 6. All are plain, being unmarked in any way.[82]

In addition to the medical arts, Komal Hok demonstrated practical crafts, such as cotton weaving, which, as to the Hopi, is generally a male occupation. With respect to Thin Leather's loom-making expertise, Russell noted that O'odham weaving "is dying with the passing of the older generation."[83] The import of this statement is twofold. First, Russell's reference to a "dying" art emphasizes the value of Komal Hok's knowledge. Second, Russell's ethnographic work is validated as an example of salvage anthropology, the purpose of which was to preserve dying cultures.

Symptomatic of O'odham weaving as an endangered art is the difficulty with which enough "Pima cotton" was procured for a demonstration on Komal Hok's model loom. During 1901 and 1902, the phenomenon of "Pima cotton" was a hybrid, an experiment, engineered by the Bureau of Plant Industry at Sacaton Village. "This loom," Russell notes, "made by the writer's old friend Kâ'mâl tkâk [Thin Leather] . . . could not spin and had to engage a woman to do that portion of the work."[84] Nevertheless, "[Komal Hok] succeeded in finishing the spinning before the writer had an opportunity to witness the process."[85] All items collected during Russell's fieldwork were eventually accessioned to the Smithsonian.[86]

Russell also credits Komal Hok with the O'odham names for the twelve-month calendar, which is different from the one provided by Azul. Russell explained that the "moons" are of "recent origin." By which Russell meant that the Gregorian calendar, which arrived with the jujkam and the spread of the Jesuit missions, was further normalized under US Office of Indian Affairs. Once again, Russell may have been underestimating the O'odham intellect. Akimel O'odham were of course aware of the phases of the moon and the changing desert seasons. Nonetheless, Russell asserts, "Not many [O'odham] have any names for them and these do not agree even in the same village."[87] What Russell did not consider was whether differing calendars represented regional or clan differences within the O'odham jeved, in which each village or village groups maintained endemic oral traditions and customs. Just because Thin Leather and Azul were living in Sacaton at the time of Russell's fieldwork did not mean that their respective knowledge came from the same source. Having said that, Russell recounted an illuminating legend about counting the moons, mamshath kuintakud: "It is said that when Elder Brother was leaving Pimería for the last time he told the people to count the tail feathers of the little bird, Gisap, [verdin] which are twelve in number, and that they should divide the year into that number of parts. He gave them names for these parts, except for the coldest and the hottest months."[88] The coldest and hottest months correspond to the rainy seasons, the most important of which is the monsoon season during July through September, when the rain ceremony, the jujkida, was performed. Another ceremony was performed during the winter.

Russell's references to the rain-making ceremony are all too brief, which may be symptomatic of both a water crisis and an oppressive Indian Office, which frowned upon non-Christian religion on the reservation. What endured was knowledge of ancestral villages, which were organized around the akimel, their river: "During the early part of the nineteenth century there were eight Pima [Akimel O'odham] villages on the Gila, according to statements made by Kâ'mâl tkâk [Thin Leather] and other old men of the tribe."[89]

> 1. Petâ'îkuk, Where the Petai (ash tree?) stands, 2. Tcupatäk, Mortar Stone, 3. Tcu'wutukawutûk, Earth Hill, 4. Os Kâ'kûmûk Tco'tcikäm, Arrow-bush Standing, 5. Ko'-okûp Van'sîk, Medicine Paraphernalia, 6. Ko'mît, Back, 7. Tco'ûtîk Wu'tîk, Charcoal Laying, 8 and 9. Akûcîny, Creek Mouth. One 5 miles west of Picacho Peak and another southwest of Maricopa station. Both depend upon flood waters.[90]

Russell also noted three Maricopa (Piipaash) villages, Hi'nâmâ, Hina Head, and Tco'ûtcîk Wu'tcîk. More specifically, Piipaash lived below Gila Crossing Village, while the "Hi'nâmâ [Xalchidom] people reside on the south bank of the Salt, east of the Mormon settlement of Lehi."[91] Akimel O'odham villages, on the other hand, "were principally upon the south bank of the [Gila] river, along which they extended a distance of about 30 miles. Some have been abandoned; in other cases the name has been retained, but the site has been moved."[92]

In *The Pima Indians*, the origin narrative, "TcÇ-Ûnnyikita [Tcu-unnyikita]," or "smoke talk,"[93] takes up roughly twenty-four pages before switching to a section on Coyote. According to Lloyd in *Aw-aw-tam Indian Nights*, Komal Hok "began by saying that these were the stories he used to hear his father tell, they being handed down from father to son, and that when he was little he did not pay much attention, but when he grew older he determined to learn them and asked his father to teach him, which his father did. And now he knew them all."[94] What Komal Hok recounted was the moral corruption around Elder brother, which was caused by the sisivani in the big houses, who believed they needed to kill their teacher and protector. So the sisivani turned to one of the survivors of the flood, Vulture (Nuwi), who "told the sun [tash] to spit on the house of Elder brother [I'itoi ki]," which is in Komadk do'ag (Grassy plains mountain),[95] in addition to spitting "on the four pools of water at the va'akî [old house] where Elder Brother kept his magic power, on his dwelling places so that heat might fall upon him and smother him."[96] Nuwi's instructions worked and Elder brother died. But who was Nuwi, such that he had the power to kill a sacred being?

> Vulture [Nuwi] was a man who transformed himself into a bird with his own magic power and had gone through the openings in the sky and thus saved himself from destruction during the flood. After he came down from the sky he wandered about the country and finally built a va'-âki, magic house, the ruins of which yet remain, south of where Phoenix now stands, between the Gila and Salt rivers.[97]

Thin Leather's knowledge of medicine and songs completed Russell's portrait of the revered elder. More specifically, Komal Hok was a "medicine man's assistant,"* a distinction that appeared during a discussion about a

---

*　　　Likely a reflection of Komal Hok's advanced age and growing frailty.

treatment for an "evil spirit" called â'mîna, which is a "disease of the throat which causes the victim to lose flesh."[98]

> The treatment consists in placing â'mîna [prayer sticks] in an olla of water to soak while the doctor [i.e., mahkai or medicine maker] or his assistant blows through a tube, called the tcunyîm cigarette, upon the forehead, chin, breast, and stomach of the patient. The tube has a bunch of feathers attached called a-an kiatûta, and these are next swept in quick passes downward over the body. The â'mîna are then taken and sucked four times by the patient, after which the end of the bundle is pressed against the patient's body, then laid flat upon his breast and rubbed. Finally, the assistant repeats the speech of Siu'u [Elder brother] at the time when that deity restored himself to life [after being killed according to Nuwi's instructions], at the same time making passes toward the patient.[99]

The three songs that Thin Leather sang consisted of a song in which "Earth Magician," or Jeved mahkai, "shapes this world."[100] Jeved mahkai, or "Earth medicine maker," figured prominently in Komal Hok's narrative. Brennan's translation mimicked biblical language:

> *In the beginning* there was nothing where now are earth, sun, moon, stars, and all that we see. Ages long the darkness was gathering, until it formed a great mass in which developed the spirit of Earth Doctor [Jeved mahkai], who, like the fluffy wisp of cotton that floats upon the wind, drifted to and fro without support of place to fix himself.[101]

Earth medicine maker then created the shegoi (creosote bush), which was implanted in the freshly made earth that Jeved mahkai molded from the muhadag (grease) from their chest (bahsho).[102] Jeved mahkai "flattened [this] into a cake."[103] Upon bringing forth "some kind of plant," the creosote bush, Jeved mahkai stood the shegoi three times on the freshly formed jeved, only to see it topple after each attempt. On the fourth try, the shegoi remained standing, as one sees it today. Jeved mahkai then sang in celebration. Brennan's translation genders Jeved mahkai in a way that was typical for the times in which he lived; moreover, the translation evinces a penchant in anthropology to treat Indigenous origin narratives like children's fables:

> Earth Magician [Jeved mahkai] shapes this world.
> Behold what he [sic] can do!
> Round and smooth he molds it.
> Behold what he can do!
>
> Earth Magician makes the mountains.
> Heed what he has to say!
> He it is that makes the mesas.
> Heed what he has to say.
>
> Earth Magician shapes this world;
> Earth Magician makes its mountains;
> Makes all larger, larger, larger.
> Into the earth the magician glances;
> Into its mountains he may see.[104]

Komal Hok also sung about rain and corn, which were likely ceremonial songs. Unfortunately, the explanation for how these songs were performed was not included. Nevertheless the rain song retains its power to evoke a sense of the extraordinary, even without naming or mentioning a sacred being. Instead the song conjures a vision of a healthy field of corn, or huun, swaying and rustling in the wind as evening approaches, which is an extraordinary image given the perilous times in which Akimel O'odham were forced to live. The song climaxed with the refrain:

> Hi-iya naiho-o! The earth is rumbling.
> From the beating of our basket drums.
> The earth is rumbling from the beating
> Of our basket drums, everywhere humming.
> Earth is rumbling, everywhere raining.[105]

The rain ceremony, or Tcutc kita (jujkida), which means to "make rain,"[106] is performed when "one of the leading men who understands the ceremony" notifies "the medicine-men, the orator or reciter, and the singer."[107] The ceremony commences with the recitation of a speech recounting when "the earth was new" and "it was shaking and rough."[108] The song calms the trembling earth, restoring the balance. In Brennan's translation the speech is recited in the first person and the present tense; moreover, the narration recalls journeys to the four directions: to Black mocking bird in the west, Blue mocking bird in the south, White mocking bird in the east, then "above me enveloped in darkness lived the magician Kuvîk [Kudvik, curved-bill thrasher]," whom one can only suppose lives to the north.[109] Both the mockingbird (shuug) and thrasher (kudvik) are songbirds, not to mention quite intelligent. What was sought at each of the four directions were "commands to control the hills, mountains, trees, everything."[110] After visiting the three mockingbirds, the seeker observed after seeing Kudvik that the "earth became much quieter, but still moved somewhat."[111]

With more work to do, the seeker then spots Grey spider (Komagĭ tokdoḍ), a "wise man," who further stabilizes the earth by sewing bundles of sticks along "the edges of the land."[112] Komagĭ tokdoḍ then proceeded to envelope the land with the powers of the three houses, which stand at three of the four cardinal directions, where dwell three different rain powers whose medicines are colored black for west, blue for south, and white for east. Kudvik, of course, lives in the north, but his home was not part of Grey spider's work. Black measuring worm (ohchwigi, inchworm) and Blue gopher (cevo) assist the seeker at completing his/her task—making the land hospitable for the people. Black measuring worm aligns the poles around which Blue gopher will cover the frame with brush, something like the "willow ki" that Russell belittled earlier. Unexpectedly, snow (gev) begins to dust the ground. Since O'odham do not have a migration legend, as do the Hopi, Zuni, and Navajo, one can only assume that the ceremonial speech is referring to a rare occurrence of snow in the Akimel O'odham jeved as opposed to a place beyond the Gila River valley. Upon lighting a ritual cigarette, an unnamed figure blows smoke in an arch towards the east. Grass (washai) appears. The speech concludes with the fruition that was brought by the medicine that the seeker gathered.

Scattering seed, he [the seeker] caused the corn with the large
stalk, large leaf, full tassel, good ears to grow and ripen. Then
he took it and stored it away. As the sun's rays extend to the
plants, so our thoughts reached out to the time when we would
enjoy the life-giving corn. With gladness we cooked and ate the
corn and, free from hunger and want, were happy. Your worthy
sons and daughters, knowing nothing of the starvation periods,
have been happy. The old men and the old women will have their
lives prolonged yet day after day by the possession of corn.[113]

During a time of famine, this speech supplicating rain is medicine
for the people's spirit. The corn song in turn evokes Elder brother, who blew
winds over Ta-atûkam, Picacho Peak, driving "the clouds with their loud
thundering."[114] In the end the rain (juhk) arrives, answering the people's
prayers, and the people then sing and rejoice.

One may wonder if Komal Hok and other O'odham who participated
in Russell's research sang and rejoiced when their knowledge and stories
appeared in print. One wonders if any of them ever saw the finished work. In
The Pima Indians, O'odham were respected yet were hardly treated as equals.
Komal Hok and his peers likely did not fully comprehend the purpose driving
Russell's field work in Sacaton. Mimilgahn tended to do strange things. Did
any O'odham confront Russell with difficult questions, and did Russell take
them seriously? Did O'odham refuse to accommodate Russell at any point?
We will more than likely never know. We do not even know from Russell's
final report what he told his collaborators about his work. What one cannot
doubt is the expertise with which Komal Hok understood the stories and
traditions he relayed and the O'odham himdag, which gave his knowledge
its meaning and value.

Should one give any credit to Russell? He is after all a colonizer.
Although Russell did not coerce any O'odham into cooperating with his
research, he nonetheless went into Sacaton based on salvaging what he could
of O'odham culture before it faded into history. In other words, Russell's
project documented what happened to Akimel O'odham, whose demise would
be as profound as the "Hohokam." Or so went the anthropological legend.
Only this time, it was the US Army that rolled over the Akimel O'odham

jeved, not I'itoi. In the absence of any testimony from Thin Leather and other collaborators, one can only speculate about their motivations. Did they feel they had a choice? Were they hoping for compensation? How did they feel about the times in which they lived? Did they believe, as did the Bureau of American Ethnology, that pre-reservation Indigenous cultures were on the threshold of extinction?

Perhaps sharing stories and traditions with Russell, Fewkes, and Lloyd was comparable to I'itoi, Elder brother, jumping into his olla when a flood swept everything away. During that time before time, I'itoi sang songs for safety and well-being as the waters tossed about his clay vessel. When the flood waters subsided, I'itoi emerged atop Chuk do'ag, Black mountain, in what became the heart of the Hia-Ced O'odham jeved, singing:

> Here I come forth! Here I come forth!
> With magic powers I emerge.
> Here I come forth! Here I come forth!
> With magic powers I emerge.
>
> I stand alone! Alone!
> Who will accompany me?
> My staff and my crystal
> They shall abide with me.[115]

I'itoi emerged into a rejuvenated land and environment cleansed of the first people's deprivations. Nonetheless he brought his medicine making power with him, which included teachings that would form the foundation for the O'odham himdag, which he would give to all hehemajkam. Similarly the books into which Komal Hok placed these oral traditions are another kind of olla. Whereas the original flood cleansed the land, leaving I'itoi alone to recreate the jeved and its people; in Komal Hok's time the flood is made of mimilgahn, which has tried to wash away the himdag, leaving Komal Hok alone to try and preserve O'odham teachings. Only time will tell if, with the aid of Komal Hok's legacy, I'itoi can recreate the jeved and its people again. In *A Pima Remembers* Webb said with genuine concern for future generations of Akimel O'odham:

I don't think that they [the legends] should be forgotten. They are a part of Pima tradition. They show what life was like in those old days and what bothered people such as floods and drought and old Ho'ok's bad manners. They show what our ancestors thought was important. They help us to understand what is important today.[116]

Then, in *A Pima Past*, Anna Moore Shaw made this appeal to O'odham consciousness:

The time has come to take pride in our Indian blood and our precious heritage. Our ancestors were not wild savages but a very religious people with a rich and varied culture . . . But beyond our material culture we have our precious values, philosophies, artifacts, legends, songs, and dances to contribute to the world. Again I have the temerity to repeat: the first step for every Indian is the attainment of pride—a pride in himself and his wonderful heritage from the past.[117]

The book in hand is the author's sincere effort at bringing Webb and Shaw's aspirations into the current generation, to share with hehemajkam, my relatives, who still take pride in themselves as O'odham and who still want to know what our ancestors learned from their ancestors.

Casa Grande Is Not a Ruin

Huhugam Narratives as a Living Part of the Land

s recounted in the previous chapter, not long after Komal Hok availed his expertise to Russell (and the Smithsonian Institution), the learned storyteller played a role in Jesse Walter Fewkes's Bureau of American Ethnology (BAE) report on the excavations of the ge'e kih (the big house) southeast of Blackwater Village, on the south bank of the akimel the Gila River. The archaeological record named this place Casa Grande Ruins. Padre Kino, in fact, is credited with baptizing this place with its historic name:

> Por noviembre de 1694 entré con mis sirvientes y algunas Justisias desta Pimeria hasta la Casa Grande, que assi le llaman estos Pimas, y es el rio caudaloso de Hila, que sale desde el Nuevo México, y tiene su origen cerca de Acoma.[1]

> In November, 1694, I went inland with my servants and some justices of this Pimeria, as far as the casa grande, as these Pimas call it, which is on the large River of Hila that flows out of Nuevo Mexico and has its source near Acoma.[2]

Fewkes visited this site over two winters, 1906–1907 and 1907–1908. Although Adolph Bandelier preceded Fewkes in visiting the site, it was Fewkes, as an American archaeologist, who set the stage for subsequent research. Although Bandelier was the first to use the term "Hohokam," which he wrote as "ho-hoc-om," in his journal, dated June 23, 1883, it was Fewkes who elevated the concept into the scholarly literature. Thin Leather was part of Fewkes's inaugural work in "Hohokam" archaeology. In this epoch-shifting moment in Akimel O'odham history, "Hohokam" developed into a term of art sourced from the excavation of the ge'egdaj kikih (big houses), not just at Casa Grande Ruins but everywhere such "ruins" were located. Consequently, Komal Hok witnessed the appropriation of O'odham oral history into the work of Bandelier, Russell, and Fewkes. Because of Komal Hok, the Akimel O'odham origin narrative affirmed how O'odham comprehended their origins, even as milgahn archaeologists debated their "discoveries."[3]

Archaeologists, beginning with Fewkes, limited their discourses to analyses of artifacts, ruins, and remains instead of referencing I'itoi. Particular attention was paid to architectural remnants, pottery shards, utensils, and canals. In this context "Hohokam" was defined by the evident decline of the big house society. Over time the Hohokam was regarded as a distinct civilization whose rise and fall were divided into discrete periods and whose historic people may or may not be related to descendant O'odham communities. Never mind that Komal Hok clearly stated that the shohshon (ancestors) that lived in the big house villages spoke O'odham neok. On the contrary, archaeologists even went so far as to portray "Pimas," based on anecdotal evidence, as knowing little of any significance. Fewkes noted: "Throughout this region [the Gila River valley] existed minor divisions of a common stock. The Pima name Hohokam may be adopted to designate this ancestral stock, to whom may be ascribed the erection of the casas grandes [big houses] on the Gila."[4] Although Fewkes did not reject outright the preposition that the "Hohokam" were ancestral O'odham, as a "scientist" he left room for skepticism about O'odham oral tradition. Whereas O'odham would never question the teachings of the origin narrative, which had been handed down for generations, Fewkes trusted only what his methods and theories told him was correct.

Thin Leather, in his subaltern role as "informant," recalled stories about the huhugam big house near Florence, Arizona, which belonged to a culture that for Fewkes was filled with mystery. Fewkes said of the aged but formidable knowledge keeper:

> The following existing Pima legends relating to Morning Green, chief of Casa Grande, were collected from Thin Leather (Ka-maltkak), an old Pima regarded as one of the best informed story-tellers of the tribe. Some of his legends repeat statements

identical with those told to Father Font, 137 years ago, a fact which proves apparently that they have been but little changed by intervening generations. . . . The following stories supplement published legends of this chief and other ancients and shed light on the condition of early society in the settlement over which Morning Green is said to have ruled.[5]

In "Casa Grande, Arizona," Thin Leather is credited with telling "How a Chief of Another 'Great House' Enticed the Women from Casa Grande" and "How Turquoises Were Obtained from Chief Morning Green."[6] Four additional legends follow, but it is unclear whether they are attributed to Thin Leather. These are "How Morning Green Lost His Power Over the Wind Gods and the Rain Gods," "The Birth of Hok," "A Creation Legend," and "A Flood Legend." Given these stories are similar to the ones in Russell and Lloyd's work, it is probable that Komal Hok was the source of all six narratives.

An unexpected insight into Komal Hok's character appears when Fewkes shared an anecdote about Thin Leather. As Fewkes tells it: "Thin Leather slept for several weeks in the west room of the [Casa Grande] ruin. The hooting of the owls which nest in the upper walls may add to the Pimas' dread of [being near the ruins], but did not seem to disturb him."[7] Fewkes found Thin Leather's attitude fascinating because among other O'odham they "had a superstitious fear of Casa Grande which at times led them to avoid it, especially at night, and many do not now willingly sleep or camp near this remarkable monument of antiquity."[8] The so-called "superstitious" attitude is common among Indigenous peoples across the Southwest regarding ancestral sites. The Diné (Navajo), for example, are taught to respect the ruins located throughout their reservation, such as in Canyon de Chelly. Customarily, they prohibit either visiting the sites or taking pottery shards and artifacts from where they are found.[9] In the case of ancestral places along the akimel, the Gila River, these vahkih* (ancient houses) were the eternal homes of huhugam that ought to be respected, just as peoples with cemeteries are expected to respect their loved ones' final resting places. With respect to Komal Hok, one can only speculate why he did what he did at Casa Grande.

---

*   Vahkih is singular, Vapakih is plural.

Did he regard Fewkes as brave or foolish? If brave, then perhaps Komal Hok wanted to match his courage. If foolish, then perhaps Komal Hok thought that huhugam would throw their gewkdag (strength) at the milghan, not him. What Fewkes likely did not notice was if Komal Hok did anything to protect himself. On the other hand, perhaps Thin Leather thought that the white men had violated the sanctity of this place so much, the power of the ancestral respect relation between huhugam and hehehmajkam was broken.

As a man of his times, Thin Leather was comparable to Sala Hina, whom Russell described as "an earnest Christian," who "had no scruples about relating all that she knew concerning the religious beliefs of the tribe." Hina's knowledge was as copious as Thin Leather's. Meaningfully, Russell noted that Hina had "undergone a long and exacting training in practical botany which rendered her a valuable assistant in gathering information concerning the economic plants of the region." Was she a mahkai? Russell did not say. What is made clear is that Hina "inherited through her father some of the Kwahadt potters' skills, which enabled her to impart valuable knowledge of the art to furnish specimens."[10] Similar to Thin Leather, Russell made references to Hina throughout *The Pima Indians*, including her knowledge of cattle, basketry, sieve-making, pottery, intermarriage, and medicine people. Fewkes, in turn, pointed out Hina's participation at the Casa Grande excavation: "At the present day Sala (Sarah) Hina, of Kwahadt ancestry, is regarded as the most expert Pima potter. She spent considerable time at Casa Grande while the excavations were in progress and copied many designs."[11]

When J. William Lloyd (1857–1940) published *Aw-aw-tam Indian Nights* in 1911, he felt fortunate to have met and worked with Thin Leather, who, in a photograph in the frontispiece, looked frailer than when he posed for Russell. Nonetheless, Lloyd portrayed Thin Leather as the last of his kind: "Comalk-Hawk-Kih, or Thin Buckskin, who was a see-nee-yaw-kum, or professional traditionalist, who knew all the ancient stories, *but who had no successor*, and with whose death the stories would disappear" (my emphasis).[12] In the course of a single summer in 1903, Thin Leather, in collaboration with Lloyd and Edward Hubert Wood, produced nineteen separate stories, beginning with "The Story of Creation," for a volume extending to 241 pages. One of the legends, "The Story of Corn and Tobacco," Lloyd read "before the Anthropological Society of Philadelphia, May 11, 1904."[13] As for the accuracy of the stories translated, Wood is identified as a "full-blooded Pima, educated at Albuquerque, New Mexico."[14] Wood's legacy, while not nearly as distinguished as Brennan's, appears in Amadeo M. Rea's *Wings in the Desert: A Folk Ornithology of the Northern Pimans* (2007).

> *To my knowledge, no creation storytellers survive today.* Only a few of the oldest Indians told me about sitting up in their younger days during the longest winter nights to hear the episodes. . . . Fortunately, a number of documentary sources, published or in manuscript, exist that preserve parts or all of the Origin Story. . . .

> In the midsummer of 1903, J. William Lloyd of New Jersey and Pima educator Edward H. Wood rendezvoused in the vicinity of Sacaton on the Gila River Reservation. The objective was a team project: the elderly storyteller Komal Hoği, Thin Leather or Buckskin, a monolingual Pima, began narrating the Creation Story, which bilingual Wood translated, while Lloyd recorded everything by pencil in English, as faithfully as possible, except for a few passages of "almost Biblical plainness of speech on family matters . . . expurgated . . . for prudish Caucasian ears.[15] (my emphasis)

In addition to *Aw-aw-tum Indian Nights*, Lloyd published *The Scripture of the Serene Life* (1900), *Dawn-Thought on the Reconciliation: A Volume of Pantheistic Impressions and Glimpses of Larger Religion* (1900), and *The Natural Man: A Romance of the Golden Age* (1902).[16] How Lloyd came to learn of Komal Hok, let alone convince him to commit to sharing his knowledge, is unknown. Did Lloyd, like Russell, contact the superintendent of the Pima Agency? In "Auto-Biographical Essay by J. Wm Lloyd" (1940), a brief but interesting account of Lloyd's work in Arizona is recounted, curiously, without mentioning either Thin Leather or Edward Hubert Wood.

> Back in 1903 . . . I had gone out to the Pima Indians of Arizona, on the invitation of one tribe to get their wonderful old legends, living with them, as one of them, and building these stories into

my "Am-Am-Tam Indian Nights" [sic] and some of the experience into "The Songs of the Desert"; on my return visiting the Grand Canyon of the Colorado and the Petrified Forest at Adama; La Veta and Denver, Colorado, Pike's Peak and the Garden of the Gods.[17]

Given that it was nearly thirty years since publishing *Aw-aw-tum Indian Nights*, one cannot dismiss the possibility of faulty memory; still, it is disappointing that Lloyd did not remember "Thin Buckskin," who shared so much of his knowledge with him. Sadly, once Lloyd took from his "Pima Indian" what he wanted—material for his publication—it was likely easy for Lloyd to forget the two O'odham men he left behind. History, however, seems to have forgotten Lloyd. Thin Leather's copious knowledge of Akimel O'odham teachings, however, is prominently displayed.

In "The Story of Vandaih, the Man-Eagle," Komal Hok provided an extensive account of the ritual customs employed when an O'dham prevails over an obga, killing him. "Even tho the act itself was most valiant and praiseworthy, [one] must be expiated by an elaborate process of purification. From old Comalk Hawk Kih [Thin Leather] I got a careful description of the process."[18] Then in "The Story of Wayhohm, Toehahvs and Tottai," the O'odham technique for fire-making is narrated with a demonstration. "But he [Thin Leather] was old and breathless, and 'Sparkling-Soft-Feather,' the mother of my interpreter, took [the two pieces of wood] and made the fire for me."[19] Thirdly, in "The Story of Ee-ee-toy's Army," Komal Hok explained how the Piipaash (Maricopas) came to live with their Akimel O'odham friends. Because of an ancient feud with the Quechan and Cocopah, the Piipash sought safety in the O'odham jeved.[20] Lastly, in "The Story of the Children of Cloud," Lloyd cites in his notes at the end of this story W. H. Emory, who led the 1857–1859 US-Mexico boundary survey commission,[21] in which "Thirsty Hawk, the Maricopa [Piipaash]," recounts a story about an extraordinarily beautiful woman who gave birth to a son, "who was the founder of a new race which built all these houses," meaning the ge'egdaj kikih.[22] Thin Leather, as an Akimel O'odham, naturally tells a different version of the woman's story. As Komal Hok tells it, the woman has Cevagi's (Cloud's) twins, not an only son, who moreover are not a "new race." Regarding Thirsty Hawk's story, Thin

Leather stated that he "knew nothing of any story of their children [meaning the twins' progeny] or of these buildings, the vahahkkees."[23] What he likely meant is that he knew nothing about the Piipaash oral tradition, as that was their story to tell, their teachings. Contravening Thin Leather nonetheless, Lloyd cites Joseph E. Johnston, who worked with Emory on the Boundary Commission, who claimed that another "Pima" told a story that corroborated Thirsty Hawk's. What Lloyd did not have was the cultural fluency to understand that each version of the story of Cloud is true to the extent that it narrates each people's understanding of their origins. If Lloyd had been more astute, he might have noticed that the Piipaash are acknowledged as friends to the Akimel O'odham well before the first canal was built. After all, the latter is in the origin narrative that Komal Hok shared with Russell.

To the Piipaash, the story of Kwe, or Cloud, teaches them their relationship with their Akimel O'odham friends, which is a relationship that goes back to the time of the ge'egdaj kikih (the big houses). Hence Thirsty Hawk's reference to the woman's son fathering the sisivani that founded these great villages. Symbolic of the Piipash's ancient kinship with their homelands along the Gila and Salt Rivers is their name for South Mountain. Whereas O'odham say "Muhadag do'ag," the Piipaash say "Vii kwxas." Both names mean Greasy mountain. Piipaash and Akimel O'odham nonetheless are distinct peoples, complete with different languages and oral traditions. As such, their diverging narratives about the woman who gave birth to Cloud's child(ren)—whether an only son (Piipaash) or twins (Akimel O'odham)—maintain their respective sense of peoplehood.

When Cloud (Cevagĭ) acknowledged his twin sons in Komal Hok's story, he sent them back to their mother, whom they yearned to see, with instructions that they should not speak to anyone along the way. When an unnamed man approached them, however, one brother thought they should ask about their mother. When the other reminded his twin of their father's instruction, the first assured his brother that asking for their mother must surely be an exception to their father's command. Unbeknown to the twins, their father was trailing them high overhead. Hearing his sons disobey him, Cevagĭ threw thunder and lightning at his disobedient children, turning them into century plants, also called "agave" in Spanish and English or "a'ud" in O'odham. [24] Another storyteller named Inasa is credited in *The Pima Indians* with yet another version of this narrative. In this recounting, the two boys encounter Bán (Coyote). Fearing Bán, the two boys tried avoiding him, but the trickster kept putting himself in their way. Cevagĭ came to his children's aid, this time punishing Coyote by assailing him with his fearful display of thunder and lightning.

> It was on the mountain top that the boys were halted by Coyote, and one stood on each side of the trail at the moment when they were transformed into the largest mescal that was ever known. The place was near Tucson.
>
> This is the reason why mescal yet grows on the mountains and why the thunder and lightning go from place to place— because the children did. This is why it rains when we go to gather mescal.[25]

What these stories teach is that it was sacred beings—Cevagĭ, his twin sons, and Bán—that established a relationship between hehemajkam and plant people, namely agave (a'ud) and mescal. A'ud is indigenous to Gagodk do'ag, the Superstition mountains, and Komadk do'ag, Estrella mountains. Inasa's story, moreover, tells of a place near Tucson, or Chuk son, which may be Ce:wi do'ag, the Huachuca Mountains, near Sierra Vista.[26] Places where one gathers plants is a common feature of sacred places.

When Komal Hok assisted Fewkes at Casa Grande, as observed earlier, he made a point of sleeping among the ruins, indicating that the O'odham himdag had undergone substantial permutations wrought by the American occupation. Since the 1854 Gadsden Purchase, waves of immigrants swept over everything, building their settlements and damming akimel, which led to the "time of famine" (bihugig). Despite having once been an important ally to the United States, an untold number of hehemajkam were now collateral damage to westward expansion. As for those who remembered how things were before, O'odham voices have been few and far between. Among the few to publish works in their own name are George Webb, Anna Moore Shaw, Alice Paul, James McCarthy,[27] Ofelia Zepeda, Barnaby Lewis, Martínez (the author of the book in hand), and, most recently, Fantasia Painter.[28] Complementing this list of published O'odham authors is an equally important list of O'odham who, like Komal Hok, availed their knowledge and wisdom to numerous papers and books dedicated to O'odham culture and history. Prominent among these are Maria Chona, who Ruth M. Underhill immortalized in *Papago Woman* (1936), and Frances Manuel, whose stories were brought together in *Desert Indian Woman: Stories and Dreams* (2001). Then there are the innumerable O'odham students like Ignacio, the boarding school student acknowledged in the previous chapter, who have written papers, theses, and dissertations. Defying the concern that Russell had of O'odham undergoing the boarding school experiment, generations of O'odham have proven the resiliency of their himdag in modern times.

When Russell contributed to the BAE's salvage anthropological enterprise on behalf of the Smithsonian, he documented O'odham suffering under the Indian Bureau. "Deprived of the rights inhering from centuries of residence," Russell marveled "that the starvation, despair, and dissipation . . . did not overwhelm the tribe."[29] Comparable crises occurred throughout the American West as territories turned into states and settlements turned into towns and cities, and the pressure on Indigenous water rights steadily rose.[30] Tragically, much damage was done before the US Supreme Court affirmed in 1908, in *Winters v. United States,* that tribes inhabiting the reservation system possessed reserved water rights, which antedated the prior appropriation system brought in with non-Indian settlement. In the words of the Supreme Court: "The government of the United States has the power to reserve waters of a river flowing through a territory and exempt them from appropriation under the laws of the state which that territory afterwards becomes." In sum, statehood does not affect the inherent right of tribes to sufficient waters to sustain that reservation.[31] Reserved water rights notwithstanding, Akimel O'odham, like every tribe in North America, were expected to vanish into the dust of history. In the Americas, excavations revealed countless remains and artifacts from the Moundbuilders to the Anasazi, making names for a bevy of diggers, such as Ephraim G. Squier,[32] Adolph Bandelier, Jesse Walter Fewkes, and Charles Di Peso.[33] In turn, Hohokam archaeology spawned major works accredited to Erich Schmidt, Harold and Winifred Gladwin, Emil Haury, Donald M. Bahr, and David Abbott.[34] Hidden in the thick of the mounting archaeological record, Komal Hok appears as barely more than a footnote. Then, again, it all depends on whose cultural perspective one privileges when recalling the story of the huhugam. O'odham have never felt obliged to justify their regard for their ancestral teachings.

Barnaby Lewis, the longtime tribal historic preservation officer for the Gila River Indian Community, argues that archaeological research has generated an archaeological fiction in which "Hohokam" signifies a category of "data" that archaeologists dug up at sites where "ruins and artifacts" are recorded in terms that are endemic to the archaeological sciences. Huhugam, to the contrary, is a kinship term.

> Huhugam does not literally mean "the things that are all used up." Huhugam specifically applies to past human life and not objects as in the generally accepted translation, "that which has perished" [citation omitted]. The term "that" [as opposed to "those whom have perished"] implies reference to an object, which is inaccurate and is not acceptable in the hearts and minds of the present-day O'odham.[35]

Archaeologists nevertheless defined "Hohokam" with a taxonomy of material culture that asserts that the "Hohokam" are a separate society that is distinguishable from other archaeological groups, such as the Anasazi, Mogollon, and Salado, that developed in the Gila River Valley in approximately 1–1450 CE. Hohokam civilization is further divided into three major periods, namely Pioneer/Formative, Colonial/Preclassic, and Classic. The Classic period, in turn, consists of four distinct eras within the years 1050–1450, during which the Hohokam civilization reached its apex, collapsed suddenly, then dispelled its population, leaving a void that the Akimel O'odham later filled. It was the Akimel O'odham whom a succession of Spanish and American explorers encountered during the late seventeenth through nineteenth centuries.[36]

Defined by linear time and the scientific method, archaeological analyses determined that Hohokam and Akimel O'odham were fundamentally different groups, divided historically and culturally, which instigated the "Hohokam-O'odham continuum." When Paul H. Ezell published "Is There a Hohokam-Pima Culture Continuum" (1963) in *American Antiquity*, he limited the debate to competing archaeological theories, which were strictly based on forensic evidence. Ethnographic reports on O'odham communities, in addition to Piipaash, are regarded as of limited value, as there are no corresponding ethnographies of the "Hohokam." Obviously, what O'odham had to say about their ancestors was discounted as irrelevant. As Ezell argued, "the body of [O'odham] tradition, legend, and mythology," may be disregarded from the scientific discourse, "because no way has been found to test the results of attempts to explain archaeological remains in the light of mythology and legend." Thus, Ezell stipulated unequivocally, "The folklore approach will not be considered here."[37] With a single archaeological blow, Ezell eliminated how O'odham, such as Komal Hok, explained their relationship with their huhugam and the big houses they built, not to mention their canals and the stories of what happened to drive people away. In the absence of O'odham narratives, Ezell surmised that the answer to the question of a Hohokam-Pima culture continuum depends solely on future archaeological research.

What Ezell did not acknowledge is that his disregard for O'odham oral history stems less from the scientific tradition and more from the Spanish colonial disposition of regarding Indigenous people as uncivilized. As Nentvig assessed the intellectual capacity of the Indigenous people inhabiting Sonora, namely "the Opata and the Pima":

> None of these nations has an alphabet, nor do they have any inclination to acquire one. . . . Thus, *without even the simplest forms of writing*, without even strings of beads or tallies which after a fashion were equivalent to writing to the Mexicans, Peruvians, and other nations, *the Sonoran tribes have no record of their past except the confused and inaccurate accounts which have been transmitted from father to son.* One can learn little from these. The Indian will relate only what he has seen and would give away his soul rather than reveal any secrets.[38] (my emphasis)

Ezell, were he still here, would likely be appalled at the accusation of racial bias. Yet considering that Ezell's dismissal of O'odham oral tradition is based on the skepticism of his predecessors—namely Fewkes and Russell (who cited Luis Velarde)—who dismissed O'odham for supposedly knowing nothing of the huhugam, then is this not bias?

Speaking of the Spanish tradition in the "New World," Ezell concludes with a reference to Henry F. Dobyns's work on the historic impact of the Spanish conquest of Tenochtitlan. Of particular interest here was the spread of disease that preceded the Spanish conquest and the latter's subsequent occupation of the lands stretching from the Valley of Mexico to the upper reaches of the Sonoran Desert.

> When we remember how soon after AD 1520 the Spaniards reached Baja California, sailed up the Colorado River, and marched through Sonora, the possibility arises that the new diseases got there ahead of them. The further possibility also exists that epidemics of new diseases contributed to sudden and marked culture changes, as a consequence of which the Hohokam culture pattern became no longer recognizable.[39]

In spite of compelling points of overlap between huhugam big house and Akimel O'odham olas kih material culture, namely ceramics, Ezell remained skeptical: "In short, although a Hohokam-Pima ceramic continuum seems to me the most probable explanation of parallels, the available ceramic evidence is not conclusive."[40] More than two generations later, Chris Loendorf published a 2017 paper in collaboration with Barnaby Lewis, also for *American Antiquity*, in which the authors affirmed that the debate continues. "Despite many decades of work, little consensus exists regarding what caused the Hohokam Collapse, and researchers still don't agree about the nature of the relationship between prehistoric and historic populations in the area."[41] Exacerbating the predicament for O'odham oral history in the scientific record is the notion that it is human nature to develop societies that over-tax the environment and create ecological upheaval. Ever since Paul Martin published "Africa and Pleistocene Overkill" (1966), in which Stone Age populations, including "paleo-Indians," perpetrated mass extinctions due to over-hunting and environmental degradation, has the theory of human destructiveness clouded opinion.[42]

The Ecological Indian (1999) is probably the most problematic work in the paleo-Indian overkill tradition. Shephard Krech III attempts to build on Paul Martin's thesis that "paleo-Indians" transformed the continents they inhabited as waves of primal migrants worked their way from the Bering Land Bridge to Tierra del Fuego, complete with instigating the extinction of an array of megafauna, such as the mastodon.[43] Moreover, remnants of this Indigenous Anthropocene, if you will, are evident in the oral traditions handed down into the present era. Among these are the "Hohokam," whom Krech regards in the archaeological terms defined by figures like Bandelier, Russell, Fewkes, Haury, and Ezell. Most importantly, Krech uncritically references sources that claim that O'odham do not know who built the ge'egdaj kikih, the big houses. In regard to which Krech asks, "Are the Akimel O'odham the descendants of the Hohokam? . . . In the last one hundred years, the Akimel O'odham themselves have lacked consensus on their relationship to the Hohokam."[44] Krech then summarizes the supposedly conflicting versions of the Akimel O'odham origin narrative. However, upon inspecting the citations, Krech relies solely on two dated sources: Adolph Bandelier's 1883–1884 survey of New Mexico, which included trips to the Gila River Indian Community, Tempe, and the Casa Grande Ruins; and, F. E. Grossman's 1871 field report for the Smithsonian Institution.[45] While both works are historically important in the history of O'odham studies and the discourse on Hohokam archaeology, these sources need to be read critically, taking into consideration the biases of the era in which they were written, the nineteenth century, and the positionality of the authors (Bandelier was a Lewis Henry Morgan-trained archaeologist; Grossman was a captain in the US Army). Krech's disregard for the historical context of his sources did not prevent him from disparaging the Akimel O'odham himdag. Under the pretense of criticizing Haury's portrayal of the "Hohokam" as "candidates for ecologically aware sainthood," Krech postulated to the contrary:

> Yet there can be no doubt that they [the Hohokam] cleared, irrigated, and cultivated fields, actions with consequences: fewer trees, more ragweed, a higher water table, possibly oversalinization [sic]. They also demanded wood for use in domestic consumption in a region where there was not much of it. . . . [Consequently] they might have deforested areas where there were few trees, as along the Gila River, especially during periods of prolonged drought.[46]

While Krech acknowledges that European and American colonization had a more devastating effect on the Gila and Salt River valleys than did their huhugam big house predecessors, it is of great concern for Krech that he dissuade anyone from regarding the huhugam big-house period as Edenic. In Krech's estimation, the impulse to romanticize huhugam big house culture is the conceit of modern man's desire for a utopian escape from the modern industrial world. "Each age," Krech reflects, "reads something different into the demise of the Hohokam." To illustrate his point, Krech makes another dated reference, this time to Frank Cushing, whose followers held an idyllic picture of the Hohokam.[47] At this juncture, one may wonder if Krech ever refers to Komal Hok. Krech fleetingly refers to the work that Thin Leather did for Fewkes and Russell. Thin Leather is noted as having affirmed to Fewkes that the people who built the Casa Grande Ruins were Akimel O'odham who spoke the Akimel O'odham neok. However, Krech rebuts this claim with Russell's observation in *The Pima Indians* that the Akimel O'odham "now frankly admit that they do not know anything about the matter." Krech ignores Komal Hok, of course, when he maintained that the huhugam who constructed the g'egdaj kikih were also Akimel O'odham and spoke their language. Comparable to Ezell, Krech did not feel obliged to take O'odham oral history seriously, especially those parts that contradicted his thesis.

Whenever Akimel O'odham are obliged to explain where the name "Pima" came from, they typically respond with a humorous anecdote about the Spanish asking either who they are or who built Casa Grande, to which they replied, "Pi 'añi mac" (I don't know). Hence, Pimas are the "I-don't-know people." Curiously, neither George Webb nor Anna Moore Shaw refer to this oral tradition in their books. Despite an admiring account of Jesuit missionary Padre Kino in *A Pima Past*, Shaw evades recounting how the "Pimas" got this name from the jujkam.

> In 1694 Father Eusebio Francisco Kino rode a dusty trail to visit the Big House. What a great surprise awaited Padre Kino! The Indians were nearly naked, wearing only breech cloths, and they had long hair and tattooed faces. The gentle padre asked them, "Who built the Casa Grande?"
>
> "Huhugam," the Pimas must have answered.[48]

Russell is credited with documenting the origin of the Spanish name for the Akimel O'odham. Or, at least, as close as one gets to the name's origin.

> The tribe known as the Pimas was so named by the Spaniards early in the history of the relations of the latter with them. The oldest reference to the name within the writer's knowledge is that by Verlarde.[49]

Russell is specifically referring to Luis Velarde's 1854 document *Descripcion del sitio, longitud y latitud de las naciones de la Pimería.* What is clear in Russell's citation is that the Spaniards were aware of what the Akimel O'odham called themselves. Velarde makes this clear at two points. First: "The Pima nation . . . call themselves Otama or in the plural Ohotoma." Second: "They call themselves Â'- â'tam, 'men' or 'the people,' and when they wish to distinguish themselves from the Papago and other divisions of the same linguistic stock they add the word â'kimûlt, 'river.' 'River people' is indeed an apt designation, as evidenced by their dependence on the Gila."[50] As for "Pima," Velarde does acknowledge that the word is derived from the O'odham neok, stating, "'the word pima is repeated by them to express negation.' This 'negacion' is expressed by such words as pia, 'none,' piatc, 'none remaining,' pimatc, 'I do not know' or 'I do not understand.'"[51] What neither Velarde nor Russell relate is the humorous anecdote told earlier, which is not to say that it is incorrect. What O'odham tell is likely how the story was handed down to this day, the consistency of which is evidence of its accuracy. As for the milgahn historical record, Kino is cited as the first to claim that the Casa Grande Ruins, and other huhugam ge'egdaj kikih, were built for "Montezuma."[52]

While Thin Leather was certain that huhugam spoke Akimel O'odham neok, what is not remembered is what sisivani, the priest chiefs who led the big houses, called themselves. Did they call themselves Akimel O'odham or another name in O'odham? Akimel O'odham social organization is village-based and consists of two major clans, Nuwi and Bán, developed after the collapse of the big houses. Those in the Nuwi clan descended from the original big house community, and those in Bán descended from the people who made up I'itoi's "army from the east." Both are O'odham.

However, these clans did not exist until after I'itoi had cleansed the jeved. If the huhugam called themselves something other than Akimel O'odham, there is no oral tradition about it. But how much did the milgahn archaeologists understand this when they began asking "who built Casa Grande?" How can "pi'añi mac" be an answer?

> The Pimas [Akimel O'odham] have long since grown accustomed to being interrogated concerning the builders of the great stone and adobe pueblos that now lie in ruins on the mesas of the Gila and Salt river valleys. However ready they may have been in the past to claim relationship with the Hohokam or relate tales of the supernatural origin of the pueblos, they now frankly admit that they do not know anything about the matter.[53]

More than others, Krech failed to consider that O'odham responses to inquiries about Sivan vahki were due to O'odham not wanting to answer milgahn questions anymore. After all, their minds appeared to be made up about them—from Fewkes to Krech and Loendorf—it was just a matter of digging up enough evidence.

As noted earlier, Kino initiated the custom of referring to huhugam as descendants of Montezuma. Pedro Font, despite being a Franciscan, did not hesitate to reinforce this doctrine:

> Determino el Sr Comandante que descansara oy la gente, y con esto tuvimos lugar de ir â registrar la casa grande que llaman de Moctezuma, situada â una legua del rio Gila y distante del parage de la Laguna, unas tres leguas al estsudeste, â donde fuimos acompañados de algunos Yndios y del Governador de Vturituc, quien en el camino nos contó una historia y tradicion que conservan de sus passados sobre dicha casa, que toda se reduce â patrañas mescladas confusamente con algunas verdades catolicas.[54]

> The commander decided that the people should rest today, and so we had an opportunity to go and examine the house that is called La Casa Grande de Moctezuma, situated one league

from the Río Gila and some three leagues to the east southeast of La Laguna. We were accompanied there by several Indians and by the governor of Uturituc, who told us on the way a tale and tradition regarding the house, handed down from their forefathers, all of which is nothing but fables mixed confusedly with truths of the catholic faith.[55]

When Kino wrote that Casa Grande belonged to the legendary Mexica leader, he used the phrase "dísese la dexaron," or "it is said," which evokes a folkloric origin, something that is common knowledge but that may lack a clear source, such as a text. Because O'odham neok is unwritten, it is of dubious historical accuracy. In other words, as Ezell might say, nonliterate folklore cannot be cross-referenced with written references. Ironically, what Kino and Font did not realize is that it was Spanish folklore that was suspect. O'odham say, as did Komal Hok, that ancestral O'odham built the ge'egdaj kikih, they spoke O'odham, and they are descendants of the first people that Jeved mahkai and Elder brother created.

Adolph Bandelier (1840–1914), as noted earlier, is credited with being the first American archaeologist to use the word "Hohokam."[56] On June 23, 1883, Bandelier recorded his visit to Casa Grande, where he spoke with unnamed Akimel O'odham. Desiderio Palma, "who speaks the Pima language perfectly," served as translator. On June 17, Bandelier equates I'itoi with Montezuma: "He [Montezuma/I'itoi] is represented as having been a great man, even the first man, and of having taught the Pima all they know." Nevertheless, as Bandelier learned from Palma, Akimel O'odham deny any knowledge about the people who dwelled in the ge'egdaj kikih. "Palma assured me that the Pima laid hardly any claim to these ruins; still they say that they were built by the people of Montezuma [I'itoi], and that when he returned, he found that these people had turned bad, whereupon he changed them into stones and destroyed the places."[57] Bandelier then notes the O'odham kinship terms for the huhugam. "The Ancients [Hohokam, huhugam] are called by them 'vi-pi-sets' great-grandparents (vi-cor, great grandmother) also 'ho-hoc-om' [Hohokam], the extinct ones ('ho-hoc,' cosa acabada)."[58] As for how O'odham remembered Bandelier, the ooshikbina for 1883 are sparse and make no reference to him or Palma.

1882–1883. Gila Crossing, Blackwater. An epidemic of measles prevailed among the Pimas and Maricopas, causing the death of many persons.

1883–1884. Gila Crossing. The Salt River Pimas went to a fiesta at Gila Crossing.

Blackwater. A drunken Pima while riding on a box car on the Southern Pacific was run over and killed.[59]

Obviously, what was important to O'odham was of no relevance to Bandelier. One may wonder if Bandelier met Komal Hok. Was the learned storyteller among the unnamed O'odham with whom Bandelier and Palma spoke? Possibly. As an archaeologist, Bandelier complemented the missionaries and Indian agents that were sent into the reservation system to transform Indigenous societies into American ones. None of them listened to what the Indians had to say about anything. Missionaries could not hear that Indians already had a religion. Indian agents could not hear that Indians already knew how to govern themselves. As for archaeologists, they could not hear that Indians already know their own history, which began with the first people recounted in their origin narrative. Because they did not listen, the missionaries thought the Indians were sinful, the Indian agents thought the Indians were like children, and the archaeologists thought that the Indians did not know about their ancient history. So O'odham just said "pi'añi mac" and let them all think what they wanted.

Privileging the Spanish invasion of the Sonoran Desert, Ezell emphasizes environmental phenomena, especially epidemics, when explaining the shift from "Hohokam" to "Pima" culture:

The differences between Hohokam and Pima cultures are just those which would follow a catastrophic reduction of population, attended by social and technological disorganization, with only a skeleton of the previous culture being retained. Assuming this to have been the case, it would seem that the Europeans reached the Pima country before Pima society had recovered from the disruption.[60]

If, as O'odham assert, the huhugam are their ancestors, then why did descendant O'odham not rebuild their civilization to its former grandeur? Even O'odham pottery to the archaeological eye seemed inferior to its "Hohokam" precursor. Obviously Akimel O'odham did not feel a sense of loss when the big houses collapsed. Perhaps the big houses represent a side to O'odham society that caused the big houses to fall. Answers can be found in the O'odham origin narrative and what I'itoi did during these times. However, the answers are not the kind that can be dug up like pottery shards in an excavation.

What Komal Hok shared with Frank Russell was less about the collapse of the "Hohokam" and more about the origins of the akimel, the river, and the hehemajkam, the people who spoke O'odham neok and for whom Jeved mahkai, Earth medicine maker, created these places, the O'odham jeved. From the first people (s*os*anac/j, s-totonigk, many ants) who perished in a flood, to the great houses that were swept away by I'itoi and the son:tal (army) he brought from the land below, to the people who returned from the ocean (ge'e shuthagi) to resettle the jeved and danced for rain, making the fields fertile once more. Variants of the origin narrative corresponded to the dialects, families, and villages that spread from the Akimel O'odham of the Gila and Salt River Valleys to the Sobaipuri O'odham along the Santa Cruz River, then eastward toward Texas Canyon, back across toward Baboquivari and the Tohono O'odham, then toward the Gulf of California and the Hia-Ced O'odham, then, finally, south to the mountains north of Hermosillo, Sonora, where the Pima Bajo dwell. Piipaash, who live north of the Gila River at Maricopa Village and at Lehi Village along the onk akimel, the Salt River, have their own origin narratives, which recall that they are related to the Mojaves, Cocopah, and Quechan along the Colorado River.

"Hohokam" is not a name but a kinship term. Huhug means someone, an O'dham (singular), who has passed on into the next world; huhugam means O'odham (plural) who have passed on generationally. Huhugam therefore are ancestral O'odham, meaning people who dwelled in the big houses and who resettled the jeved. In turn, the latter's descendants (Akimel O'odham) are people that juhkam and milgahn explorers, missionaries, soldiers, and migrants encountered when they passed through O'odham land.

> In the O'odham traditional view, Huhugam is used in referring to O'odham ancestors, identifying a person(s) from whom an individual(s) is a lineal descendant. The O'odham family tree is inclusive of all O'odham. This has been related not by one particular person, but has as its basis the Creation story that places the existence of life on earth from time immemorial.[61]

What matters most, at least to O'odham, is the kinship relation rather than the artifacts, such as pottery shards or the ruins such as Casa Grande. Just as there is a point at which one's lineal predecessors disappear into a mist of forgotten names and half-remembered stories, so too are entire communities distilled into memories of long-ago ages. As George Webb remarks in *A Pima Remembers*: "No one knows where they came from, or what became of them. I think, as all Pimas and Papagos do, that we are their descendants."[62] As for what remains of the big houses, Webb states in his version of the origin narrative: "The great house of Blue Hawk is still there as the great army of tribes left it, in ruins. It is called Casa Grande."[63] So these "ruins" are a monument to Elder brother's "army," who succeeded in cleansing the jeved. Among the Akimel and Tohono O'odham, as Webb explains, one can see Elder brother's legacy.

> In these two tribes there two clans. You can tell who belongs to one clan or the other by the way people speak to their parents. Those who refer to their father as *va'v* or *ma'm* belong to the Buzzard [Nuwi] Clan. Those who call their father *'apap* or *apki* you will know belong to the Coyote [Bán] Clan.[64]

Regarding which clan is descendant from I'itoi's army and which is from the big house people, Webb explains this in the way he recounts the fall of the big houses.

> The first village they [I'itoi's army] came to was near Blackwater. There, in a tall four-story adobe building lived a chief who was

called Blue Hawk. The great army of tribes camped outside the walls of Blue Hawk's big house, and their chiefs met how to conquer it.

They could not think of a way. So Old Man Coyote said that he would help them.[65]

As Komal Hok teaches, it was Buzzard (Nuwi) who taught the sisivani in the big houses how to kill I'itoi.

When O'odham recount their origins, there is an account of where the people of the big houses came from—they came from the akimel—and what became of them—they resettled the land as they returned to their river-valley homeland, with some choosing other lands either along the way or by continuing farther. For O'odham, there is no problem with the so-called Hohokam-O'odham Continuum. There is only an archaeologist's problem with O'odham history.

> The historic translation of Huhugam as recorded by ethnographers and archaeologists basically accepts an interpretation provided by O'odham informant(s) in 1908 [*The Pima Indians*]. The recorded translations that are attributed to the O'odham word Huhugam are incorrect. The limited knowledge of the English language on the part of the informant(s) [namely, Thin Leather] and the context of the conversations may account for the misleading interpretations.[66]

Anna Moore Shaw, in her 1974 book *A Pima Past*, respectfully acknowledges the archaeologists' timeline as the context in which she shares her knowledge about Akimel O'odham teachings. Shaw struggles nonetheless at reconciling the archaeological record with O'odham oral tradition. At one point, she awkwardly suggests that archaeologists—such as Haury, whose Snaketown excavation during the mid-1960s reshaped "Hohokam" archaeology—proffered the theory that huhugam and contemporary O'odham are related, or more specifically, that the Akimel and Tohono O'odham have a common ancestor, "whom the Pimas call *Huhugam* (Those Who Are Gone)."[67] In other words, Shaw affirmed in Haury's work what O'odham have always known, that huhugam are ancestral O'odham. Krech, of course, found Haury's validation of O'odham oral history to be naïve. As for Casa Grande Ruins, Shaw states matter-of-factly that they "were built sometime in the thirteenth century by a small ancient band called the Salado."[68] Yet in *Pima Indian Legends*, like other O'odham storytellers before her, Shaw says it was "See-van Vah-Ki," who foresaw the arrival of "Se-eh-ha" (I'itoi) and the downfall of the big houses, and that "the Aki-mal-Aatom (River People)," not the Salado, "lived in fear and anxiety" of I'itoi's return.[69]

So, in the end, where does all of the foregoing leave us with respect to O'odham teachings? I'itoi, huhugam, and ge'egdaj kikih are not archaeological concepts based on linear time and scientific theories of social decay or evolution. O'odham origin narratives are nonliterate expressions of a nonlinear conception of the jeved around them. O'odham narratives, moreover, are webs of stories radiating outward across generations of related people, held together by a common tradition of storytellers, such as Komal Hok, George Webb, and Anna Moore Shaw. Analyzing these narratives with scientific or positivist concepts only reduces these narratives to being little more than folklore or fairytales, in the diminutive sense of these terms.

In the end, the future is huhugam, not "Hohokam." As far as most O'odham are concerned, they already know all that they need or are meant to know about their ancestors, their huhugam, based on their oral traditions. Analyzing pottery shards or geological strata is a western scientific conceit, in which a people's privacy and the integrity of sacred places is sacrificed for the purpose of scientific inquiry and the presumptive right of non-Indigenous institutions to know about another people's ancestors. In contravention to the scientific agenda, the discourse on O'odham history must reaffirm the values that Komal Hok taught us through his storytelling.

In the meantime, as the Phoenix metropolitan area continues to grow and the stress on Arizona's water supply intensifies, the lessons that ancestral O'odham learned centuries ago may have to return to enlighten the current denizens of this desert. For what huhugam endured was a collapse in their sustainability as a large agrarian civilization. Perhaps the ancient canal builders over-taxed the river, grew their crops too large, and were unprepared for a prolonged drought, which led to panic and social strife. Perhaps I'itoi's "army" was less of a conquering army and more of a rebellion. Perhaps, like the Tower of Babel, the big houses reached too high, as the leaders cared more about their wealth than their himdag. Whatever the details, the hehemajkam, the people were compelled to leave their river valley so that the land might heal itself, making its riverine environment suitable for human habitation again. Having learned I'itoi's lessons as recounted in their origin narrative, O'odham reinvented themselves as people who lived in small roundhouses called olas kih made of cottonwood, arrowwood, and cattail reeds atop an earthen floor. They were still farmers, but on a smaller, more sustainable scale.[70] Unlike Krech, who was only focused on criticizing his anthropological peers for romanticizing Indigenous precolonial culture—what he derisively called the "ecological Indian"—the O'odham did not teach that their ancestors were ecologically pure or perfect; instead, they bore the lessons that come with learning from the land over countless generations, including mistakes that were sometimes catastrophic, in addition to accumulating the knowledge and wisdom that enable a people to overcome calamities and to thrive anew.

For the Akimel O'odham, the story of the people of the big houses are a part of a single narrative, in which the sisivani who led the building of the great canal system were integral to the O'odham's understanding of how to live in balance with their jeved and all that is contained therein, from the akimel to the dodoag, the mountains that set the boundaries of their homeland. In a land of extremes, where droughts are complemented by magnificent monsoons, respecting the power of the land is essential. With that in mind, the big houses are monuments to the sacrifices that their ancestors endured as I'itoi, Coyote, and Buzzard wandered the land, making the world that Jeved mahkai, Earth medicine maker, created into a place where the people, the O'odham, can live and one day become huhugam for the generations ahead.

CHAPTER THREE

Earth Medicine Maker Shapes This Place

Kinship as the Origin of Ethics

I n the two previous chapters, Komal Hok's narratives are elevated above the limitations of Russell's ethnographic recordings into a living body of literature. Critical to this process, recounted earlier, was José Lewis Brennan, an O'dham intellectual who deliberately intervened into Russell's field research as Thin Leather's translator. Consequently, Komal Hok is to O'odham literature what Homer or Hesiod was to ancient Greece, a singer and mythmaker for the generations. Komal Hok is also like the pre-Socratics, such as Anaxagoras, Thales, or Heraclitus, someone whose teachings evoke cosmological wonder and whose vision of life and nature will continue to inspire insights into the O'odham himdag. Having said that, one must be cautious about insisting upon parallels between Greek and O'odham thought, lest it seem that one is privileging Western philosophical discourse and its roots in ancient Greece. My intentions are quite the contrary.

When one considers the history of philosophy during the so-called Age of Discovery (from the fifteenth to the seventeenth century) and Enlightenment (from the seventeenth to the eighteenth century), there is little that can be regarded as intersections between Western philosophy and Indigenous traditions. In Hobbes's *Leviathan* (1651), Locke's *Second Treatise on Government* (1689), and Rousseau's *The Social Contract* (1762), each philosopher evokes a "state of nature," which was less about portraying Indigenous peoples and more about creating a philosophical fiction. Hobbes, for his part, saw in tribal people a propensity for savagery; Locke saw the origin of property; and Rousseau saw an Edenic form of natural equality.[1] None ever traveled to the Americas, let alone learned anything from any Indigenous persons.

In that way they are the utter opposite of Russell, Fewkes, and Lloyd, who at least spoke with Indigenous knowledge-keepers and their translators José Lewis Brennan and Edward Hubert Wood. Instead, spurious references to tribal people abound for the purpose of supporting political theories, be it an ecclesiastical commonwealth, a democratic republic, or a social contract. Inevitably, the state of nature and the people who inhabited it must give way to a higher, more European, form of thinking.

Since Plato's *Republic*, philosophers have presumed to know what was best for the human condition and its need to control its baser instincts. Alas, as the history of global colonization has shown, it is easier to find fault in others than it is in oneself. Accordingly, Spanish, French, Portuguese, British, and American conquerors sought to reform or save droves of Indigenous peoples, who they saw as slaves to their depraved habits, the most egregious of which was sloth. Indians, or indios, *as a race* refused to covet, hoard, and exploit. They insisted on sharing everything. This lack of industry would be the undoing of Indigenous cultures. Proponents of assimilation argued passionately that the only way to save Indians from destruction was to force them to assimilate into white American society. Senator Henry Dawes (R-MA) infamously stated in 1884, in response to the custom of collective Indigenous landholdings:

> They [Indians] have not got as far as they can go, because they own their land in common. It is Henry George's system,[2] and under that there is no enterprise to make your home any better than that of your neighbors. There is no selfishness, which is at the bottom of civilization. Till this people will consent to give up their lands, and divide them among their citizens so that each can own the land he cultivates, they will not make much more progress.[3]

Yet it is precisely this natural impulse to share the land and its bounty that is at the heart of Indigenous land relations, which are based on kinship ties and the responsibility that relatives feel for one another, that differentiates Indigenous communities from the republics, city-states, principalities, kingdoms, nation-states, and colonies that define western civilization. The lack of sharing, to the Indigenous mind, only leads to poverty, social decay, and strife—all of the ills that Americans bemoan but find impossible to resolve.

Before colonization and the slow erosion of ancestral knowledge, generations of O'odham were taught that Jeved mahkai made *this place* and that it was I'itoi who shaped the hehemajkam. What hehemajkam built, grew, and worshipped as they followed the sisivani, the chief medicine people, including the errors of their ways, was recounted in the origin narrative that Thin Leather knew, for which he was greatly respected. As Lloyd claims on Thin Leather's behalf in *Aw-aw-tam Indian Nights*, the aged storyteller "had no successor," implying somewhat presumptuously that it was up to persons like him to preserve O'odham oral tradition. Since Komal Hok's generation, Hohokam archaeology has grown and become a distinguished area of specialty, as recounted in the previous chapter. Because of the abundance of research produced, O'odham have to respond to the reports and theories that archaeologists have developed about ancestral O'odham. Knowing one's oral tradition is not enough. Saying "pi'añi mac" is not enough. When referring to huhugam and the ge'egdaj kikih, one has to also know that "Hohokam civilization" built "14 irrigation networks with an estimated aggregate length of 300 miles [that] watered 400 square miles of agricultural land and settlements," which sustained a population in the tens of thousands.[4] Just as Dawes stated that Indians needed to become more selfish, archaeologists have obliged us to become more scientific.

Despite my earlier comparison between Komal Hok and the ancient Greeks, the modern philosophical community has made scant reference to Indigenous peoples, let alone acknowledge them as worthy of philosophical contemplation. Instead the anthropological discourse took over the topic of Indigenous cultures and languages. Franz Boas and Alfred Kroeber, for example, were major influences who focused on Indigenous cultural demise as unique but endangered specimens of human evolution. What Boas added to the discourse on early human history was turning attention away from evolution and towards migration and dissemination. Boas wondered in particular whether diffusion can be sustained across wide swaths of geographic distances.

In short then, the method which we [American ethnographers] try to develop is based on a study of the dynamic changes in society that may be observed at the present time. We refrain from the attempt to solve the fundamental problem of the general development of civilization until we have been able to unravel the processes that are going on under our eyes.[5]

As for the philosophical community, what mattered more than cultural differentiation was the synthesis of these differences into a unified system of thought. One need only examine Hegel's swift disregard for the Americas in his *Philosophy of History* (1858), in which the Mesoamerican and Incan empires are mentioned succinctly before being vastly overshadowed by the ancient Greeks and Romans.[6] As for Karl Marx, except as a journalist, he did not examine the colonization of the Americas as a dedicated topic in any of his works on political economy.[7] Noteworthy is the last chapter of Friedrich Engels's *The Origin of the Family, Private Property and the State* (1884), titled "Barbarism and Civilization," in which Engels refers significantly to the Haudenosaunee as portrayed in Lewis Henry Morgan's *The League of the Ho-dé-no-sau-nee or Iroquois* (1851) and *Ancient Society* (1877). In North American scholarly circles, however, Indigenous people have been largely absent. Fleeting exceptions were Ralph Waldo Emerson's 1836 letter to President Martin Van Buren on behalf of Cherokee Nation, which was being unjustly forced out of its historical homeland by the 1830 Indian Removal Act, and Henry Thoreau's 1842 Indian journals, which did little more than conjure a Longfellow-like image of the Indian's demise in New England.[8] Things took an interesting turn when the burgeoning field of psychology developed an interest in the "primitive mind."

When Sigmund Freud equated "savages" and "neurotics" in *Totem and Taboo* (1913), anthropologists became fixated on the "deviant"[9] thinking of tribal people.[10] Freud's treatise *Totem and Taboo* appeared as anthropology was turning toward cultural relativism, as indicated in Franz Boas's *The Mind of Primitive Man* (1911) and the *Handbook of American Indian Languages* (1911). Cultural relativism purported to reject the scientific racism of its predecessors such as Aleš Hrdlička, whose phrenological studies of Indigenous cranial remains were premised on the theory that racial traits corresponded to physical features.[11] Boasians instead pivoted toward the phenomenon of culture as something that arose organically as a given people adapted to a given place, which is to say, a particular environment. As such, each people is an indigenous people, insofar as their culture is an adaptation to their environment. Thus, Akimel O'odham are *of the akimel*, the river. Tohono O'odham are *of the tohono*, the desert. And Hia-Ced O'odham are *of the hia-ced*, the sand dunes.

As observed earlier, Akimel O'odham's first extended appearance in the western intellectual tradition was in Frank Russell's 1904–1905 report for the Bureau of American Ethnology (BAE). *The Pima Indians* was a standard field report for its generation, which consisted of an inventory of cultural traits divided into major categories, namely Technology, Esthetic Arts, and Sophiology. In turn, the major categories were further divided into an array of subcategories. In the case of Sophiology, which is where the "Creation Myth" is located, Russell inserted sections on medicine men, types of disease, and a host of songs about various animals. In 1911 J. G. Frazer, of *Golden Bough* fame, cited Russell's report at length in *Taboo and the Perils of the Soul*. Of particular interest was the ritual purification of an O'dham warrior after having slain an enemy in combat. Komal Hok provided information about this custom in *Aw-aw-tum Indian Nights*. Then, in 1913, Freud quoted Frazer in *Totem and Taboo*, thus initiating a discourse on the "primitive mind" that has recurred in the anthropological literature.[12] The most influential example is Claude Lévi-Strauss's *La Pensée sauvage* (The Savage Mind) (1962), whose thesis that all humans possess an "untamed mind" challenged the Western convention that technological advancement indicated evolutionary advancement. Even people in so-called advanced societies must rely on the same ancestral intellectual traits as those from comparatively undeveloped peoples. Therefore Indigenous peoples, like Komal Hok, are just as capable of "philosophical" thinking as any of their Western counterparts, however different their respective cultures might be.

The philosophical project is engaging with the world through an analysis of language and ideas for the purpose of understanding the nature of the array of beings perceived by the senses, intellect, or intuition—be it eidetic, phenomenal, or pragmatic—insofar as the reflective mind is conditioned by the social environment in which it developed. It does make a difference if the resulting discourses are limited to a particular social institution—such as the Western philosophical community—to the exclusion of others, such as the Indigenous communities of North, Central, and South America. In the case of Indigenous philosophical traditions, because they are nonliterate,[13] their respective concepts of the world are expressed through narratives and ritual teachings, such as origin narratives and oral histories. Such autochthonous expressions not only include legends and folklore but also prayers and songs, all of which commonly form the basis of a given people's ceremonial customs. The latter is the case with the Akimel O'odham, as documented in *The Pima Indians*, which is augmented with a range of ethnographic treatises, such as those by Ruth M. Underhill and Donald M. Bahr.[14] With respect to these sources, this raises a question about philosophical expression, specifically, must philosophy be *written* by an *individual* thinker in a discourse that is aware of itself as "doing philosophy" in order for that expression to be accepted as philosophical? While an adequate answer to this question is beyond the scope of this chapter, it is nonetheless important to introduce this issue. For one cannot appreciate Indigenous philosophical traditions unless one dispenses with the ethnocentric assumption that philosophy must be the singularly written product of the Western abstract intellect. Only then will a space open for nonwritten expressions that are the creation of collective wisdom and experience. Moreover, one does not need to privilege the Western philosophical tradition in the first place for Indigenous philosophy to be philosophy.

At its most basic, philosophy, as a discrete form of thinking, signifies the communication of wisdom from teacher to student, as exemplified by Plato's accounts of the Socratic dialogs or Aristotle's peripatetic lectures, in which topics like justice, metaphysics, and the good were discussed. In this respect, Indigenous oral traditions are also teachings, which are handed down from elders to youth, and which teach one how the world was formed, how the first people were made, and how to sustain a balanced relationship between a people and their homeland. When philosophizing entails a certain level of critical thinking, meaning doubt or skepticism, Western philosophers and Indigenous thinkers begin to part ways. The radical break with tradition that Socrates initiated—in which his questions cast doubt on the political and religious orthodoxy of his times—would lead to Descartes's skepticism and Nietzsche's atheism, not to mention the existential crisis of modern European man. Indigenous peoples, however, were focused on maintaining their world in balance, as did their ancestors. They did not doubt the wisdom of their oral traditions; they respected it.[15] Consequently, because Western philosophy, as an intellectual culture, depends on analyzing, critiquing, and potentially rejecting previous ideas and systems, Indigenous philosophies are preempted from partaking in this dialogue. Hence, a common assumption in the philosophical community is that Indigenous philosophies are the provenance of anthropology, not philosophy. Unfortunately, a philosophical community that regards only its own tradition as philosophy cannot see that Indigenous thinkers analyzing, critiquing, and often rejecting the discourse of anthropologists is also philosophizing. In this way, asserting one's respect for Indigenous teachings is a form of philosophical resistance, which is as poignant as Nietzsche's declaration that "God is dead!" or Kierkegaard's "leap of faith."

Akimel O'odham's respect for their jeved, which sustains their lives, is more than a belief that these places are inhabited by spirits whose names are invoked in their origin narratives and ceremonial customs; it is knowledge about these lands derived from generations of intimate interaction. In the Technology section of Russell's BAE report, there are subsections on "Plants used for food," "Medicinal plants," and "Animals used for food." Integral to Indigenous experience is knowledge, in the form of stories and songs, about how to live with the places in which one dwells. Like Russell, others over the years have intervened to "preserve" O'odham teachings. In the recent past, Gary Paul Nabhan has published books and articles on O'odham plant knowledge, such as *Gathering the Desert* (1986) and *Enduring Seeds: Native American Agriculture and Wild Plant Conservation* (2002). Amadeo Rea has compiled three superlative volumes: *At the Desert's Green Edge* (1997), *Folk Mammalogy of the Northern Pimans* (1998), and *Wings in the Desert* (2007). Most recently, Jared Orsi published *Peoples of a Sonoran Desert Oasis: Recovering the Lost History and Culture of Quitobaquito* (2023). These are in addition to the historically important works that have appeared since the 1930s, beginning with Ruth M. Underhill.

With this in mind, the objective of the present discourse is to intervene into the discourse on environmental ethics—which is dominated by non-Indigenous thinkers, including those of great historical importance such as Rachel Carson and Aldo Leopold—and assert an O'odham-centered agenda for reflection and analysis. Although environmental ethics is still a minor subfield of Western philosophical ethics, the topic of the environment has always been of major importance to Indigenous communities. Ever since the first trappers, miners, ranchers, and prospectors began looking to make money from exploiting sacred places have Indigenous peoples worried about the environment. So this is why this project matters, but not because of what it may contribute to mainstream environmental ethics. What one can learn today from the O'odham himdag with respect to the environment is how to critique the environmental impact wrought by industrialization—such as climate change—from a local, which is to say O'odham, perspective. Indeed, it is only from an O'odham perspective that one can begin to see the challenges confronting O'odham communities as their relationship with their jeved is disrupted by the upheaval of colonization—not just in the historic past, but also as part of their current affairs.

The Gila River Indian Community, which is the modern name of the Akimel O'odham reservation—the other reservation is the Salt River Pima-Maricopa Indian Community—has long battled local, state, and federal authorities over environmental justice issues pertaining to freeway expansions, urban development, and water rights. All of these are the consequences of illegal land and resource loss due to the encroachment of settlers onto the O'odham jeved, which the American government pursued under the pretense of holding title to Arizona—including Indian lands—under the articles of the 1848 Treaty of Guadalupe-Hidalgo.[16] In light of this unfortunate history, colonization is not just an O'odham or Indigenous people's issue, it is an issue for all of humanity. More to the point, the same land that settler-colonial nations like the United States have seized from Indigenous nations and exploited for national aggrandizement is the same industrially assaulted land that must somehow sustain the non-Indigenous populations now occupying these lands. The environmental crisis that Lynn Townsend White Jr. alerted his readers to in "The Historical Roots of Our Ecologic Crisis" (1967), has long been in a crisis state for the people who still depend on the riverine environment along the akimel (Gila River) and onk akimel (Salt River).

Although changes to the Akimel O'odham environment began with the introduction of Spanish trade goods such as wheat and cattle during the eighteenth century, it was not until the Americans took political control of the New Mexico Territory after its war with Mexico (1846–1848) when substantial and devastating changes occurred. In 1859 the new political order was articulated in the Gila River Indian Community reservation, which was established through presidential executive order, the boundaries of which would be altered under pressure from settlers in 1879.[17] In response, Headman Antonio Azul, mentioned earlier, would work to restore as much of Akimel O'odham land as possible, largely on the basis of the services its scouts rendered against the Apache.[18] Significantly, the Gila River—the life blood of the community—was dammed upriver at Adamsville in 1868, instigating a water crisis that would ensue until the turn of the current century.[19] Arizona, moreover, which entered the union on February 14, 1912, steadily depleted its water table as its population grew and its agribusiness expanded, thereby putting the state in competition with California and Nevada over the Colorado River.[20] Throughout it all, the Akimel O'odham barely eked out a living.[21] Thus, it is within this historical context that one must understand the Akimel O'odham values regarding their environment that, on the one hand, are reaffirmed in their oral tradition and their ceremonial customs but, on the other hand, have been impacted by the political, economic, and even religious forces of the American settler-colonial state.

At this juncture, the foregoing discourse on the Akimel O'odham is more of a political critique of Indian-white relations than a philosophical discourse on the O'odham himdag. However, as made relevant in the earlier chapter on Komal Hok, reflecting on O'odham land relations is impossible without also reflecting on the deliberate harm that American settlers inflicted on the O'odham jeved, not to mention the hehemajkam and himdag that the land, and only *this* land, sustains.

The O'odham himdag has undergone waves of colonization, which O'odham have resisted, adapted to, and (sometimes) been overwhelmed by. In light of this, the literature that informs the discourse on the O'odham himdag as a form of environmental ethics is a product of historical forces, many of which are beyond O'odham control. At the same time, this is not to say that only a colonized version of the O'odham himdag endures in the present era, but rather that it bears the scars of its survival. Some scars, like language declination, are still fresh. Thus the knowledge that O'odham like Komal Hok have shared with anthropologists and other researchers exhibits a conscientious choice to retain this knowledge as part of their community, albeit in colonized media such as books and papers. Even the book in hand is a part of the contemporary O'odham practice of knowledge keeping.

Komal Hok is distinguished among his fellow collaborators, not only for how much he knew of the O'odham himdag, but also for his reputation as a distinct O'dham thinker.[22] More typically, references to O'odham stories and teachings in the Spanish archival record, such as Kino and Font's diaries, were recorded anonymously. However, when Thin Leather contributed to Russell's BAE report, then more expansively in J. William Lloyd's book, the O'odham himdag came to life. Like an O'odham Hesiod, Komal Hok evoked Jeved mahkai (Earth medicine maker), Bán (Coyote), and I'itoi (Elder brother) as they created the first people and the land in which the people built their villages, farmed their fields, and installed an impressive canal system that harnessed their akimel and onk akimel, nourishing their valley homes.[23] Ultimately, the origin narrative is about the rise and fall of huhugam, ancestral O'odham, who lost their way when the sisivani, the chief priests, thought their teacher, I'itoi, was harming their society, so wanted to kill him. In the end, what I'itoi teaches about the himdag is not a renunciation of that jeved in which the ge'egdaj kikih rose but lessons learned about the himdag from that experience, which took untold generations to develop.

Because Akimel O'odham do not have a scientific tradition—at least, not in the sense recognized by Western intellectuals—their origin narrative has been relegated to fable, folklore, and fantasy, which is to say it is regarded as a cultural relic of a premodern, prescientific people. In this case, the flood narrative is no more historically accurate than the one found in Gilgamesh, and the ceremonies based on that "myth" are no more effective than a Druid festival at Stonehenge.[24] At this point one might raise the age-old debate between faith and reason, in which rational thought as defined by Western intellectuals is based on the principles of Aristotelian logic, thereby prohibiting anything that defies the rules of that logic, one of the most important of which was the rule of the excluded middle. So either science is correct or mythology, but not both.

Of course, Aristotle and the logical tradition he initiated in the *Organon* and the *Metaphysics* were products of their time and place, namely fourth century BCE Macedonia. What Aristotle sought to achieve, beyond articulating the rules for a correct syllogism, was a form of argument that was axiomatic and far less rhetorical than what characterized the thinking of the Sophists, who appealed more to the emotions and the senses. Such formulaic reasoning and analysis interestingly became the basis of both the Medieval arguments for the existence of God and the scientific thinking initiated during the Renaissance by Descartes in his *Discourse on the Method* (1637) and Galileo Galilei's *Discourses and Mathematical Demonstrations Relating to Two New Sciences* (1638).

The first rule of thought stipulated in the Cartesian tradition is that the aim "should be to direct the mind with a view to forming true and sound judgements about whatever comes before it," thus inaugurating a tradition of skepticism regarding Christian religious orthodoxy, in which Galileo stands as a hero of free thinking.[25] However, whereas Galileo's scientific challenge to Church teachings over the nature of the universe is celebrated as a profound act of resistance to religious dogma and oppression, the same is not true when the scientific attitude, if you will, is applied against Indigenous customs and values. In the latter case, the derision of Indigenous knowledge as "primitive" has been a part of the colonization and oppression of Indigenous peoples as morally and culturally inferior to Europeans. This belittling attitude toward Indigenous cultures would be enshrined in American case law in 1823, namely *Johnson v. M'Intosh*.[26]

With respect, then, to what the references to Aristotle, Descartes, and Galileo mean to this discourse on Akimel O'odham teachings, it is not to say that what Komal Hok recounts is based on invalid or illogical premises, but rather that Western thinkers were affirming a type of knowledge, intrinsic to Western intellectual society, for which they developed an effective practice that they named "the scientific method." What scientific thinkers from Russell to Krech could not apprehend is that the O'odham origin narrative is also a form of knowledge. Rather than reducing the object of inquiry down to its component parts and analyzing its nature and function, as Descartes would have one do, an origin narrative is a holistic and noninvasive means to understanding the created world. Thus Komal Hok teaches that before the first people were made, "Earth medicine maker" must make the earth, the jeved, which they do by rubbing their chest with their fingers, then forming the "dust" into a flattened "cake."[27] In *Aw-aw-tum Indian Nights*, what Earth medicine maker rubbed off their chest was muhadag, "perspiration, or greasy earth."[28] Jeved mahkai then planted the creosote or greasewood bush (shegoi), which symbolized the kind of jeved that was taking shape.[29] Insects soon followed, in particular "some black insects," "the termite," and "a gray spider." Together they helped Earth medicine maker make the "water, mountains, trees, grass, and weeds," above which, covering it all was the sky, "shaped like the round house [kih] of the Pima." It would not be until after the sun and the moon, along with the stars, were made "when the earth was thus prepared for habitation." At which point, Earth medicine maker made, as Komal Hok recounted in Brennan's biblical-sounding translation, "all manner of birds and creeping things."[30] With regard to how various creatures learn, while each acquires knowledge in its own way, all creatures require a place in which to learn, experiences from which to draw, and a teacher to guide one. According to the O'odham way of thinking, every creature has its himdag, its way of being.

In the case of the first humans, they bear the traits of their creator who, in the Akimel O'odham origin narrative, tried and failed at creating the sun and the moon; each was placed in what turned out to be the wrong direction, until they tried the right direction, the east, thereby generating the days and nights that persist to today.[31] Similarly to humans, Earth medicine maker went through trial and error. The first people were made from clay, which was gathered from the akimel, or Gila River. These first people, s*os*anac/j (many ants), multiplied until they overran the land, leaving themselves with a scarcity of food and water. Tragically, "they began to kill one another and to eat human flesh." Out of pity for their distress, Earth medicine maker determined that he had to "destroy all." So they grabbed the sky with their staff and pulled it down, "crushing to death the people and all other living beings." Because of the destruction, everything that was created before had to be created anew, including the people, whom Komal Hok identified as s*os*anac/j, which may be translated as either "the beginning of something" or "the base of something." S*os*anac/j may be expressed metaphorically as "many ants," which evinces their carelessness at reproducing and devouring resources. They learned the first lesson of the himdag.[32] These s*os*anac/j are the people whose descendants, the Akimel O'odham, will refer to as huhugam. Thin Leather refers to them as "the Pima nation," implying kinship between the generations.[33] At the same time, s*os*anac/j are fated to be destroyed by I'itoi, Elder brother, who is later called Siuuhu or S-e'ehe.[34]

Elder brother sprung from the earth, the jeved, appearing not long after Coyote, who came from the moon as it was setting behind the tohavs, the white brittlebush.[35] Elder brother's emergence moreover, marked the beginning of a new era, as his power challenged that of Earth medicine maker. I'itoi, for example, shortened the lifespan of the first people so that they would not overrun the earth as before. A shortened life was the teaching that these hehemajkam had to learn as a part of their place in this jeved. However, Elder brother's teachings did not end with making the hehemajkam aware of their mortality. Earth medicine maker's people were still prone to overindulgence. The s*os*anac/j's became wealthy. One day, "Elder Brother created a handsome youth, whom he directed to go among the Pimas, where he should wed whomsoever he wished." As the youth proceeded with his philandering, the girls he wed gave birth to children, each one taking fewer months than the previous to gestate, until one was born from the youth himself at the "time of marriage."[36] This child, more specifically, would bring about the flood that destroys the s*os*anac/j homeland.

In preparation for calamity, Elder brother began making a large olla (pot) out of "either bush or gum."[37] All the while, the first people grew restless and alarmed, in addition to distressed. "South Doctor" (Vakolo mahkai) set out to disrupt Elder brother's designs on the hehemajkam. Vakolo mahkai "had power similar to that of Elder Brother. South Doctor [Vakolo mahkai] was noted for his knowledge of all things and his skill in reading signs." He instructed his daughter to accept the youth that Elder brother sent around to wed girls like her. The daughter was reluctant, but her father explained that she needed to do this so that "a divine plan might be accomplished." As expected, the youth came for Vakolo mahkai's daughter. Before long, the mahkai and his wife were stirred by the sudden cries of an infant. Assuming their daughter had given birth, they rushed to see their grandchild. To their dismay, they encountered their daughter telling them that she was "not the mother,"[38] but rather that the child came straight from him, the youth, not from her. Feeling ashamed, the youth absconded with his child and returned to Elder brother, who was finishing his olla.

On the way back to I'itoi ki, the youth abandoned his child. But Elder brother knew what the youth had done, so asked him for his child. Elder brother also knew that Vakolo mahkai wanted this aberrant birth to happen. Abruptly, the child's cries "shook the earth." In response, Jeved mahkai assembled hehemajkam and warned them that a great flood, a ge'e wi'inthag, was approaching. Earth medicine maker then took their staff and struck the ground, which opened a tunnel to the "other side," to a place far below this place, this jeved, where people would find safety. Only some of the people, though, followed Earth medicine maker to this unknown place.[39] Wherever Jeved mahkai led the hehemajkam, it was beyond the known boundaries of the Akimel O'odham jeved. Perhaps farther than the known boundaries of the Tohono, Hia-Ced, and Sobaipuri O'odham jeved. Such a path may have led to multiple places. Perhaps to the lands where the Pima Bajo—Óob O'odham, Ó O'odham, and Taramil O'odham—now dwell.

What this narrative teaches about the s*os*anac/j's relation with the homeland that Earth medicine maker created is that their many-ants way of being was inappropriate and exposed them to forces beyond their control. In the original jeved, in which Jeved mahkai planted creosote, s*os*anac/j did not know disease or death, so they multiplied to the point of exhausting their food and water. In desperation, they preyed on each other. When the jeved healed, Elder brother sent his "youth" among the people to sow distress. Perhaps the hehemajkam were overgrowing their fields, taking too much from the jeved. Perhaps these people took too much pride in their power over the jeved. Because the jeved is a living being, it knew how to restore the balance. Natural forces cleansed the land. Out of calamity, though, the O'odham himdag emerged, which is the way for hehemajkam living in every part of the O'odham jeved to live in harmony with the jeved O'odham call home. For the s*os*anac/j, their fate was to learn foundational lessons of himdag. When Earth medicine maker opened a tunnel into which the people could seek safety, he sang over hehemajkam as they took to the path they prepared:

> Weep, my unfortunate people!
> All this you will see take place.
> Weep, my unfortunate people!
> For the waters will overwhelm the land.
> Weep, my unhappy relatives!
> *You will learn all.*
> Weep, my unfortunate relatives!
> *You will learn all.*
> The waters will overwhelm the mountains.[40] (My emphasis)

When Komal Hok shared his knowledge of the origin narrative, for someone like Russell it was a relic of a bygone era when a nonliterate people living in grass huts and digging with sticks believed the world was no bigger than the horizon of their own experience. Muhadag do'ag was the edge of everything. And the akimel simply disappeared into the distance. For Komal Hok, he had dedicated his life to knowing and telling these stories. Which are not mere stories, but timeless teachings that are relevant for as long as there are O'odham around to hear these things. Because the origin narrative is about the environment in which the people live today, there are reminders in the landmarks, animals, and other natural phenomena of what happened *here*. For example, among the birds that survived the flood was the "Vipisimal," the hummingbird.

> If anyone harms the little Vipisimal to this day the flood may come again. Accidental injuries to the bird must be atoned for; if it be killed, its tail feathers must be kept for a time to avert disaster; if it is found lying dead, it must be buried and appropriate gifts must be placed upon its grave.[41]

From the scientific perspective, the O'odham hummingbird tradition is nothing but an ungrounded superstition, a naïve belief that harming or disrespecting a hummingbird may literally cause a flood. *Post hoc ergo propter hoc*, as the logicians say. From the point of view of a people who must sustain themselves in their homeland, it is practical wisdom. What would it mean if O'odham became a society in which deliberately harming hummingbirds was acceptable? O'odham customs about hummingbird are not childlike beliefs in magic. They are about the tangible and delicate balance between people and place—O'odham and O'odham jeved—which are lessons that developed as the first people became huhugam, which taught their O'odham descendants.

Canals in particular distinguished ancestral O'odham in Elder brother's creation, as these are what made the big houses possible. What is typically overlooked in the archaeological record is that a powerful medicine woman, a mahkai, assisted the people when they needed a canal cut into the onk akimel, the Salt River. Komal Hok calls this woman Th'oachudam Oks, or "White-eater-old-woman," which Lloyd and Wood translated as "Wampum Eater."[42] What is fascinating is that hehemajkam are not remembered as designing the canal system, but rather a medicine woman with extraordinary powers.[43] For the hehemajkam at Papago Park, which today straddles the cities of Scottsdale and Tempe, they were in view of the distinctive red rock hills, Vav do:dadk (Rocky outcrops). It was here that hehemajkam "tried to build canals, but were not successful, because of the hard rocks and soil." Naturally, the people turned to their Elder brother for help, and he did his best to make the land soft enough for them to dig their canal. He had taught them to make digging sticks (giikĭ) out of ironwood (ho'idkam), but his efforts failed. So, I'itoi advised the people to see his "sister, who also had great power." When White-eater-old-woman availed her abilities to the people, "she finished all the work in a single night."[44] In the *Aw-aw-tam Indian Nights* version, "Wampum Eater" brought fog, kohmhai, with her, which she left at the mouth of the desired canal, adjacent to the riverbank. She then blew a "seev-hur-whirl," a bitter wind, from the mouth of the canal up through the rocky hill. As the wind "tore up the bed of the canal," the still hovering fog "dammed up the river and the water ran thru the canal." In this way did the people acquire their canal. After this, I'itoi's sister returned home without speaking further with the people.[45] "From that time on," though, Elder brother once again set out to put these hehemajkam through another ordeal. He "began to do mischief, such as marrying young women, then deserting them for others. People began to be jealous of him and planned to destroy him."[46] I'itoi's destruction, however, would hasten the end of the canal builders and the big-house way of life.

I'itoi's work over the jeved begins when a rattlesnake bites and kills a rabbit. At the time, I'itoi had taken pity on the snake, which did not have its fangs and was being taunted by Rabbit. So I'itoi "pulled a hair from his own lip to cut in short pieces to serve as teeth for [Snake]." Rabbit's death shocked the people, who grew upset with Elder brother. They did not appreciate I'itoi's act of compassion.[47] Still, Rabbit's death marked a change across the jeved. During Rabbit's cremation, which the Piipaash taught them, Bán (Coyote) stole and ran away with Rabbit's heart. As the people pursued him, Bán left a trail of his misdeed across the Akimel O'odham homeland. As Komal Hok tells this story, it was in Komadk do'ag, the Estrella Mountain range, where Coyote stopped at "Anûkam Tcukwoanyik, Place of the Uprooted An Bush." Then at Kihâtoak, or Quijotoa, Coyote dusted off the ashes covering Rabbit's cremated heart. Lastly and most importantly, Coyote stopped at Muhadag do'ag (Greasy mountain), where Coyote spilled grease from Rabbit's heart while he consumed it.[48] These places mark the boundaries of the Akimel O'odham homeland,* which Jeved mahkai made, but which are now empowered with new meaning because of what Coyote did there.

Because people were still angry with Coyote, he fled to far-flung parts, where he took advantage of a girl from another tribe whose kinsmen possessed powerful medicine. When they learned of how Coyote used his cunning to violate their young relative, they became angry and used their power to take away the animals that O'odham hunted. These animals hid in a cave northeast of Waw giwulk, Baboquivari Mountain. Coyote had to work hard to free them again. In another story, a boy who grew up misbehaving around his grandmother nonetheless earned renown as a hunter because of the enchanted bow that he used. When the boy married, he was approached by a gambler of ill repute. Because of the gambler's medicine, hehemajkam were unable to defeat him. One man, "a powerful doctor," however, in exchange for sending his son and daughter to work for Elder brother, obtained assistance at sabotaging the gambler's power. What Elder brother unleashed on the people in return for his aid, alas, was a greater menace. Elder brother instructed the man's daughter to lure the gambler into imbibing a concoction that looked

---

*   The reference to Quijotoa indicates that O'odham homelands overlapped. Quijotoa, Giwho do'ag, is today located in Tohono O'odham Nation.

and smelled like pinole, but which was actually a potion that turned the gambler into a man-eagle, Vandaih, who began hunting people whenever game was scarce. When the people implored I'itoi for help, he took a long time to respond to the people's pleas because Vandaih was his relative. Eventually I'itoi showed the people how to prevail over this creature.[49]

The O'odham himdag, as expressed in Komal Hok's stories about I'itoi, is more than the set of customs that anthropologists like Russell and Underhill inventoried in their reports. It is knowledge that emerges as humans, hehehmajkam, adapt to their desert environment. In a sense, each generation has to adapt anew. Each generation must learn through experience like their ancestors. What they learn is that, just as the birds that survived the flood did so because of the nests that they built, so too have the O'odham endured calamity because of their round houses, or olas kikih. Symbolically, the olas kih is the himdag, which is knowledge handed down through the generations. As mentioned in the introduction, *himdag*'s root is *him*, an O'odham verb meaning "to walk," "walking," or in some manner "moving along." While the stem, -*dag* or -*thag*, signifies "belonging to" or "being related to," as well as "enrooted." Most often *himdag* is translated as "a way of life," "culture," or "traditions." *O'odham himdag*, as used in the current discourse, evinces a particular group of hehemajkam—such as Akimel O'odham—and *their* way of doing things. It is beyond the scope of this chapter, not to mention the author's fluency in O'odham neok, to engage in a linguistic analysis of *himdag* and its relation to other O'odham concepts and values, such as *thoag/doag* (mountain), let alone how O'odham syntax shapes the way in which O'odham see and experience their environment. But what can be derived from the story about Coyote and I'itoi is the manner in which human folly was essential for establishing himdag in the places named in the origin narrative.

When Ho'ok, the clawed monster, appeared, she soon exhibited a predilection for human flesh comparable to Vandaih's. She thus became notorious for snatching children and taking them to Taht-kum, north of Picacho.[50] Once again, the people turned to Elder brother for help. Following instructions, Ho'ok was lured to a dance where she was put to sleep with enchanted cigarettes that I'itoi made for her. While under the tobacco's spell, the people dragged her to the cave where she kept her victims and burned her alive. But when the fire shocked Ho'ok out of her comatose state, she smashed into the ceiling, opening a crack that permitted her escape. Once aloft, Ho'ok became a giant hawk who remembered what was done to her. So she killed hehemajkam whenever she had the chance.

One day Ho'ok attacked a woman making pottery. But the woman evaded capture. Missing her target, Ho'ok crashed into the fire the woman was using to fire her pots. The people thought Ho'ok had finally been destroyed. Unexpectedly, the pot began to boil over, killing people with scalding water. The pot continued to boil all day, ceasing at night only to resume at sunrise. Once again, the people sought help. This time they recruited two men, Toehahvs and Geeahduk Seeven, who took their clubs and shields and smashed the pot. As choohookyuh (amaranth) spilled from the pot, an old man and his orphaned grandson, who were there to watch the battle, ate up the food and turned into bears (jujudami)—one black, the other brown. Now people had to figure out how to kill these creatures. By their own reconnaissance the hehemajkam figured out how to distract the bears with balls made from o-nook palm tree. Once distracted, hehemajkam shot the bears with arrows.[51] At long last their turmoil settled down. Did the hehemajkam think that they did not need I'itoi anymore?

When Elder brother caused unrest by taking women who had just been through their coming-of-age ceremony only to abandon them, he also shot arrows through the people's crops, causing them to wither. These things happened near Muhadag do'ag, where I'itoi lives.[52] Because of his privations, people conspired to kill I'itoi. However, Elder brother's medicine was strong. Each time they killed I'itoi—first with their clubs, secondly with fire, thirdly by boiling him, and fourthly by pushing him off a high cliff—he was seen the next day, walking among the people and making mischief. Finally, after another unsuccessful attempt, this time by drowning, Nuwi (Vulture) called people together. Nuwi reminded everyone of Elder brother's immense powers, explaining why hehemajkam could not subdue him. Nuwi then revealed that he possessed the necessary powers, which Earth medicine maker gave him. So it was Nuwi who killed I'itoi, which he did with the help of the Sun (Tash), which lent Nuwi his me'akud (weapon).[53] Because the weapon came from the Sun, the heat engulfing the land became increasingly hotter each time Nuwi shot at I'itoi. As I'itoi ran, looking for a place to escape, the heat found him at every turn. To his dismay, each place I'itoi hid had no respite to offer, as every cool place became devastatingly hot. Exhausted, I'itoi had no place left, eventually succumbing to Nuwi's assault.[54]

As expected, I'itoi eventually returned—which he did with the rain (juhk)—and when he did the canal-based civilization that the first people created along the banks of the akimel and onk akimel crumbled. Driven by purpose, I'itoi gathered strength, and as he did, the land and waters that were completely dry at his demise sprung back to life. In the meantime, I'itoi gathered medicine, including items from which to fashion a bow and arrows. When I'itoi was prepared, he looked for the Sun, following its path. I'itoi also sought Jeved mahkai, who lived with the people, hehemajkam, that followed them into the tunnel that opened when the flood was imminent. Upon finding Earth medicine maker, Elder brother recounted his travails, including his deaths. Because of what happened, I'itoi explained to Jeved mahkai that it was time to assemble the powers that would overcome "the enemy to my people and to the earth." Earth medicine maker offered help. Indeed, so many people assembled to follow I'itoi that when they began marching back to the akimel and onk akimel valleys, not all of them made it out of the tunnel before the earth sealed up.[55] The ones left behind may be the Pima Bajo, or Lower Pima, which the Akimel O'odham call Chuhwi Lo'atham, Jackrabbit eaters.[56] Komal Hok says that I'itoi's son:tal (army) was made up of O'odham speakers.[57] Webb, in *A Pima Remembers*, describes the invading force as "a great army of tribes" "from the east." From where they came or why they wanted to conquer the big houses is not explained in Webb's version.[58] Shaw's version names "Se-eh-ha," another name for I'itoi, as leader of the assembled army. "'[Se-eh-ha is] going down to join his brother Juvet-Makai (Earth Medicine Man). They will come and wage war against us,' warned See-van Vah-Ki, a man who possessed great ability to foresee the future."[59]

As Elder brother led the people to their destination it took many years to find their way. As they journeyed, Elder brother created the deer, sihki, because there were none before and the people needed something to eat. Because of this, people learned how to hunt deer, which did not always go very well, and the people became hungry again. So they found a mahkai who knew deer medicine but whose power could hide the deer just as effectively as it could lure them. Consequently, the mahkai with deer medicine had mischievously hidden the deer. Nonetheless, he agreed to help the hunters, and they found game. Another mahkai helped when a pestilence broke out, which he treated by killing a doe and having a dance. Only after these events did I'itoi and his army return to the akimel, where they begin vanquishing villages around the big houses.

From the Casa Grande Ruins to Komadk, I'itoi led hehemajkam up the Gila River. What is remarkable is the display of extraordinary powers exhibited by various mamahkai (medicine makers) on both sides of the conflict. While the conquest is replete with images of warriors, weapons, and slayings, the episodes are punctuated with natural catastrophes, such as earthquakes, thunder, and fog, each one instigated by mamahkai whose powers derived from these phenomena. Just as the mahkai who knew deer medicine could control the deer, so too were there mamahkai able to control earthquake, thunder, and fog through their knowledge. Taken altogether, I'itoi's conquest of huhugam vapaki (ancient houses) evokes a narrative in which great social strife is occurring along with tremendous environmental upheaval. Underscoring this is the determination that I'itoi had for slaying Nuwi, who was responsible for killing him earlier. So I'itoi sent Eagle (Ba'ag) and Chicken-Hawk (Wishag) to find his nemesis, which they did. They then brought Nuwi back to I'itoi, who scalped him—which one can see today. However, like I'itoi, Nuwi eventually returns to life. Thin Leather's conquest narrative continues into what is today called Fort McDowell, along the Verde River (which the Yavapai call Haka'he:la), then turns westward to the Colorado River (Weg akimel), where the conquest meets its end. In time, people return to the akimel and onk akimel valleys, and as they do different bands claim different lands for their home. Most people, in Komal Hok's narrative, reclaim their O'odham jeved, which was where jujkam found them centuries later. Some of the returning O'odham continued up into the Rio Grande Valley, where they became the Rio Grande Pueblo communities.[60] In Shaw's version, I'itoi's army "marched, fighting and destroying. Whenever a fertile area was reached, a small number would express their wishes: 'We like this place and wish to make our homes here.' Se-eh-ha's reply was, 'You may settle here. Though the distance divides you from the rest of your tribesmen, nevertheless you will be related.'"[61]

Archaeologists, unsurprisingly, have largely ignored O'odham narratives on the rise and fall of huhugam big houses (vapaki), privileging their theories and assumptions instead. Through it all, O'odham have held to their oral histories, including their account of their huhugam, regardless of what the latest archaeological research may have to say about it. At one level, one might regard this dispute as another instance of the confrontation between science and religion, in which a community of believers (O'odham) refuses to accept scientific fact (archaeology). O'odham elders from Thin Leather to Anna Moore Shaw, however, do not necessarily reject the analyses, theories, and conjectures of their archaeological counterparts. O'odham do not dwell in the darkness of primitive superstition. They simply do not have any doubt that they are recalling their ancestors' experiences, which was based on a deep understanding of their jeved, in which they have dwelled for innumerable generations.[62] Therefore O'odham see archaeologists as telling the stories of their own experience with the land, in which they see "Hohokam," who mysteriously vanished, never to return. But this is not the O'odham experience, let alone what they know about these things.

O'odham do not abide by the Western notion of history in which a linear timeline is used to assemble data into a narrative documenting origins, developments, and declines such that each item is indexed according to a specific point in time—hence archaeologists' reliance on dendrochronology and stratigraphy. Therefore the origin narrative, which is dateless, does not shed light on the historiographical elements of the scientific perspective, because that is not its purpose. Because the origin narrative is about the first people, the ones that I'itoi taught their himdag, then more important than explaining the historicity of pottery sherds and ruins is the story's account of who the O'odham are, their relation to their huhugam, and how their himdag *defines their kinship* with Earth medicine maker, Elder brother, Coyote, and their jeved. With respect to the decline and fall of the big houses, other than offering evidence for how Indigenous people were as ecologically destructive as their Euro-American counterparts (as Krech argues), Elder brother's conquest of the big houses demonstrates what O'odham have learned from their transformative experiences.[63] What happened between Elder brother and the first people was due to his deliberate mischievousness, as he violated the trust and virginity of various young women who had just been through their coming-of-age ceremony, transgressing their integrity and bringing shame and resentment to their families. Yet what did I'itoi symbolize as a sacred being among the O'odham? When I'itoi was not troubling the minds of ancestral O'odham with his misbehavior, he sent terrifying creatures to prey over the jeved, not too far from their villages. Their himdag was taking shape. Over the generations, I'itoi nurtured ancestral O'odham into who they are as Akimel O'odham, from shortening their lifespans to teaching them how to make digging sticks from ironwood. I'itoi also sent his sister when they needed help building a canal across difficult terrain. At the same time, he introduced challenges, sometimes traumatic, that forged them into a strong people, from the flood that wiped out the first people's village to giving Snake the fangs that killed Rabbit, not to mention sending the array of monsters that preyed on them. Life, O'odham history, is a maze of obstacles; but at the end, awaiting them is I'itoi.

In the story of I'itoi's sister White-eater-old-woman, the canal that she dug near Vav do:dadk for the first people helped them to become as prosperous as other villages. Such a leap of imagination gave hehemajkam control over their akimel—signified by the digging stick. The more miles of canals that the hehemajkam constructed, the vaster were their fields, which led to greater crop yields. The increase in food supply led to population growth, which during times of drought may have resulted in social distress.[64] While not all huhugam villages are named in Thin Leather's story, their expanse between two distant points along the Gila River, then outward across the Phoenix Valley and up into Fort McDowell, indicates a hitherto unheard-of civilization. In the wake of the collapse of the big houses, the Akimel O'odham established a culture, a himdag, that still relied on agriculture—even utilizing the old canals—but on a smaller, sustainable scale.[65]

In conclusion, the events recounted in the origin narrative—which continue much further than the summary provided—established the Akimel O'odham himdag, which is about respecting the jeved and the akimel as living beings and as gifts from Jeved mahkai. As such, when O'odham show respect for wipismal (hummingbird), it is not because of a naïve belief that such a tiny creature can cause a flood. Their concern is for developing in oneself an attitude toward their jeved that sees everything as part of the whole. Because O'odham himdag is about maintaining healthy kinship ties with land and community, both human and nonhuman, the values expressed in the origin narrative are as pertinent today as they were for the first people. In the current era of climate change—or what many are calling the Anthropocene—I'itoi may need to cleanse the land again. In the meantime, O'odham have been subjected to the intense forces of colonization as American settlers occupied land they presumed to own by right of conquest, thereby usurping political and economic control from the villages dwelling along the akimel and onk akimel. Fortunately, despite Rea's dire assessment that no one is left who knows the whole origin narrative, O'odham have followed Komal Hok's example and have preserved their knowledge of these ancestral teachings.[66] This author counts himself among his relatives. For as long as the land sustains our hahashañ, the saguaros that O'odham believe hold shoshon spirits, the O'odham jeved will endure.

CHAPTER FOUR

Hahashañ

Brief Reflections on an Ancestral Plant

When Juan Nentvig wrote about his observations of the Sonoran Desert in *Rudo Ensayo* (1764), he referred to the saguaro fruit, which the Opata called "ychivo." The O'odham said "bahithaj." Jujkam like Nentvig called it "pitahaya." In Nentvig's words, "Pitahaya . . . is foremost among the wild fruits of Sonora, equally relished by Spaniards and gente de razón as well as the aborigines."[1] Likely overwhelmed by the diversity of the saguaro cactus population, Nentvig also said, "the saguaro, which I have seen only in the Pimería Alta, has a taller and thicker stalk than the plant which bears the pitahaya, but the fruits of these plants differ only in that the saguaro's is sweeter than the pitahaya."[2] What Nentvig likely also did not realize is what these hahashañ meant to the O'odham. Wherever one sees hahashañ, saguaro cacti, one knows that they are in the O'odham jeved. From what is today southern Arizona to northwestern Sonora, Mexico, hahashañ spring from the earth, the jeved, across areas that Akimel O'odham, Tohono O'odham, Hia-Ced O'odham, Sobaipuri, and Pima Bajo recognize as ancestral land. Everywhere that O'odham believe that I'itoi has his home, his ki, namely South Mountain, Baboquivari Mountain, and Sierra Pinacate, hahashañ forests abound. Naturally there is oral tradition about this. The fruit of the haashañ, its bahithaj, marks the beginning of the O'odham year. Its ribs are used to make calendars sticks (ooshikbina). Olas kikih (O'odham houses) and watto (ramadas) are also made with saguaro ribs. Hahashañ, most importantly, are shohshon (ancestors) about whom there are stories that explain the kinship tie that O'odham have with their hahashañ relatives. In these narratives hahashañ were once children who either misbehaved or ran away before transforming into plant people. The haashañ, as a person, also has a himdag.

When Jeved mahkai made this place, they created the different species of cacti that inhabit the plains, riverine areas, and mountain slopes that give the O'odham jeved—which the Spanish named "el desierto de Sonora" and divided between Pimería Alta and Pimería Bajo—its distinct character among the world's desert regions. Symbolic of this place is the haashañ, the saguaro. According to the Arizona-Sonora Desert Museum, just west of Tucson, the saguaro "is one of the defining plants of the Sonoran Desert. These plants are large, tree-like columnar cacti that develop branches (or arms) as they age, although some never grow arms. These arms generally bend upward and can number over 25. Saguaros are covered with protective spines, white flowers in the late spring, and red fruit in summer."[3] Amadeo M. Rea, in *At the Desert's Green Edge: An Ethnobotany of the Gila River Pima*, wrote extensively about hahashañ. More than botanical phenomenon, the haashañ embodies the spirits of O'odham, bearing sustenance, its bahithaj, which is central to the annual harvest ceremony, or wiigida.

> Blooming time and the arrival of White-winged Doves and Long-nosed Bats correspond. Each flower opens late in the evening, closing the next afternoon. Insects, bats, doves, woodpeckers, and even flycatchers are attracted to these flowers. . . . Blossoming time is staggered, with dozens of flowers in various stages of development crowning the tip of each arm. The egg-shaped fruits mature during late June and early July . . . the greenish fruit splits open, revealing the dark red pulp with its mass of black seeds.[4]

In the stories that Komal Hok shared with Frank Russell, he included two compelling tales about the haashañ. In one, an O'dham boy and his grandmother lived together because o'obga (Apaches) had killed the boy's father and abducted his mother. This left the boy (ceoj) and old woman (oks) to fend for themselves, which was hard. They did not get along. Nonetheless, when the boy said that he wanted to rescue his mother (je'e), his grandmother (hu'ul*) feared for him. Despite the grandmother's worries, the boy set out on his quest to the Apache camp where his mother was held. Following close behind, the grandmother sought to bring the boy back

---

*   Hu'ul is one's maternal grandmother; Ka:k is one's paternal grandmother.

home before the obga, the enemy, spotted and killed him. However, when the old woman was just about to catch the boy, he turned into a saguaro, a haashañ. After evading his grandmother, who was forced to return home, the boy snuck into the Apache camp and found his mother. The boy disguised himself as a little dove (hohhi) and plotted his mother's escape. Mother and son spoke quietly in O'odham. Nevertheless, the Apaches overheard them and knew that the bird belonged to their captive's tribe. Confronting them, one of the Apache seized the dove from the woman and crushed it, tearing the wings apart. At that moment the feathers transformed into a raging flock of hawks (vivisig), attacking without mercy. Making their escape, the hawks turned back into the boy. "But when they reached the place where the grandmother turned back, they could go no farther. They turned into saguaros, one on each side of the road."[5] Second, a story that Russell titled "The Naughty Grandchildren":

> An old woman had two bright grandchildren. She ground wheat and corn every morning to make porridge for them. One day as she put the olla on the fire outside the house, she told the children not to fight for fear they would upset the water. But they soon began quarreling, for they did not mind as well as they should, and so spilled the water, and the grandmother had to whip them. They became angry and said they were going away. She tried to make them understand why she had to whip them, but they would not listen and ran away. She ran after them, but could not catch up. She heard them whistling and followed the sound from place to place, until finally the oldest boy said, "I will turn into a saguaro, so I shall last forever, and bear fruit every summer." And the younger said, "Well, I will turn into a palo verde and stand there forever. These mountains are so bare and have nothing on them but rocks, so I will make them green." The old woman heard the cactus whistling and recognized the voice of her grandson; so she went up to it and tried to take it into her arms, and the thorns killed her.
>
> And that is how the saguaro [hashañ] and palo verde [kuk chehethagi] came to be.[6]

William Blackwater, in turn, tells a different story in *O'odham Creation and Related Events*, which consists of oral histories collected by Ruth Benedict in 1927. Donald M. Bahr, cultural anthropologist and author of numerous works on the O'odham, edited these accounts. In Blackwater's narrative, the story follows a little girl (chehia) whose mother enjoyed playing toka, the women's field hockey game, to the point of neglecting her daughter. Uncared for, the girl followed her mother from village to village. At one of these villages, the girl asked the other children to show her a tarantula (hiani) hole, because she had never seen one before. At her behest, the children led her around the desert until they found one. The little girl abruptly placed her foot over the hole and began sinking into the ground. Alarmed, the children told their parents, which caused the girl's mother to look for her daughter. But when the mother attempted to pull her daughter free from the tarantula hole, she sank further. "She sank down into the earth. A giant cactus [ge'e haashañ] grew up over that spot."[7]

Instinctively, the saguaro moved farther and farther from the people in Blackwater's tale, until it "came up at Carrying Basket Mountain [Giwho do'ag]. It grew there and blossomed and bore fruit. Only the birds could reach it to get at the fruit." Attracted to the bounty, the people sent Raven (Hawani) to collect the fruit for them, and when he returned the people let the harvest sit and ferment. When some of them drank too much of the fermented juice, they began fighting. After this incident the people put the seeds in a sack and instructed one of the men to scatter them "in the mountains." Along the way, the man ran into Bán (Coyote), who heard about the drinking and was on his way to the village. Disappointed at the news that the fête was over, Coyote asked the man what he had in his bag. After some coaxing, the man handed the bag over to Coyote, telling him not to open it. "Coyote took the bag and threw it high up into the air. The seeds blew all about, and that is why the cactus grows in every direction. Some of Coyote's seed is still in the ground, and that is why we still see some cactus just beginning to grow."[8]

According to the white man's calendar, "July" is the middle of summer, equidistant from the beginning and end of the year. For O'odham, jukiabig mashath ushers in the big rains, the monsoon, and the start of a new cycle of life in the desert. During the previous month, the saguaro fruit (bahithaj) ripened, forming the substance of the ceremonial wine (nawait) that signifies the commencement of the harvest ceremony (wiigida). When Underhill recorded Tohono O'odham songs and stories for *Singing for Power: The Song Magic of the Papago Indians of Southern Arizona* (1938), she focused one of her chapters on the wiigida. Contrary to the bacchanalian impression that the "drinking ritual" had on mimilgahn, one O'dham elder said: "Do the whites not understand . . . that we have no water except for what comes from the sky? We have no canned food, so we need the corn to feed our children. We have no automobiles, so we need hay for our horses. Why then do they say we should not drink the cactus liquor?"[9] Without the wiigida and its ritual winemaking, the summer rains would not bless the land. Thus, drinking the cactus wine is a moral imperative. "It is the duty of every man to drink his fill of this liquor; to drink to a saturation, even as the rain-soaked earth is saturated. In accordance with the rules of Papago magic [ceremony], which always imitates the desired event, this act will bring the rain to moisten the earth."[10]

While Underhill wrote in the dated language of "sympathetic magic," a term coined by James G. Frazer in *The Golden Bough*, she nonetheless evokes O'odham himdag, which is premised on what Irving Hallowell referred to as "animism" in his work with the Ojibwe. More exactly, the O'odham mamah-kai (medicine makers) regard the jeved as populated by spirits, beings that possess a mind (wehsig), or a soul (thoakag), or strength (gewkdag) that if disrespected can make one sick. In a 2020 message about "a prayer walk and pilgrimage to offer ocean water to [A'al vaipia]," Quitobaquito Springs, which was under assault from recent political developments along the US-Mexico border, the chairman of the San Xavier District of Tohono O'odham Nation referred to this site as "a living being that is a very sacred place to us."[11] A'al vaipia, also known as Quitobaquito Springs, is in the middle of Organ Pipe National Monument. Chuchuis, or senita cactus, euphoniously called "organ pipe" in English, inhabit this terrain alongside the hahashañ.

While not everything in the jeved is dangerous in the sense of causing ká:cim múmkidag (staying sickness), one can nevertheless cause harm to oneself and others by straying from one's himdag, as everything is related. With respect to hahashañ, when Rea asked Sylvester Matthias, an Akimel O'odham from Komadk, he said: "They say haashañ is a good friend, harmless. Want to serve people, like kui [mesquite]." At the same time, harming hahashañ is unconscionable. Joe Giff, another Komadk elder, reacted with sincere disapproval at the thought of using hahashañ for target practice, which is a recurring problem: "It would be wrong for us to do something like that, to injure, . . . to shoot at a Saguaro, because that would be like shooting at a *person* . . . the Saguaro *is* a person" (emphasis in original). Making an indirect reference to the stories recounted earlier, Giff added: "That's where Saguaros come from; in the stories it was somebody who turned into a Saguaro, so that would be forbidden, to do that."[12]

In Underhill's 1934 essay on the "Papago Calendar Record," which is about the calendar sticks (ooshikbina), she notes that the "only standardization is in the quadrennial feast of the wiigida (prayer stick festival), represented by a puncture in the middle of the year space."[13] Made from saguaro cactus ribs, the ooshikbina regularly recorded the ceremonial life of the hahashañ, in addition to the events deemed most significant in the life of the calendar-stick keeper's village. As a sign of the hashañ's importance, the saguaro fruit harvest in July marks the beginning of the O'odham year. Russell, in *The Pima Indians*, observed that "At that time [harvest] . . . the mesquite beans are ripening, as well as the cultivated crops. It is the season of feasting and rejoicing."[14] Ooshikbina also preserved the changes that occurred throughout the jeved. While himdag evokes an O'odham sense of goodness (ape'akam) and a climate of well-being (ap'ethag)—especially when the prayed-for rain arrives—neijig (calamity), disaster, tragedy, and foreboding may suddenly swoop over the horizon like a monstrous bird looking to prey upon the people.

When the mimilgahn (Americans) annexed Texas in 1845, it initiated an era in which mimilgahn began sweeping across the desert in pursuit of the gold mines in California. After the 1854 Gadsden Purchase, "southern Arizona" was overrun with milgahn settlements that transformed the jeved with roads, railroads, farms, ranches, dams, and canals. The Arizona Canal and the Salt River Project superseded the huhugam era of the big houses in terms of developing the akimel. During the 1870s to 1920s, as recounted earlier, Akimel O'odham endured a time of famine (bihugig) as their access to their akimel, the Gila River, was repressed due to the encroaching towns of Adamsville and Florence, which was soon followed by Chandler and Mesa. The calendar stick at Gila Crossing Village for 1870–1871 stated: "The canal at Tempe was built by the Mormon settlers."[15] The calendar stick for Salt River Village stated for 1896–1897: "The Maricopa and Phoenix railroad was extended from Tempe to Mesa . . . during this year."[16] Change was not only material, such as canals and railroads, but also spiritual. A church at Blackwater Village (1896–1897) and a Catholic mission at Gila Crossing (1899–1900) were established. Hehemajkam, I'itoi's people, were forced to change with the times: "Hwela, named for agent Wheeler, was baptized this year [1885–1886] as the first Christian convert among the Pimas."[17]

The O'odham himdag transformed as Christian missionization, a shrinking land base, and economic decline forced the O'odham's relationship with their hahashañ to the margins of their community. As for the fate of the saguaro, Arizonans regularly see reports of the symbolic plant's perilous status. In 1977 Warren F. Steenbergh and Charles H. Lowe stated in "Ecology of the Saguaro": "Comparison of saguaro densities in these plots [Organ Pipe Cactus National Monument and Saguaro National Monument] in 1941 and 1975 shows a decrease in saguaro numbers at all sites."[18] Meaningfully, in order to give their field observations some further ecological depth, Steenbergh and Lowe made reference to the Tohono O'odham calendar stick record. In a subsection titled "Freezing and the historical record—the last 200 years," O'odham climate data, if you will, is documented:

> Historical observations further complement the record of such events. Of particular significance are such accounts as recorded on Papago Indian calendar sticks.
>
> 1848—In this year happened an almost unbelievable thing. Cold weather of unheard-of intensity swooped down on the Papagos [Tohono O'odham] and almost snuffed them out. Snow fell to a depth of three feet on the level and as deep as the tops of houses in drifts, and lay on the ground for many weeks. Cattle and horses could not find food under the snow and the People [hehemajkam] could not find firewood. There was great suffering because the People had always been accustomed to warm winters.

1870—Snow again fell to a remarkable depth. It remained on the ground only two days before melting away.[19]

Then, as recently as April 12, 2021, the Phoenix Desert Botanical Garden published an article titled "A Disappearing Icon," in which readers were alerted: "If left unchecked, invasive grasses, combined with climate change, may have dire consequences to saguaros across large portions of Arizona. Fortunately, efforts are ongoing to mechanically remove invasive grasses from prime saguaro habitats."[20] O'odham, of course, are equally concerned for the hahashañ, as are the various conservation groups throughout the region. Integral to the O'odham response to the environmental crisis is maintaining the saguaro fruit harvest. In 2019 the *Arizona Daily Star* published a story about Tanisha Tucker, a Tohono O'dham keeping alive the tradition taught to her by her mother, Stella, and her great-great-aunt, Juanita Ahil. An important part of Tucker's work is passing along her knowledge to children: "The kids took turns carrying the poles, and it took some effort to dislodge the fruit and remove the pulp from the pod. They were told to give thanks to the saguaro by leaving the empty fruit pod at the base of the cactus. By the end of the morning, some had their hands and shirts stained red from the fruit."[21]

Tucker's story is relevant to the discourse on O'odham himdag in that it is consistent with the origin narrative that Komal Hok recounted and what O'odham calendar-stick holders recorded on their ooshikbina. Unfortunately, just as Rea observed that he was unaware of any O'dham possessing the origin narrative to the extent that Thin Leather did, so too is this author unaware of the jujkida, the rain making ceremony, which follows the wiigida, the harvest ceremony, being performed anywhere.[22] However, this may have to do with the author being an Akimel O'dham from the Gila River Indian Community and a family that took up the Presbyterian way generations ago. What references there are to the jujkida and wiigida in the published literature is limited to the Tohono O'odham jeved.[23] Russell did make a brief but significant reference to the "rain-making ceremony" in *The Pima Indians*, cited earlier. Otherwise, as Edward S. Curtis observed in *The North American Indian* (1908):

The disintegration of their tribal laws and customs has almost put an end to Pima ceremony; yet parts of a Rain-making Ceremony [jujkida] and Harvest Dance [wiigida] are sometimes given in the more isolated districts, under strict secrecy. Many of the older men and women are still familiar with nearly the entire category of Pima rites, having participated in them in their youth.[24]

Significantly, Curtis's brief chapter on "The Pima" divides the O'odham summer ceremonies into jujkida (rain ceremony), which Curtis writes as "chóchkĭta," and wiigida (harvest ceremony), or "víkĭta." However, Russell only refers to "tcutc kita," the rain ceremony (jujkida) as a religious event. The reference to the wiigida is listed under "Festivals" and labeled "saguaro harvest festival," in which the "drinking of navait or saguaro liquor" is highlighted as one of the "arts of pleasure." Referring to "drunken orgies," Russell points out that "the Government has prohibited 'tizwin drunks,' as they are called by the whites, though they are still surreptitiously held."[25] Given the brevity of Russell's ensuing description of this "festival," it is likely that Russell did not witness any of these "surreptitiously held ceremonies." Instead he emphasizes that the ceremony is on the decline, more so due to milgahn coercion than to O'odham choice.

> Through the influence of the missionaries, the native police under the [Indian] agent's orders, and the actively exerted influence of the more intelligent men in the tribe, the custom is dying out. The subchief, Kâemâ-â [Coy-e-mau, Rattlesnake-head], at Gila Crossing has been a zealous advocate of temperance for a number of years, and it is not unlikely that the folly of such debaucheries was apparent to some members of the Pima community during preceding generations before outside influences were brought to bear upon them.[26]

Contrary to the milgahn belief that the wiigida was morally depraved, O'odham participation in the wiigida was regarded among O'odham as a moral imperative. The wiigida keeps the rain pouring down, replenishing the O'odham jeved from the akimel to their fields and into their bodies. Given that O'odham can only rely on themselves for keeping the wiigida viable and the wiigida's connection to the O'odham himdag, the moral imperative is based on the kinship ties that all O'odham have with one another as families, as villages, and as a people. However, the O'odham himdag is not limited to the wiigida but applies to every aspect of O'odham culture. More to the point, every ritual and ceremonial action is oriented toward "bringing the clouds down" and keeping the rain pouring. "It was Earth Medicine Man [Jeved mahkai] who made the earth," Joseph Giff was recorded saying in "Pima Blue Swallow Songs of Gratitude." Furthermore, Jeved mahkai "then made people[;] then gave them knowledge[,] whatever people would have for knowledge[,] to help each other in life[,] and make their life continue."[27] At this juncture, it should be clear that the O'odham origin narrative is a primary source of this knowledge. Among Tohono O'odham, as Underhill observed:

> Young people were ceaselessly trained in the [Tohono O'odham] moral code [or himdag], whose principal tenets were industry, fortitude and swiftness of foot. Industry was a woman's virtue, without which no girl could hope to be kept as a wife. Fortitude was a virtue of both sexes and Papago [Tohono O'odham] life, which was so frequently on the verge of starvation, brought it to the foreground. The augury on all auspicious occasions was: "You will be hunger-enduring, thirst-enduring, cold-enduring."[28]

Furthermore, O'odham were expected to be generous with each other, as well as soft-spoken and patient. Within O'odham society one of the most reproachable vices is stinginess or greed (banmadag), as it is prone to undoing the social fabric that keeps kinship ties healthy and strong. In a sense, hehemajkam ought to be as generous as the land itself, which avails its bounty in the form of rain and that which the rain nurtures, such as the hahashañ.

During the salt pilgrimage, onamed (to gather salt),[29] Tohono O'odham men (cecoj) and boys seeking to become men venture into the riverless desert plains when the sky is dominated by the sun and its heat. They go on this possibly perilous journey not only for the salt ('on), but also for the sake of having visions and bringing back the rain (juhk) from the ocean (ge'e shuthagi). Hehemajkam wait for summer when the tide has receded enough to gather the much-desired gift. Visions are sought especially by young men who are likely on their first salt pilgrimage. They hearken a message on their direction in life. A young man may have a vision about being a hunter (o'oitham), a runner (melchutham), or a medicine maker (mahkai). This is the way to distinguishing himself and gaining respect. "Though they take canny means to compass the journey safely, they make no attempt to minimize its hardships." Moreover, as Underhill further observes in *Papago Indian Religion*, the hardships "are emphasized to the last degree and used as an occasion for heroism. . . . They fast voluntarily, almost to starvation. They run until men have been known to die from the effects. . . . The salt pilgrimage is, in fact, very like a war party. . . . It is as though the [Tohono O'odham], who had so little to do with war, had transferred some of the magical elements connected with it [war] to this safer and more regular form of ordeal."[30]

This discourse on O'odham ceremonialism relates to the discourse on hahashañ in that abundant hahashañ forests are a sign of a healthy jeved. A sign of changing times are the reports of saguaro population decline caused by colonization, economic development, and resource-straining population growth. From an O'dham perspective, the situation demands a renewal of our himdag. O'odham spiritual life has always been focused on supplicating rain. Ceremonies like the wiigida and salt pilgrimage are saturated with rain speeches, songs, and prayers. As Underhill notes:

> [Tohono O'odham] songs deal with the holiest of all things to the desert people, rain. To them rain is [endowed] with a life-giving loveliness: it is life itself. The songs deal with the animals who flash to and fro on the desert, at home in its ways as man can never be. They deal with the springing beauty of the corn and they speak almost with the amazed rapture that the birds and animals might feel, had they found this means to make food grow at their feet, instead of having to hunt for it over the thirsting desert.[31]

At the same time, admonishing O'odham to remember their himdag is insufficient for renewing the jeved. Mimilgahn are obliged to change their culture of excess. When O'odham offered friendship to the mimilgahn when they traveled through their jeved, they did not ask them to stay and overwhelm the akimel with their settlements. For the O'odham himdag to truly thrive, mimilgahn must decolonize their relationship with the jeved. When the hahashañ are abundant once more, then both O'odham and mimilgahn will know that they are restoring the balance between humans and the environment that the himdag required ever since Jeved mahkai planted the first shegoi in the earth.

CHAPTER FIVE

When Coyote Stole Rabbit's Heart

An Environmental Ethic for the O'odham Himdag

I f hahashañ embody ancestral spirits as implied by the previous chapter, then hahashañ are not only sentient beings but also worthy of an ethical response. So, then, what is the origin of ethics? One may immediately think of Martin Buber's I-Thou concept, which he distinguished from I-You and I-It. As Buber explains, these are the three types of existential relationships one can have with another person. Simply put, Thou is akin to God, You is friend or relative, and It is stranger or object. When one is in a deeply caring, as opposed to casual, relationship, then one is likely in an I-Thou relation, which Buber affirmed one can have with anyone if one opens oneself to the other's humanity, to their godliness, if you will. This is challenging, of course, in the modern era, in which war, disease, social collapse, mass migration, and refugee camps cause more and more people to be regarded as Its, as objects, at the moment when they need to be respected for their thouness most urgently.[1] With the trauma of modern history in mind, one may also think of Emmanuel Lévinas's related concept of the Face, in which the Face behind one's physical face, which bears the image of God, transcends one's physical identity and demands a response, which Lévinas thought of as the source of responsibility. This is the true origin of ethics.[2]

O'odham are a part of the modern world that inspired the insights of Buber and Levinas, as are all Indigenous peoples. They are also a part of a unique history, which includes the American conquest of northern Sonora, namely the Pimería Alta, which became New Mexico Territory after the 1846–1848 war between the United States and the Mexican Republic. While that globally impactful conflict was not as devastating as the world wars that dominated the first half of the twentieth century, from an O'odham perspective the US-Mexican War, complete with the Treaty of Guadalupe-Hidalgo (1848) and subsequent Gadsden Purchase (1854), was more than enough to completely change the course of O'odham history. Although, as illustrated earlier in reference to the calendar sticks, this did not change the O'odham perspective on their own village-based histories. Nonetheless, what this means for the present discourse on ethics is that O'odham were rendered strangers in their own jeved. They were not only non-citizens under American law but also possessed less humanity than the milgahn settlers who took more and more O'odham land and water.

The ethical dilemma in which O'odham found themselves was defined by a world not of their own making, complete with an upheaval in the political order, as the O'odham jeved was now divided in two and controlled by two separate settler-colonial nations, the United States and Mexico. Also, O'odham himdag was disrupted, first by land cessions hehemajkam were forced to endure as milgahn farms, ranches, mines, and forts appeared. As for O'odham below the southern border, they remained a part of the O'odham jeved insofar as their lands were accessible to relatives on the American side. Nonetheless, the US-Mexico border has had a corrosive effect on O'odham kinship ties, as O'odham encountered pressures to adopt the milgahn border into their sense of homeland and peoplehood. This intervention into the O'odham mind intensified once the reservation system was fully installed and overseen by the Office of Indian Affairs, which deployed its superintendents to make decisions on behalf of their "wards." The latter included how the jeved would be managed as an economic resource. Indian reservations, after all, were under the auspices of the US Department of the Interior.

The western discourse on ethics is a discourse on how to manage human behavior, which is based on theories of human nature, society, and morality. Plato's Idea of the Good, Kant's moral imperative, Mill's greatest good for the greatest number, Nietzsche's transvaluation of values are highlights in the history of western ethical thinking. Through these works, and others like them, readers are challenged to think about the definition of key concepts (such as good, evil, and power), reflect on the meaning of moral principles (know thyself, act only if you will it to become universal law), as well as contemplate a world without meaning (God is dead). For many in the western intellectual tradition, the critical thinking intrinsic to philosophical analysis sits in contradistinction to two extremes: the amoral universe of science, which is bereft of human agency, and the dogmatic cosmos of religion—namely, Christianity—in which human will is limited to orthodoxy. Philosophy defies the tenets of conventional thinking by asking questions that set the norms of society on edge, such as when Socrates disturbed the minds of Athens's youth, which led to his legendary sacrifice as recounted in the *Phaedo*. Nonetheless, Socrates notwithstanding, philosophy is a literary genre developed over time by white men who valued the idiosyncrasies not of dialog and communitas but of self-reflection, objectivity, and critique. Philosophy, moreover, as a written tradition, lends itself to the musings of the inner voice. In a sense, every philosopher is Descartes, exploring the limits of the cogito and searching for the boundaries between knowing and unknowing, in which even the existence of God can be doubted—at least hypothetically. But what is the cogito anyway but another social convention, a philosophical trope spun from the Cartesian imagination? Descartes may be revered in the western philosophical tradition, but what did he know beyond the French Catholic world in which he lived? For that matter, what did Plato, Kant, Mill, and Nietzsche know about the world around them that was not European? What did they know that did not come from a book? Equally important, how do such lives and writings look to someone who does not identify as a European or with any facet of western civilization, including the primacy of literacy, but rather as an Indigenous person whose radical doubt puts the status of western civilization into dispute? What becomes of the discourse on ethics? Are we not now without a moral compass? Are we not mere savages without the Bible and Aristotle? My questions are meant to be ridiculous. On the other hand, one may wonder what Komal Hok might have thought.

In the context of the present discourse, Akimel O'odham evokes a world—the more appropriate word is jeved—beyond the reach of western theory. As Europe entered the Late Middle Ages when the Continent was besotted with the Black Death, the Mexica, or Aztecs, in southern México constructed their ancient capital, Tenochtitlan, and wrote the codices that formed the basis of their civilization. In turn, ancestral O'odham, or huhugam, entered what archaeologists labeled the Classical Period,[3] during which sisivani (chief priests) built great houses (ge'egdaj kikih) along the akimel, the Gila River, and the onk akimel, the Salt River.[4] For O'odham, Christianity and the Spanish Empire rode in with Eusebio Kino, a Jesuit priest of Italian descent, in 1694 to establish a mission system in the Pímeria Alta that was meant to parallel the one in Alta California. As anthropologist Eric R. Wolf might have said, the Akimel O'odham appeared in Kino's travel journals as a "people without history."[5] However, the racialized biases of anthropologists, historians, and missionaries need not be recounted here. What is important to note is that when the Spanish entrada arrived in Akimel O'odham land, the O'odham did not enter western history, but rather the Spanish (jujkam) entered O'odham oral tradition.

When Kino met the people living along the Gila River, he nevertheless saw the land as terra incognita: "In 1694 [Kino] reached the Casa Grande [ruins] in company with native guides [likely Tohono O'odham][6] who had informed him of the existence of [this place]. Absolutely nothing is known about this expedition except that, according to O'odham oral tradition, a mass was said within the walls of Casa Grande."[7] Otherwise, historians have long varied in their analyses of the archival record regarding Kino's inaugural journey to "el Río de Hila." In Fewkes' account of the historical background of the Casa Grande Ruins, he surmised, relying on Mange's version:

> The first known white man to visit Casa Grande was the intrepid Jesuit Father Eusebio Francisco Kino. . . . In 1694 Lieut Juan Mateo Mange . . . was commissioned to escort the missionaries on their perilous journeys. . . . In June of that year, while making a reconnaissance [sic] toward the northeast from Kino's mission of Dolores on the western branch of the Rio Sonora, Mange heard from the Indians of some casas grandes, massive and very high, on the margin of a river which flowed toward the west. The news was communicated to Kino and shortly afterward was confirmed by some Indians who visited Dolores from San Xavier del Bac, on the Rio Santa Cruz below the Indian village of Tucson. In November (1694) Kino went from his mission on a tour of discovery, finding Casa Grande to be as reported, and saying mass within its walls.[8]

Since Kino traveled northward from the Altar River, he inevitably encountered O'odham villages along the Santa Cruz River, which placed him in Tohono O'odham and Sobaipuri O'odham lands. Kino asked these O'odham their name before reaching Casa Grande, meaning that he learned something of the O'odham, including what they called themselves, before reaching the Casa Grande Ruins..[9] More important, as a Jesuit, Kino obliged himself to learn O'odham neok, though he was probably not fluent, hence the inaccuracies in his accounts.[10] As for the O'odham name for the Spaniards, jujkam, it evokes a people arriving from the south, so is also applied to Mexicans.[11] Jujkam is etymologically related to juhk, the word for "deep" and "depth," as in a deep place or a land below. Jujk, in turn, is related to jujk, the word for rain, which travels up from the south (wakoliw) in the form of the summer monsoons. In a sense, Mexicans are the "people from where the rain begins."[12] Thus, jujkam have a place in O'odham sacred geography.

With respect to the question of what becomes of ethics in the absence of western philosophy and religion, the implication of Spanish-O'odham history is that one must ask whose land or environment it is before initiating a discourse on environmental ethics. In the case of the Sonoran Desert, it is the home of not only O'odham but also Comcaac, Mayo, and Yoeme, as well as Opata and Raramuri. From the Spanish or Mexican perspective, the answer to the question "Whose land?" is whoever has political or colonial control over the territory in question. For O'odham and other Indigenous peoples, the answer lies in their oral traditions, in which customary boundaries are expressed. An environmental ethic on occupied Indian land may require a rethinking of the colonial institutions of border, territory, government, and sovereignty. Thus the division of the O'odham jeved between two settler colonial nations, the United States and México, is the consequence of three centuries of colonization, meaning the deliberate actions of three colonizing nations (Spain, Mexico, and the United States) to occupy and exploit ancestral Indian land. There is no right of conquest. There is only the historic problem of conquest. Therefore, in the transborder region of Arizona and Sonora, an environmental ethics must begin not only by acknowledging that O'odham jeved is occupied but also by proclaiming that the restoration of O'odham land relations, or himdag, requires decolonization. O'odham communities must pursue—and non-O'odham must support, as a moral imperative—more environmental sovereignty over their homelands, especially sacred sites.

At this juncture it is important to remember that O'odham neok does not have a word for either "world" or "worldview." Jeved, which has been evoked numerous times, refers simply to land, earth, and soil. O'odham were aware of places beyond the O'odham jeved, but those places were given to other peoples by their creators. Environmental ethics, as a nonindigenous intellectual field, be it applied or theoretical, tend to be premised on the assumption that what is articulated in principle is universal, meaning relevant to all humans, regardless of the differences that distinguish human communities. We all need drinkable water. We all need breathable air. We all need food security. Such prepositions lend credibility to the presumption that environmental ethics is global. After all, does not the global warming crisis necessitate a global response? An O'odham environmental ethic, however, based on local land relations and cultural exclusivity sounds counter-intuitive.[13] Yet, if global warming is the consequence of colonization,[14] which is also global,[15] then is it not sensible that the antidote is anticolonial, site-specific, and indigenous? This means an O'odham environmental ethic, specifically their himdag, is necessary for O'odham land, their jeved.

When Kino visited Casa Grande in 1694, he joined others who pondered the origins of the great adobe houses.[16] Europe, of course, was home to a plethora of ruins. Some stood as monuments to well-documented civilizations, such as the Parthenon; while others, like Stonehenge, evoked an unknown people lost in the mist of history. Both known and unknown ruins equally marked the decline of a historical epoch and collapse of the civilization that once flourished where now only a few stones remain. So, what about Casa Grande?[17] An unfortunate consequence of the teleological theory of history is the presupposition that once a civilization declines it can never be reborn, especially if overtaken by a more powerful nation. According to Russell, as cited earlier in chapter 2, O'odham queried about Casa Grande stated that "however ready they may have been in the past to claim relationship with the [huhugam] or relate tales of the supernatural origin of the pueblos, they now frankly admit that they do not know anything about the matter."[18] Curiously, Russell cites J. R. Bartlett, a member of the US Boundary Survey Commission, to corroborate his assertion:

[Casa Grande], as well as the ruins above the Pimo villages, are known among the Indians as the "houses of Montezuma," an idea doubtless derived from the Mexicans. . . . We asked our Indian guide who Montezuma was. He answered, "Nobody knows who the devil he was; all we know is, that he built these houses."[19]

Was Montezuma a synonym for I'itoi, Elder brother? While Russell noted that "Hohokam" referred to "the race that occupied the pueblos that are now rounded heaps of ruins in the Salt and Gila river valleys," he failed to comprehend these houses as integral to the story of I'itoi, who taught O'odham their himdag. As also observed with great frustration, generations of archaeologists, from Jesse Walter Fewkes to Emil Haury and Paul Ezell, puzzled over the relationship between the "Hohokam" and the "Pima," often dismissing O'odham oral tradition as unscientific.[20]

It is time once again to turn to Thin Leather, Komal Hok. Although other O'odham mamahkai (medicine people) and kekelimai (elders) have shared their knowledge, as cited in numerous books and papers on the O'odham written by scholars such as Underhill and Bahr, Komal Hok is distinct for sharing the whole epic in two historically important sources.[21] Moreover, adding to Thin Leather's historical importance as an O'odham storyteller is Rea's earlier observation of the dearth of any men and women like Thin Leather in the present era. So it is worth mentioning that the Akimel O'odham origin narrative persists today as a source of knowledge largely because of him.[22] At the same time, there are still mamahkai availing their medicine to people suffering from illness. There are still kekelimai guiding the young and not so young. There are O'odham working in the fields of education, art and literature, music and dance, and other media that give expression to O'odham voices. And there is at least one O'dham, the author of this book, who has a degree in philosophy. Such an array of modern adaptations may at a glance appear to be signs of O'odham assimilation into modern Western society, but upon closer examination they are signs of O'odham resistance. As a living society, O'odham are aware of their colonization, which is a kind of wandering sickness, 'Oimmeddam mumkidag (something harmful from beyond the jeved), yet possess the instinct for life preservation.

Hehemajkam, as ordinary people, are a part of the contemporary world. So too is the O'odham jeved. Therefore Komal Hok's legacy is more than historical; it evokes a himdag that endures today, even under layers of milgahn colonization. Thus, the wia'i (ruins) that were "left behind" by huhugam (ancestral O'odham) at places like Sivan vahki (Casa Grande) are not the vestiges of a fallen civilization—or "that which has perished," which was Haury's translation of "Hohokam"[23]—but the landmarks of a contemporary O'odham world. Prominent among revered places defining the Akimel O'odham jeved is Muhadag do'ag, Greasy mountain, which the Americans christened "South Mountain." This is one of the places where I'itoi ki, Elder brother's house, is located. I'itoi ki is commonly known as the man-in-the-maze symbol.[24] Each O'odham community regards a different mountain as where Elder brother's house can be found. Tohono O'odham point to Waw giwulk, Constricted rock, or Baboquivari Peak. Hia-Ced O'odham regard Chuk do'ag, Black mountain, or Sierra Pinacante, as I'itoi's home. As for the Sobaipuri O'odham, it is unclear where they place I'itoi ki.[25] Our focus here is Greasy mountain, in the heart of the Akimel O'odham jeved.

When Thin Leather recounted the origin narrative, he lived in Ge'e kih (Big house), or Sacaton Village, north of Sacaton Mountains, along the south bank of the akimel, the Gila River. As Komal Hok tells the story, after Jeved mahkai cleansed the land of the first people, who turned on each other when they over populated their jeved,[26] they[27] made all things anew, including the first people, s*os*anac.[28] However, not all was as before. Springing from tohav (white brittlebush) was Bán (Coyote), a trickster who embodies childish impulses and playfulness.[29] Also springing from the earth was I'itoi, later known as Siuuhuu, a powerful mahkai whose powers were comparable to Jeved mahkai. I'itoi, in fact, declared to Jeved mahkai that he would "destroy" the s*os*anac.[30] In a sense, Coyote and Elder brother mark a change from one world to the next.[31] As such, Elder brother's appearance suggests that he is here to fulfill a destiny embedded in Jeved mahkai's creation, a natural part of its growth and maturation. More to the point, what the first people lacked when Jeved mahkai made them, I'itoi would provide, namely their himdag.

As may be recalled, I'itoi created an unnamed "handsome youth" who "wed" with whomever he pleased.[32] The unnamed youth impregnated women with children whose gestation was each shorter than the previous.[33] Eventually, a child appeared at birth without a mother. "This was the child that caused the flood which destroyed the people and fulfilled the plans of Elder Brother."[34] However, the flood would not strike until I'itoi completed a nawaitakud ha'a, the "jar or olla"[35] he made for himself. Jeved mahkai gathered people together and described "the calamity that would befall them."

> [Jeved mahkai then] thrust his staff into the ground. . . . Some of the people went into the hole, while others appealed to Elder Brother. Their appeals were not heeded. . . . Coyote . . . was [then] told to find a big log and sit upon it. . . . Elder Brother got into his olla and closed the opening by which he entered, singing in the meantime.[36]

After the flood, Jeved mahkai saved themself in their "reed staff,"[37] floating to a location "somewhere in the east."[38] Bán (Coyote) wound up at "Driftwood Mountain," whose location is also unknown, though it is likely in the south.[39] I'itoi, on the other hand, "came to rest beyond Sonoita [sic], near the mouth of the Colorado river. The olla (nawaitakud ha'a), now called Black mountain (Chuk do'ag), may be seen there to this day."[40] Chuk do'ag, as noted earlier, is where the Hia-Ced O'odham say that I'itoi ki exists.[41]

After locating the center of the world, I'itoi, Bán, and Jeved mahkai sat down to make the creatures to inhabit the land, which was still "wet and muddy." After Bán and Jeved mahkai cast their creations into the water and to the west, respectively, as I'itoi instructed, Jeved mahkai suddenly sank into the earth. When I'itoi grabbed hold of Jeved mahkai, he was not strong enough to keep them from disappearing, leaving I'itoi's hands covered in "blood and dirt." When I'itoi shook his hands clean the blood and dirt scattered, spreading disease "over the land and in the water."[42] I'itoi then flung the Apache (the O'ob) to the other side of the mountains, where they now live, which made them angry (baga). In turn, I'itoi divided the people into four tribes. In addition to the Apache, he made the "Wä-akĭ Âp [Wa'akih O'ob?] . . . the Maricopas, and, lastly, the Pimas."[43] Not long afterward, I'itoi decided mysteriously "to do mischief [among the O'odham]."[44] At this juncture, as may also be recalled, the last time I'itoi helped the people was when he assisted them with building canals. However, this does not mean that I'itoi abandons his hehemajkam.

The lessons that I'itoi brings to the O'odham began with giving Rattlesnake (ko'owi) their fangs, which they used to bite Rabbit (tohbi), which caused the first death (muhkig). Moreover, it was during Rabbit's cremation that Bán stole Rabbit's heart, or ibdak, and ran away to Komadk do'ag, Grassy Plains mountain, which the jujkam named Sierra Estrella. When people went after him, Bán fled to Muhadag do'ag: "Again the people overtook Coyote, and he ran northward across the Gila, where he ate [Rabbit's] heart, and as he did so the grease fell upon every stone of the mountain, which accounts for its appearance and the name it bears to this day—[Muhadag], Greasy mountain." Finally, when he had his fill, Bán ran away "to live in the sea in the south."[45] Bán nevertheless would always return when there was trouble to be made, which meant turmoil, disruption, or chaos with a purpose. As Komal Hok further recalls the downfall of the big houses, I'itoi alternates between playing a direct and indirect role. Suffice it to say, hehemajkam endure difficult lessons, such as when they learn to hunt and fend for themselves, which is made all the more difficult when Bán's randy behavior causes the game to be chased away. Also, a sivani named Feather-breathing, who had strong powers but was childlike, built a vahkih along the onk akimel, the Salt River, where a gambler named Väntre came to live. Väntre's name is not O'odham. From where he came is a mystery.[46] Nonetheless, when Väntre begins preying on the people, I'itoi knew what to do and intervened to eliminate the monster from terrorizing O'odham villages. "Elder Brother," Thin Leather recalls, "then went home and told the people how to conduct themselves when they had killed an enemy." Once I'itoi taught the Akimel O'odham the enemy purification ceremony, "the people about Baboquivari wished to have Elder Brother come to them."[47]

At this point, Komal Hok focuses on Casa Grande. During a women's field hockey (toka[48]) game, a "little green lizard"[49] appeared at the sivani's daughter's feet, under which "green stones"[50] were found. Women began wearing these as jewelry, which sparked envy in Tas Namkam (Meet-the-Sun), who sent a parrot[51] to eat the stones. The people had never seen such a creature,[52] so fed it more stones. When the sivani, Si'al Cehedag (Morning

Green), became angry and lashed out, Meet-the-Sun retaliated by sending a young man with a football (songiwul), which he gave to the daughter. When she hid the ball up her dress, playing a trick on the young man, it went into her womb and impregnated her. "The people wished to destroy the child, because it had long claws instead of fingers and toes; its teeth were long and sharp, like those of a dog."[53] Ho'ok,[54] as this child was called, began preying upon everything, including children. I'itoi, once again, intervened to save the people. "After killing [Ho'ok] Elder Brother made his home at Baboquivari for some time."[55]

In time, I'itoi began his mischief again, and in earnest. "He sang the song of the menstrual period and accompanied it by reviling the family of the young girls. At last the people could endure his pranks no longer and drove him away."[56] Like Bán, when he stole Rabbit's heart, I'itoi fled to Muhadag do'ag. Four times the people killed him. Four times I'itoi revived. So the people called a council, where they determined to seek assistance from Nuwi, the vulture mahkai that lives in Komadk do'ag.

> Vulture was a man who transformed himself into a bird with his own magic power and had gone through the openings in the sky and thus saved himself from destruction during the flood. After he came down from the sky he wandered about the country and finally built a va'-aki, magic house, the ruins of which yet remain, south of where Phoenix now stands, between the Gila and Salt rivers.[57]

Nuwi used his medicine to compel the sun to overheat I'itoi's house like a volcano. When the calamity was over, I'itoi was little more than a skeleton. However, yet again I'itoi rose, alarming the people who wanted him slain. "Elder Brother sank through the earth and found the people that Earth Doctor [Jeved mahkai] had assisted to reach that side in order to escape the flood. Elder Brother told the people there of his ill treatment and asked them to come through and fight with him and to take the land away from the Indians."[58] Thus, the decline and collapse of the big houses began. Once again, it is worth mentioning that the hehemajkam that returned with I'itoi were likely another branch of the O'odham, such as the Pima Bajo. Given that O'odham regard these people as their ancestors, huhukam, it only makes sense that I'itoi brought people who spoke some dialect of O'odham neok with him.

Casa Grande was the first to fall. Then the big house at Santan.[59] From there, I'itoi's army went to Sweet Water.[60] At each village I'itoi's allies sang a song. At Casa Blanca,[61] I'itoi's warriors sang of their concern at confronting such a powerful place: "It will be difficult. It will be difficult. To capture this pueblo. With its magic power." Each big house has a sivani, a chief priest. "[Chukchu Tadai Sivan at Casa Blanca] was the most powerful of all the chiefs who ventured to oppose [I'itoi's army]."[62] Komal Hok then describes an epic battle between Chukchu Tadai (Black Roadrunner) and I'itoi, in which each controlled natural phenomena like rain and wind. In the end, the Casa Blanca sivani was defeated. And in his heart, the victors found a small green stone, like the ones that Meet-the-Sun coveted. The next battle was against Nuwi. I'itoi headed to Gila Crossing. When Nuwi was captured, I'itoi scalped him, leaving the bald head that distinguishes him today. Afterward, big houses in Mesa and Tempe (Oidbad) also fell. Eventually, the fighting stops and I'itoi vanishes from Thin Leather's narrative.[63] Komal Hok concludes with an anecdote about a young man searching for food in the mountains near the Salt River valley for his pregnant wife, who "would eat nothing but green plants and game found in the mountains," meaning that she was not satisfied with the crops that her Akimel O'odham family grew. While out there, away from their village, the man was surrounded by O'obga (Apaches) and killed. When his remains were recovered, like Rabbit before Bán stole his heart, "they [were] burned to ashes." One day, the young man's son Ka'kanyip would avenge his father's death.[64] Thus do the Apaches that I'itoi created as one of the first four tribes return to the O'odham origin narrative, establishing the rivalry that persisted at the time the colonizers invaded the jeved along the akimel and onk akimel.

In the aftermath of the ge'egdaj kikih, Akimel O'odham emerge as a people of the olas kih, the small roundhouse that predominated across the O'odham jeved until the Americans' arrival in the 1850s.[65] The himdag that I'itoi embodied is adapted anew to the sacred places that Jeved mahkai made, which were cleansed multiple times. Now the hehemajkam (the people), without sisivani, sowed their fields, maintained their villages, and gathered for the wiigiida (saguaro cactus harvest ceremony), which beckons the jegos (summer monsoons) to rejuvenate the jeved.[66] The cactus fruit (bahithaj), which is turned into ceremonial wine (nawait), symbolizes this renewal. The story that Thin Leather relayed to Russell and Lloyd teaches that the civilization the sisivani built collapsed because they strayed from their himdag. Instead they killed I'itoi. So I'itoi sank into the earth and sought Jeved mahkai's people to assemble an army to rid the land of sisivani, which I'itoi's "mischief" exposed as corrupt. The people of the olas kih, of course, can still lose their way and abandon their himdag. This is something that contemporary O'odham wonder about, as they are no longer people of the olas kih but dwell in modern housing, complete with the technology and infrastructure that undergirds such a society.

The O'odham jeved is ill again,[67] and has been since American settlers stole the akimel from the hehemajkam only a few years after they were placed on a reservation in 1859.[68] Their Tohono O'odham cousins were at one time reduced to a handful of villages surrounding San Xavier del Bac Mission, while others were pushed away from their sacred mountain Baboquivari. Hia-Ced O'odham and Sobaipuri, in turn, were presumed to have vanished either due to disease—the Hia-Ced O'odham suffered a yellow fever epidemic in 1851—or due to relentless Apache attacks, which is what drove the Sobaipuri away from their lands around Dragoon. For decades, Indian agents pressured all O'odham to abandon their himdag and take up the ways of Americans, who called themselves a Christian nation. When, for example, US Army veteran Charles H. Cook rode into Sacaton Village, which was home to the "Pima Agency," on December 23, 1870, he did so at the behest of the Board of Indian Commissioners,[69] which oversaw "Indian civilization" at a time when the Gila River community was undergoing a crisis due to severe water shortages caused by upriver settler damming.[70] The Presbyterian mission did not see itself as causing the water crisis, but rather the Army. Instead the mission perceived itself as a humanitarian intervention motivated by the Gospel. Cook stated: "It was not until several months after I reached . . . Sacaton that I learned [of] others beside myself, who were anxious to have the gospel and christian [sic] civilization brought to a people, who are perishing for want of it."[71] In other words, Cook saw his work as charitable, as did Kino when he colonized the Tohono O'odham and Sobaipuri O'odham jeved with this mission system.

The Presbyterian Church, nevertheless, as an agent of federal Indian policy, was quick to express disdain for hehemajkam that clung too closely to their himdag, especially mamahkai. Cook's colleague and contemporary Reverend Isaac T. Whittmore, in particular, did not hesitate to despise medicine men that he regarded as obstacles. "Ever since the missionary [Cook] began work[ing] here [at Gila River]," Whittemore recounted, "these . . . medicine men have been an annoyance and hindrance to his work."[72] Ultimately, *Among the Pima* is about how Cook's congregation grew at the expense of the O'odham himdag, complete with churches at Sacaton, Casa Blanca, Bapchule, Gila Crossing, and Maricopa.

> Many [Akimel O'odham] come regularly to church a distance of from two to twenty miles, and not a few twenty or thirty miles. In summer, when churches in town are closed from the intense heat, these overflow with a multitude who are attracted, not by the eloquence of the preacher or by the exquisite rendering of chants by a well trained [sic] choir, or soul-stirring peals of the organ, but from pure love to God and delight in the service of preaching, prayer and praise. This influence on a people just emerging from heathenism and breaking up old superstitions and vices, and instead of them, leading an industrious and virtuous life, must far exceed that of churches in town on a civilized people.[73]

While the Gila River Indian Community today has gained political sovereignty, including water rights,[74] their freedom is still limited by the same settler-colonial power—the United States—that drew the reservation boundary in 1859.[75] As stated earlier, one cannot articulate an Indigenous environmental ethics without first acknowledging that the land is stolen and occupied. Only the colonizers can afford to be color-blind, ahistorical, and transcendental. It is time, then, for I'itoi to assemble his army once again and cleanse the O'odham jeved.

Restoring the O'odham himdag, however, is not something that Akimel O'odham would will to become a universal law, except among themselves. Like other Indigenous groups, O'odham do not proselytize nor expect other people to adopt their way of doing things. The O'odham himdag is not an organized religion. In the western intellectual tradition, religion is an institution governed by a set of beliefs oriented around a supreme being whose will for the people he created is expressed in a sacred text. As a text-based institution, religions—as opposed to being religious—are defined by the rules, beliefs, and missions that distinguish them from one another. The goal of the Presbyterian Home and Foreign Mission, the entity within the US Presbyterian Church that organizes its global missionary work, in North America was to bring the gospel to the Indians while organizing the frontier into presbyteries. Cook, in *Presbyterian Home Missions* by Sherman H. Doyle, is recognized with the highest esteem:

> [Cook's] success has been marvelous. "Fourteen hundred Indians baptized is a fine record. Old men and young, mothers and grandmothers, warriors and medicine men, with children claimed in covenant, are written by name in his book of baptism." [citation omitted] Five church buildings have been erected under his care and through him thousands have heard the gospel, and hundreds been developed in Christian life and service. . . . What a record for one man. "Father" Cook is a great man, a patriarch among thousands of people, welcome in many villages.[76]

Even today, Presbyterian Mission is guided by influencing people's faith, beliefs, and values.[77] With respect to Cook's legacy, while the "apostle to the Pimas"[78] passed away long ago in 1917, the role he played at disrupting the O'odham himdag lives on in O'odham language declination and cultural loss. Consequently, an O'odham environmental ethic is not about encouraging non-Indigenous people to appropriate the O'odham himdag, but about creating the cultural and political space in which O'odham can revitalize their himdag. In addition to acknowledging that the O'odham jeved—which the US seized from Mexico in its illegal 1846–1848 war of aggression—is expropriated, an environmental ethic appropriate to this jeved must be premised on a nonlinear, nonwestern concept of history in which progress, manifest destiny, and the Anthropocene does not guide our thinking about the needs of this place.

What American society, on the other hand, must will to be a universal law is the revitalization of Indigenous communities and cultures. Discourses on land management, conservation, and ecological restoration must open to an O'odham-centric worldview in which O'odham can exercise their communal values free from outside interference. This will allow America, as a colonizing nation, to do the greatest amount of good for the greatest number of Indigenous people. An anticolonial environmental ethic will enable Indigenous peoples to recover their original land relations. For O'odham, this means reclaiming their relationship with Muhadag do'ag, Waw giwulk, and Chuk do'ag. *The O'odham himdag is not a religion, but higher than religion.* Whereas in the western tradition, a religion is a man-made institution and thereby prone to moral corruption, the O'odham himdag springs from the jeved (earth) just as I'itoi (Elder brother) sprung from the earth. Only when the akimel and onk akimel are cleansed of the "big houses" that the Americans have built on ancestral O'odham land, from their churches to their great cities, will the O'odham himdag be back in balance.

Missionary of Sorrows

Charles H. Cook and a Time of Bihugig

A s noted in the earlier chapters, Akimel O'odham have been living under the influence of American protestant civilization since Charles H. Cook founded his churches during his 1870–1917 years as Presbyterian missionary for the Pima Agency. This was in addition to generations of influence, albeit indirect, wrought by the Spanish mission system, in particular San Xavier del Bac, Tumacácori, and Guevavi, and the early years of American occupation ushered in by the 1848 Treaty of Guadalupe-Hidalgo, the 1854 Gadsden Purchase, and the California Gold Rush that brought innumerable migrants across "southern Arizona." Even when O'odham claim to not be Christian, such as the author of the book in hand, they still must engage with a Christianized—the better word may be Americanized—himdag. Whereas the previous chapter was aspirational and yearned for a renewal of the O'odham himdag, this chapter reflects on O'odham spirituality as largely influenced by Christian missions, from Kino to Cook, which sought to colonize the O'odham mind. Of particular interest in the present discourse is the relation between the Akimel O'odham of the Gila River Indian Community, which was controlled by the Pima Agency in Sacaton Village, and the Presbyterian Church, which was assigned to Gila River under the auspices of the Board of Indian Commissioners.

When Antonio Azul, the most revered Akimel O'odham leader of his time, was baptized into the Presbyterian Church in 1893, an estimated 1,800 other O'odham joined him in making the conversion.[1] As a moral force in the community, Azul had long set a standard by which other O'odham could gage the appropriateness of any plan of action. At first, O'odham were reluctant to listen to Cook. After all, when Cook arrived at the Pima Agency in Sacaton in 1870, O'odham were engaged in a struggle to protect their water rights, which were overtaken by white settlers upriver. Perhaps because of the suffering he saw around him, Azul began accepting Cook's advice that he and his people should learn the white man's education. "After that first group of Pimas was baptized," Anna Moore Shaw writes in *A Pima Past*, "Christianity spread like wildfire among the Pimas. Within five years the converts had helped build a little adobe church, where they could sing hymns and worship every Sunday."[2] For two centuries prior, O'odham learned to adjust to the encroaching presence of jujkam and mimilgahn. All the while they maintained their integrity as a distinct people. During the 1870s to 1910s, Akimel O'odham remained content at persevering in their customary, pre-Christian ways. So what drives a whole people to convert? Was it a revelation, mass hysteria, or the simple realization that they had changed so much that they decided to give in to what seemed like the logical conclusion?

William James in *The Varieties of Religious Experience* (1902) observed conversion as a process, "gradual or sudden, by which [an individual] self hitherto divided, and consciously wrong inferior and unhappy, becomes unified and consciously right superior and happy, in consequence of its firmer hold upon religious realities."[3] James then distinguished two forms of conversion. First, there was the "volitional type," which resulted from a gradual buildup, "piece by piece, of a new set of moral and spiritual habits." Second, there was the "type by self-surrender," which is a more rapid transition, such that the conversion seems to take place at an unconscious level.[4] While one ought to be cautious at portraying O'odham culture and history as mere illustration of James's theory of conversion, it is important to recognize that in order to understand the O'odham decision to convert to Christianity one has to consider to what extent they were coerced into making this choice, as well as to what extent they genuinely saw it as their own choice to make. O'odham were not merely the hapless victims of Manifest Destiny, which culminated in Grant's Peace Policy, subsequently bringing the Presbyterians into O'odham villages. Rather, Christianity among O'odham was the result of a way of doing things, the O'odham himdag, which had always accommodated changes in the "environment," meaning their jeved, which includes not only flora and fauna but also new people and ideas. By the time the mimilgahn appeared, O'odham across their jeved had adjusted to a substantial jujkam presence, sometimes choosing to rebel against Spanish control. The 1751 Pima Rebellion is legendary in this regard.[5] Even under extreme duress, such as the time of famine, O'odham thought of themselves as retaining their inherent sense of tachchui (self-determination).[6] However, it was not just the mimilgahn (Americans) that caused a sea-change in the O'odham jeved.

"At the time . . . Kino began his energetic work . . . in 1687," Edward Spicer writes in *Cycles of Conquest* (1962), "there was already a Spanish frontier of settlement bordering on the Pimas."[7] Long before there was a Pimería Alta, Jesuits began missionizing the Yoemem, the Yaquis, the Yoreme, the Mayo, and the Opatas.

> In 1610 the [northern] border was advanced to Rio del Fuerte [sic], so named after the fort of Montesclaros there erected; and now the Jesuits began the conversion of Mayos and Yaquis. Thirty years later San Juan Bautista was founded in Sonora Valley, already made known by expeditions which had passed into the northern regions. All this country west of the Sierra Madre was ruled by a military captain appointed by the viceroy, but subject in civil matters to the governor at Durango.[8]

According to Nentvig, "having heard that others had become Christians, the Pimas Bajos travel south to receive instruction in the Faith, thus becoming the first Sonorans to be converted."[9] By the time Kino died in 1711, he founded some twenty-six missions. Although, Kino lacked the resources to found a mission in the Gila River Valley due to its distance from the main centers of Spanish power, not to mention a general decline in support for Kino's missionary system, he did visit O'odham at Casa Grande ruins, near modern-day Coolidge, Arizona, where he said mass in 1697. According to Anna Moore Shaw, Kino's "joy was complete when he noticed the Pimas imitating the sign of the cross. The docile Pimas of the Gila Valley readily accepted Father Kino and his Christian teachings. They came to love him and his gentle ways."[10] Obviously, Shaw's perception of Kino and his mission system was sanitized by the generations of colonization. Also, O'odham of the Gila and Salt River valleys, though a part of the Pimería Alta, were beyond the reach of Jesuit missionization. At different times, the Jesuits wanted to establish a mission among the Akimel O'odham.

> [Padre Augustín De Campos] explained to his superiors the urgent need for more Padres. . . . He had suggested in a report to the viceroy that a Spanish colony and one-hundred-man presidio be planted on the lower Gila. Kino, too, had advocated a town at this spot, which he called San Dionisio.[11]

Fortunately, Akimel O'odham were spared the encroachment of both Spanish settlers and the oppressive political policies that turned Indians into peons for Spanish interests. Consequently, the 1751 Pima Rebellion and the exploits of Luis Oacapicagigua only minimally affected the river people. Instead, O'odham in the Gila and Salt River valleys evaded this fate even though Kino visited their villages a total of six times, during which he created a willingness among them to accept missionaries into their jeved. The promised mission, however, never arrived. Throughout the wide stretches of the O'odham jeved, Jesuits were incapable of meeting the numerous requests for missions. In the end, Kino only got as close as the mission at San Xavier del Bac, just south of Tucson in the Sobaipuri O'odham jeved. Kino laid its foundation in 1700, and its construction was not completed until 1797.[12] With respect to the Akimel O'odham, Kino left his only legacy, which disappeared over time, when he presumed to name the akimel that defined this part of the jeved.

> Father Kino, at the suggestion of Padre Adam Gilg, named the river Gila *Rio de los Apostolos* and, returning along its valley to the San Andres Mission which he had visited before, called the villages of the Yuma and Papago Indians after the names of several Apostles: San Pablo, San Petro, San Tadeo, and San Simon.[13]

Kino supposedly baptized innumerable hehemajkam during his six sojourns, according to his own account. Whether or not any of the O'odham understood what this meant at the time is uncertain. Some historians speculate that O'odham sought baptism as a way of accessing

Spanish material goods.[14] What is certain is that Kino's place in O'odham oral tradition, especially among the Akimel O'odham villages, is virtually nonexistent. "After the death of Kino, in 1711, no Spaniard is known to have reached the Gila or even to have entered Arizona for a period of more than twenty years."[15]

Much more than saving Indian souls, the Spanish were interested in the economic potential of the region. Until the arrival of the Americans, O'odham throughout the Pimería Alta were more influenced by wheat, tools, horses, and cattle arriving in their community by way of San Xavier. Concurrent with the mission system, nonetheless, was change in their material culture that obliged O'odham to think about their changing relation with their jeved, now under Spanish colonial control. As Winston P. Erickson observed in *Sharing the Desert: The Tohono O'odham in History*:

> With the acceptance of Father Kino, the Tohono O'odham opened the door for more intensive missionary work by the Jesuit priests. When asked for assistance, more missionaries moved into the region, and it became necessary to establish more churches and farms. The area they chose to settle was along the Altar River, where the O'odham cultivated fields with irrigation canals like those of the Sobaipuris and the Gila River Pimas [Akimel O'odham]. Once they had established missions, the priests invited the O'odham to work on the farms, exposing them to both the teachings of Christianity and European methods of farming and of raising cattle and sheep.[16]

Despite the reference to the Sobaipuri and Akimel O'odham who maintained their indigenous agrarian culture during this time, the Tohono O'odham were directly pressured to accept the Spanish notion of land ownership. Contrary to what O'odham are taught, land was now to be coveted, owned, and exploited for personal gain. Customarily, O'odham families "had the right to use the fields, and . . . a family's ability to cultivate the land determined the size of the field. Families also had the right to gather in areas where certain foods, such as saguaro fruits, were abundant. Because they used what they needed and shared any surplus food they harvested, the O'odham had no need for private property."[17] The mission system, as an economy, disrupted the O'odham himdag. Whereas O'odham sustained themselves with a sharing economy, with no currency, only trade, the missions instituted a kind of Lockean concept of individual ownership based on labor and making the land productive. Labor and property, moreover, are now monetized in Spanish reales. The jeved was no longer a gift from Jeved mahkai in which sacred places and I'itoi's teachings defined one's sense of home; but an alien landscape in which O'odham competed for resources against an occupying nation.

Like all missions to the so-called New World, what the priests wanted most of all was to colonize the hearts and minds of the people they "discovered." With respect to Akimel O'odham, Fathers Francisco Garces and Pedro Font resumed Kino's practice of saying mass at Casa Grande Ruins sometime between 1768–1776. Font wrote of this, calling the O'odham he met "Gileños" after the fact that they lived along the Gila River:

> I said mass [on 1 November 1775], which was attended by some Gileños Indians who happened to be there and who gave evidence of considerable attention, good behavior, and silence. They sought to imitate the Christians in crossing themselves, which they did awkwardly enough, and in other things.[18]

After saying mass, Garces recounts meeting O'odham at "San Juan Capistrano de Uturituc." Garces firmly believed that the O'odham were anxious to welcome the Spanish Catholic mission into their homeland.

> After we had dismounted they all came in turn to salute us and offered their hand to the Commander and the three Fathers, men and women, children and adults. Indeed they all gave token of much satisfaction at seeing us, touching their breasts with their hand, naming God, and using many other expressions of benevolence.[19]

Font noted that O'odham, like converts farther south, said "Dios ato m'busiboy," which he supposed to mean "May God aid us." Other than mimicking what they thought Garces was saying, it is indeterminable what the O'odham might have uttered. What is clear is that Garces was deluded by his self-importance and probably heard what he wanted to hear. After all, his mission was dependent on the generosity of the Spanish Crown for its funding. Unsurprisingly, Font was delighted with what he believed was O'odham willingness to accept Christ as their savior when his hosts erected a lodge for them, complete with a large cross in the front.[20] Taking O'odham generosity for compliance, Garces overlooked the possibility, as did Kino before him, that the O'odham were attempting to minimize the uninvited intervention of these jujkam by making them into allies.

As the O'odham jeved became a part of New Spain, O'odham spiritual culture, especially around the missions, tended to adapt Christian elements into their himdag, which is different from converting, their agreement to baptism notwithstanding. O'odham began, for example, referring to "Jeoss," which is derived from the Spanish *dios*.

> When there was no earth, no heaven, nothing but darkness, the only person that was here was Jeoss. Jeoss had no form, no flesh, no bones, and was nothing but pure spirit, like the wind. This Jeoss planned out a way that he could form an earth on which to rest his soul. This earth that he formed was really the heavens (damkatchim, something over above).
>
> He made a person up in damkatchim [heaven] who was nothing but light. The next person that Jeoss created was a man who came down and made the world where we now are.
>
> Now here's what this Jeoss was singing:
>
> "Earth Doctor, Earth Doctor," (Juut makai; also known as Earth Medicine Man)
>
> "You make the earth now,
>
> "And started it going."[21]

In his 1988 paper "Pima-Papago Christianity," Bahr claimed that by 1850, O'odham had "Christianized their paganism, not by centralizing Jesus, but by centralizing a Jesus-like, murdered man-god figure," namely I'itoi, Elder brother.[22] It is debatable how much of what Bahr saw is based on a

Christian-influenced O'odham narrative. It is equally likely that—in lieu of an O'odham-created, pre-1850 version of their origin narrative—Bahr was simply projecting his own cultural bias onto the narratives recorded by others, from Pedro Font to Russell. In other words, Bahr may have underestimated the extent to which O'odham storytellers adapted Christian words and symbols into O'odham thinking without sacrificing their authenticity as O'odham. The O'odham himdag is not an orthodoxy in the sense of asserting a set of core beliefs that must be heeded lest one risk condemnation as a heretic, but rather customs and values developed over time between people sharing a common language and community. Therefore it is probable that as new relations arose with jujkam, O'odham narratives appropriated new notions of sacred beings consistent with the holistic nature of the himdag. Jeoss is neither superior to Jeved mahkai nor their replacement but rather another name for the same being. Just as sacred places have multiple names in different Indigenous languages, so too may the spirit that made the earth have different names. Saying "Jeoss," then, implies acceptance of Christianity into one's sense of place, such that cheopi (church) is a site where O'odham relatives gather, Mihsh'kih if they are Akimel O'odham, Sahnto kih if they are Tohono O'odham.

At the same time, Christian adaptations emerged, including an O'odham Catholicism comparable to the Yoemem and Yoreme Catholic traditions and an O'odham Protestant tradition among the Gila and Salt River communities.[23] It was not uncommon for Tohono O'odham to sing Spanish hymns and recite Latin prayers along with O'odham curing songs when seeking relief for a sick relative. "Baptism by 1856," Bernard Fontana notes, "was something that could be performed twice: once by a native medicine man and again by a Roman Catholic priest. Indeed, it may be that the 'native' name-giving ceremony of Pimans was a Catholic-inspired one."[24] Similar to Bahr's thesis, Fontana presumes that cultural decline and diffusion is at work in O'odham communities, such that Christian baptismal ritual necessarily filled a void in O'odham spirituality. One should be cautious, even skeptical, about assuming that the similarities between disparate cultures must be the result one people exerting influence over another. There was undoubtedly an unbalanced power relation between New Spain and the O'odham—which became more severe when the Americans entered the O'odham jeved.

However, this does not preclude the possibility that O'odham originated the rituals and beliefs that Bahr and Fontana are referring to as Christianized.

Still, O'odham saw Christian baptism as similar to their own, especially when it came to being a charm for protecting children from harm, such as snake bites, lightning strikes, or illness. O'odham parents and godparents customarily named their children within their first year. When it is time for the naming, they gather before sunrise on four successive mornings in front of the house in which the child lives. Each one holds the child for a moment as the sun rises. The gender of the child determines whether it is the godfather or godmother who names the child.

> Beads were formerly held up to receive the first rays of sunlight, and were then placed about the child's neck. Gifts of clothing, food, baskets, and the like were also made by the godparents, who 'think as much of the child afterwards as its own father and mother. . . . The parents in their turn reciprocate by naming the children of the couple that acts as godparents to their own.[25]

Unlike their Christian counterparts, O'odham did not believe that the naming ritual was a way of saving the child's soul from damnation. The naming ritual purported to bless the child's path in life, meaning his or her himdag. The child was now a part of their family, village, and clan (Bán or Nuwi). O'odham taught that upon death an owl (chukud) would take them to the "Land of the East" where the "Home of the Morning" was located. Once the soul (thoakag) crossed a great chasm separating the jeved from the village of the dead, the soul found itself in a place where it can "feast and dance." In preparation for their journey, O'odham buried their dead with personal belongings, which they took to the other side. O'odham bury their loved ones with their belongings to this day, even though most funerals are conducted according to Christian ritual customs. Because O'odham expected to make this journey, they did not think of where they headed upon death as a place where there was "spiritual reward or punishment for conduct in this life." Unsurprisingly, the absence of a fear of damnation was one of the reasons why Americans believed that O'odham were in desperate need of missionization.

Although O'odham were generally regarded as the "most civilized Indians in the United States,"[26] because of their friendly relations with mimilgahn who passed through their jeved, not to mention being superb allies against the Apaches, there was still a presumption that O'odham were primitive both in terms of technology and society. Captain F. E. Grossman, who was appointed Indian Agent in charge of the Arizona Territory in 1869, wrote an ethnological report on O'odham "History and Traditions," as well as observations of their "Religion," "Burial of the Dead," "Marriages," and their "Weapons and Manner of Fighting." Under "Religion," Grossman surmised O'odham customs in rather disparaging terms.

> It is certain that their religion does not teach them morality, nor does it point out a certain mode of conduct. Each Pima, if he troubles himself about his religion, construes it to suit himself, and all care little or nothing for the life hereafter, for their creed neither promises rewards in the future for a life well spent, nor does it threaten punishment after death to those who in this life act badly. They have no priest to counsel them, and the influence of their chiefs is insufficient to restrain those who are evil-disposed. The whole nation lives but for to-day, never thinks of the wants of the future, and is guided solely by desires and passions.[27]

Because of the moral lassitude that Grossman perceived, he was not hopeful that O'odham would ever convert to Christianity, concluding, "it is believed that all efforts to christianize the Pimas would fail, not because any of them would oppose such attempts, but because they all would be entirely indifferent to the new teachings."[28] Grossman's assessment appears to contravene Bahr's earlier opinion that O'odham had Christianized their "paganism" by this point. If there was any syncretism, it contradicted Bahr's characterization.

Prior to 1850, O'odham were a prosperous people, at least according to O'odham standards of wealth, which meant an abundance that could be shared and traded. Akimel O'odham stand out in this regard, as their huhugam-influenced agrarian culture enabled them to thrive with milgahn goods.[29] They had adapted wheat (pilkañ), metal tools, cattle (haiwañ), and horses (kakawiyu) so well into their culture that they were able to provide a buffer against the Apaches and situate themselves as a geopolitical force in the Sonoran Desert. Between trade and protection, O'odham distinguished themselves from others in the region. All of this began to change, though, when mimilgahn began settling Arizona. Gone were the days when the only mimilgahn were the occasional missionary (ah'atha) seeking the nominal convert or just passing through to California. When Arizona became a territory in 1863, it began the process of becoming a state, which it would eventually achieve in 1912.

Because of Arizona's statehood aspirations, mimilgahn began accessing the Salt and Gila Rivers that were otherwise irrigating O'odham farmlands, which the akimel had done since the era of the big houses. Despite Grossman's earlier condescending remarks about O'odham's need for land and especially water, he immediately recognized the dire circumstances in which O'odham would find themselves if the rivers ran dry.[30] By 1870 settlers had assumed control of the land upriver from the reservation, where they opened large canals, "and were wasting water rather than returning it to the Gila." This period "marked the end for Pima economic stability and the way of life they had known for centuries."[31] But what looks like only an economic crisis was really a spiritual upheaval.

For centuries O'odham gathered to perform the wiigida, a ceremony that beckoned the summer monsoons (jegos), the torrential rains that annually rejuvenate the jeved, along with it the lives and beliefs of the people. The rain (juhk) was more than a natural phenomenon, it was a sacred power. Performing this ceremony was a way of keeping the world running as it was meant to. Tohono O'odham scholar and poet Ofelia Zepeda recounts in her foreword to *Singing for Power* that her mother claimed that the rainy season came because they remembered to perform wiigida. When asked what would happen if they ever forgot this ceremony, Zepeda's mother "insisted, 'at o e-padc,' literally translated as 'it will ruin itself." Zepeda explains: "I took *it* to mean the world. The world [jeved] will be ruined if the ceremony is not continued."[32] So when did O'odham begin forgetting their wiigida?

Although the ooshikbina (calendar sticks) referenced throughout this discourse were based on an O'odham sense of time, beginning with the saguaro cactus fruit harvest that preceded the jujkida, occurrences of the wiigida in O'odham oral history is sparse. Ooshikbina recorded exceptional events for the villages that kept these traditions, meaning developments that were symbolic of the group's well-being. In this context, wiigida are as normal as O'odham harvesting their crops. Explicit examples of wiigida in the calendrical record, therefore, arise only when they are a part of an exceptional event in village history. Russell notes in *The Pima Indians* that at Salt River in 1836–1837, "at the beginning of this year [meaning summer] the fruit of the giant cactus was gathered and a large quantity of liquor prepared from it. All the men became intoxicated—*too drunk to be on their guard against an attack from the Apaches*" (my emphasis).[33] Lumholtz, in *New Trails*, only recorded one calendar stick, held by an unnamed Hia-Ced O'dham, in which there are multiple references to a "fiesta," but nothing clearly indicating the wiigida. C. H. Southworth also only recorded one calendar stick, which was kept by Juan Thomas, in which once again there is no clear reference to the wiigida.[34] Lastly, in Underhill's "Papago Calendar," recorded at San Xavier del Bac, a calendar stick was kept by Jose Santos.[35] Fortunately, Underhill, unlike her peers, was interested in capturing the nuances of this cultural tradition, meaning that she provides her reader a fuller narrative, as opposed to the brief notations of other records.

The wiigida in Underhill's text is referred to as the "prayerstick festival," which she defines in *Papago Indian Religion* as "instituted by I'itoi during his march of conquest," which is a reference to the demise of the big houses, as recounted by Komal Hok. During I'itoi's cleansing of the O'odham jeved, he placed prayersticks, according to Tohono O'odham oral tradition, at "Archie" (Gu-achi) and "Quitovaca" (Giwho do'ag). The hehemajkam following him were instructed to resettle these places. As for Underhill's reference to the wiigida as the prayerstick festival, she explains that "wiikita" is made up of the "word *wiiki*," which means "bird down," and "*ta*," which means "made." Thus Underhill concludes that "which is made of bird down is a prayerstick, and the *wiikita* was the time, above all others, when prayer sticks were used."[36] Lumholtz, it is worth mentioning, used the prayersticks as a way of determining that the Hia-Ced O'odham had become an "extinct" branch of the "Papago," which was indicated by the declination of prayersticks at Sierra Pinacate, which is where Hia-Ced O'odham say I'itoi ki, Elder brother's house, is located.[37]

Between the years 1858 and 1865, the "prayerstick festival" is mentioned three times and the "drinking ceremony" once, which were observed at "Narrow Place" and "Burnt Seeds."[38] Then, for 1876–1877, it states, "There had been no prayerstick festival for ten years because there had been no rain, and no crops."[39] Nevertheless, the wiigida resumed that same year, honoring the end of a long drought. In subsequent years, 1878–1879 and 1886–1887, the wiigida appears in the calendar-stick keeper's narrative, disappearing from mention in the remainder of the calendar stick, which ends in 1931. Collectively, Russell, Lumholtz, Southworth, and Underhill offer modest but meaningful references to wiigida. What is inestimable are the parts of oral histories that were omitted by each anthropologist as they edited their manuscripts for publication. Consequently, the calendar stick record cited here is like a once formidable edifice worn away by time and the elements—not to mention the indiscriminate interference from outsiders—in which one's imagination must fill in the spaces left blank by circumstances. Regardless of the written sources cited here, they only capture a partial view of a once thriving tradition.

Nonetheless, these ooshikbina still retain the voices of ancestral O'odham who witnessed the transformation of their jeved in terms that can only be explained from an O'odham point of view, meaning the O'odham neok, origin narrative, and himdag. This is not to say that such a perspective is homogeneous. Quite the contrary. From historic times, O'odham have exhibited a diversity of opinions, values, and experiences. Not only are there different O'odham communities and dialects, but also the Akimel O'odham, Tohono O'odham, Hia-Ced O'odham, Sobaipuri O'odham, and Pima Bajo have experienced colonization differently, and these families and individuals recount differing collective and unique stories about the O'odham jeved. Because of kinship, O'odham see their stories and experiences as overlapping with each other. Before transitioning back to the discourse on the Presbyterian Church in the Akimel O'odham community, it is worthwhile to observe some of the examples of historical changes that impacted these places and peoples.

When Presbyterian missionary Charles H. Cook arrived with his wife Anna at the end of 1870, they came at a time when Akimel O'odham were at their most vulnerable. Arizona then was considered a "dangerous place," not because of the O'odham but because of Apache retaliation against settler aggressions in their homelands.[40] Cook nevertheless was invigorated by the calling he felt to bring the gospel to the O'odham. "My health was excellent," Cook later wrote, "and the journey, especially that part of it when I had little or no means of my own, through the wild Apache country, had benefited me greatly."[41] Despite his zealousness, it would be fifteen years before Cook saw any converts. On the one hand, O'odham were too distracted by their immediate concerns for survival to pay attention to Cook; on the other, O'odham mamahkai and headmen were suspicious of this milgahn's intentions. Indeed, missionaries and the medicine people perceived each other with mutual disdain. In an essay on O'odham manners and customs, the Reverend Isaac Whittemore shared his biased observations about Cook's endeavors: "Ever since the missionary began work here, these medicine men [mamahkai] have been an annoyance and hindrance to his work."[42]

> They [mamahkai] are ambitious, artful, and unscrupulous, and in this vicinity have done more to destroy the efforts of Indian agents to improve the condition of the Indian, both in school-work and their moral elevation, than all other undermining and checking influences combined. Nearly all are low, vulgar, licentious, and dishonest, and spare no pains to keep the tribe from every good and honorable work.[43]

Rather than criticize federal Indian policy, let alone the local super-intendency, Whittemore placed the blame for O'odham hardship on their mamahkai. Whittemore's disparaging opinion of Akimel O'odham was corroborated by the superintendents that ran the Pima Agency in Sacaton. According to Grossman in his 1870 report to the commissioner of Indian Affairs:

> They [Akimel O'odham] are still self-sustaining; that is, they produce an abundance of food in their fields—enough for their own consumption and enough for the purpose of barter. They

do not kill travelers and emigrants, like the Apaches, but the obliging, hospitable, and honest Pima of yore, who kindly assisted the Americans who passed through his lands in those days, has disappeared, and now owners of herds of cattle rarely ever pass this reservation without losing more or less stock.[44]

In sum, when one examines the references to Gila and Salt River in subsequent superintendent reports, the O'odham become less of an allied nation with the United States and more of a source for social issues, which the Office of Indian Affairs had to address. In other words, O'odham became just another part of the so-called Indian Problem.

Interestingly, Cook's mission at Gila River went completely unnoticed by calendar-stick keepers. Instead, at Gila Crossing, they remembered the first canal built at Tempe by the Mormons. At Blackwater, they remembered the time that some o'obga (Apaches) came for water at Santan, where O'odham scouts followed their trail. One of the O'dham was mortally wounded. The following year there was a measles epidemic that afflicted all villages. O'odham mamahkai did not know how to treat this disease, and many died. In subsequent years calendar-stick keepers recounted drought, disease, and more o'obga alongside telegraph lines and the Southern Pacific Railroad. Finally, in 1885 at Gila Crossing, Hwela was baptized as the first Christian convert among Akimel O'odham. The year after this, the first "adobe houses" were constructed, also at Gila Crossing. Their owners, by virtue of changing over from the olas kih, became entitled to one wagon each. Consequently, men had to accept cutting their long hair, which before they only did when they were in mourning. A year later the "Sonora earthquake" occurred.

> The shocks were so severe as to be destructive to property and human life. At Tombstone, Ariz, the severe shocks lasted ten seconds, and the vibrations continued for a full minute. The earthquake was felt throughout the southern part of the Territory, and many ranchmen firmly believe that the drought of the last few years, which has transformed the grassy mesas into a desert waste, is due to that earthquake.[45]

During 1894–1895, Cook led the construction of the Gila Crossing Presbyterian Church, which occurred during June, when O'odham should have been harvesting saguaro cactus fruit. Cook's church was dedicated in December, twenty-five years after the Presbyterian missionary first set foot on Akimel O'odham jeved. During this time there was an eclipse of the moon, and a mahkai who despised milgahn progress died in jail after being arrested for drinking *tizwin*, a nontraditional alcoholic beverage made from mescal.[46]

Cook, for his part, only focused on his mission, not the economic injustices of the reservation system, let alone the social issues caused by colonization. As far as Cook was concerned, he found hungry and naked Indians who above all needed a school. Presumed in this objective was the obsolescence of O'odham teachings and the himdag. So Cook opened the school that still bears his name in 1871. However, it was a generation before he could call it a success. "To educate the intellect only," Whittemore asserted, "and leave the heart untouched, is to do but little for the Indian." Whittemore lauded the two churches that Cook founded at Gila Crossing and Blackwater, noting excitedly that "both of these are full every Sabbath and frequently crowded." Whittemore does not hesitate to commend O'odham for their newfound devotion, commenting on the often-long distances they traveled to attend church. Such commitment, even during the searing heat of summer, when temperatures regularly rise above 100° F, was a divine sign of O'odham deliverance to Christian civilization. Whittemore especially perceived the profound influence that "preaching, prayer and praise" had on O'odham attitudes, creating what he saw as a genuine delight for church worship.[47]

> This influence on a people just emerging from heathenism and breaking up old superstitions and vices, and instead of them, leading an industrious and virtuous life, must far exceed that of churches in town on a civilized people.[48]

Despite Whittemore's rather condescending praise for O'odham faith, he goes on to claim that the work ahead remains difficult because of the racial obstacles that are endemic to Indians.

The Indian mind and heart is [sic] virgin soil, never working but when properly cultivated; though slow in development and requiring great patience, yet when thoroughly wrought upon by the Holy Spirit, yields more ample returns and sometimes more rapid, than a gospel-hardened soil.

The Indian belongs to the great human family. He is below his white brother in mind, morals and heart culture, ie, the representative of the cultured man, but certainly not below his ancestors in the dark ages, before the dawn of christianity.[49]

Regardless of the loss of land and water and the consequent poverty and starvation that O'odham were suffering, Whittemore's implication is clear: the current generation of O'odham should count themselves as fortunate. For they are the ones who will live to benefit from the arrival of civilization into their homeland.

What Whittemore could not comprehend was that the reasons that O'odham had for "converting" had less to do with "seeing the light" and more to do with survival. This is a factor that is amiss in the discourse on conversion that James introduced at the beginning of this chapter. When O'odham were practicing their himdag free from outside interference, they were pursuing a way of doing things that I'itoi set for them. Once the Akimel O'odham jeved was stricken by drought, it was as if I'itoi had shot one of his arrows through their cornfields, causing them to wither. Their akimel and the juhk, their river and the rain, lost their vitality. The years of famine, of bihugig, had begun. Accepting Cook's offer to convert was comparable to when O'odham asked Kino to send his missionaries so that they could be baptized as medicine against suffering. The adoption of Christian signs and rituals did not occlude them from preserving their traditional values, namely sharing, working hard, and making time to gather and feast. However, these values would now be tied to their relationship with the Presbyterian Church. As Edward H. Spicer summarizes the accomplishments of Cook's missionary work:

Gradually a transformation in village life took place, centering around the new religious organization. Annual revival meetings took the place of old ceremonies. Christian mythology and theology replaced older beliefs and the strict morality of the Presbyterians tended to reintegrate the disintegrating villages. The church affairs were almost entirely in the hands of the local Pimas, and ministers were trained to do the preaching.[50]

Over time, generations of O'odham grew up believing that Presbyterianism was the only religion that Akimel O'odham had ever known. On a personal note, when the author of the book in hand once asked his mother about "Pimas that practiced the old ways," she said that "there weren't many" and that "they lived near the mountains," meaning Komadk do'ag. Despite what Cook or Whittemore thought, Akimel O'odham never lost their connection with their himdag, not entirely. Aside from mamahkai that continued to practice their healing rituals, albeit in a more subdued and limited fashion, O'odham still regarded themselves as an agrarian culture, complete with connections going back to the huhugam who built the ge'egdaj kikih, the big houses. The Pima constitution talked about in chapter 1 is an example. At the same time, O'odham are cognizant of enduring significant loss under American colonization, most importantly their loss of water. On this point, Sally Giff Pablo quotes Alexander Lewis, who was governor of the Gila River Indian Community during the early 1970s: "In the past our people worked the land. But then it happened that the water was gone and no longer could anything grow again on their land because gone was the water, and we [must] see things differently now. From this poverty approached the O'odham."[51] When the time of famine (bihugig) began in the 1870s, the mimilgahn did not have words for genocide or crime against humanity. They would not learn these things until Nazi Germany killed millions of white people for being Jewish did they, slowly, begin to understand. Instead, during the O'odham bihugig, the mimilaghn thought that sending them missionaries was the answer.

By the time Governor Lewis said these words in 1973, Akimel O'odham had long grown accustomed to Presbyterianism as an integral part of their society. In fact, during the time that this author's grandfather, Simon Lewis, served as minister at the Gila Crossing First Presbyterian Church, the Gila River Indian Community regularly saw appreciable numbers of congregants attending church. If anything, O'odham were more concerned with their tribal economy and education than they were with saving their himdag from Christian persecution. Webb recalls fondly in *A Pima Remembers*:

> The Pimas of this time were faithful Christians. All week they would work on their farms and at the end of the week they would go down to the river to wash their clothes and bathe. They would do odd jobs such as cutting wood, so that nothing unnecessary was left to be done on Sunday. On Sunday they would hitch up the team to the spring wagon and pile in it and go to church.[52]

Suffice it to say, Webb was a man of his times. In Spicer's introduction to Webb's book, Webb is recalled as the one-time employee of the "Indian Agent at Sacaton," in which he managed "farm operations" until he "enrolled in the Cook Bible Institute." Born circa 1893, Webb was a young man during the Progressive Era that drove the Society of American Indians agenda. "In 1934 George Webb was elected representative from Gila Crossing to the first Tribal Council."[53] In that capacity, Webb was a part of tribal government when the "Constitution and Bylaws of the Gila River Pima-Maricopa Indian Community, Arizona" was approved by the US Department of the Interior on May 14, 1936. Unsurprisingly, Webb held Cook in high esteem. "Our minister, Mr Charles H. Cook, was a fine man."[54] As observed earlier, when Anna Moore Shaw published her two books, *Pima Indian Legends* (1968) and *A Pima Past* (1974), one would be hard-pressed to see these works as symptomatic of an Indian Protest movement, which reached its climax during the late 1960s and early 1970s. However, insofar as the "Red Power" movement was about revitalizing Indian peoples' pride in their ancestral teachings, any affirmation of these teachings is a part of this movement. Having said that, it was commonplace for O'odham born before World War II to be conservative in their adaptations of milgahn ways, such as going to church, and reject identifying with the Red Power movement.

"Although I have long strived to preserve our old Pima ways," Anna Moore Shaw claims in *A Pima Past*, "the poverty, grueling work, and bloody battles are things I do not miss!"[55] What the O'odham community has always most valued is living in balance with their jeved as relatives who share in the gift bestowed on them by their creator, whether they say "Jeoss" or "Jeved mahkai." From either perspective, the milgahn exploitation of the land poses a challenge to the O'odham future. As of the early 1970s the Akimel O'odham and their Piipaash friends were still struggling for their water rights, although the crisis had lessened considerably since the height of the bihugig, when Thin Leather was alive. What is remarkable about Shaw's statement is her acceptance of reservation life, specifically as an assertion of self-respect. "Our reservation life today," Shaw affirmed, "is varied, rich, and rewarding."[56] In Shaw's defense, she was quite aware of the social inequities that were burdening her community, particularly with respect to its land and water rights. She was also current with everyday developments of the Salt River Pima-Maricopa Indian Community, where she lived out her life with her husband, Ross. During those years, among other endeavors, she edited the newsletter *Awathm Awahan*. As Shaw said of her role, "In order to solve our difficulties we must be aware of them, and we do not skip lightly over serious issues in the pages of this monthly news organ. Stories discussing the activities of the BIA, the Tribal Council, the Community Action Program, the Land Board, and various community committees are frequent." [57] Nevertheless, Shaw refused to look at her reservation community, her family and neighbors, "through the eyes of a prejudiced white."[58] There is always someone like Whittemore out there.

For persons like Shaw and Webb, Akimel O'odham conversion to Presbyterianism may be regarded as an example of Vh-Thaw-Hup-Ea-Ju, or "It must happen." Vh-Thaw-Hup-EaJu is not a matter of giving in to fatalism but instead is the fruit of mindful deliberation.[59] Despite how much of the world around one may be beyond hehmajkam* control, an O'dham and their community (kihhim) can still assert themselves within the circumstances they must confront. "Our ancestors learned that it is good to take time to meditate," as Shaw quotes her elders, "to know what you want and where you are going. Only then should you do it very slowly. Thus making fewer errors."[60] In the end, O'odham continue to deliberate over what they want and where they are going. But, as it has always been, it is *their* deliberation to make. Even in an era mimilgahn are calling the

---

* Hemajkam is singular, hehemajkam is plural.

Anthropocene, which signifies the havoc they have wreaked over the jeved such as climate change, O'odham maintain a space, a path, a himdag, in which they still control the narrative that Jeved mahkai initiated when they sang this place into existence.

> Earth Magician shapes this world.
> Behold what he can do!
> Round and smooth he molds it.
> Behold what he can do![61]

CHAPTER SEVEN

Elder Brother Still Dwells Here

I'itoi Kih as a Symbol of Renewal

I f one reflects on the previous six chapters, the O'odham himdag may appear to be in tatters, a historic casualty of centuries of juhkum and milgahn colonization, not to mention the current era of globalization that has turned the US-Mexico border region from a site of international affairs, most importantly trade and immigration, into a site of racialized violence in which Indigenous and Mexican people are targeted by US federal forces under the pretense of "border security." As Roberto D. Hernández characterizes the contemporary US-Mexico border in *Coloniality of the US/Mexico Border*:

> The reemergence of . . . civilian patrol groups [such as the Minutemen], particularly after September 11, 2001, also meant an increase in anti-immigrant hostilities, and in some cases outright physical violence. However, when viewed historically, a continuum emerges: one that geographically, discursively, and corporeally follows a trajectory from early notions of "the frontier" to current images of lawlessness associated with the border in the American imaginary.[1]

While the impact of the US-Mexico border and the policy issues it causes for O'odham, especially Tohono O'odham Nation, is beyond the scope of this discourse,[2] it is worth noting the effect that the border has had on the O'odham himdag. For example, while kinship ties are still important, the O'odham sense of ihmigi (kinship) between O'odham in Arizona and O'odham in Mexico is strained by the political and linguistic divide.

Consequently, when many O'odham in Arizona think of their relatives in Mexico, they see Mexicanized Indians who have assimilated the cultural traits of the surrounding mestizo community. In turn, O'odham in Mexico often see Americanized Indians spoiled by the trappings of the very rich nation that dominates the region.

In her excellent analysis of Indigenous identities across the southern border, Christina Leza observes in *Divided Peoples*: "While some U.S. O'odham may learn Spanish as a second or third language, particularly those who travel to Mexico to visit family and friends in Sonora O'odham communities, Spanish is not a language typically learned in U.S. O'odham homes." Consequently, one may see the "othering of Spanish-speaking peoples," which can lead to prejudice within the O'odham community. As Leza further observed among activists working on behalf of border communities, such as Alianza Indígena Sin Fronteras, "Mexican Indigenous peoples are often described as 'those people' or 'those Mexicans.'"[3] Unfortunately, such condescending language can lead to much more derogatory sobriquets. This is a tension that has built up over generations of living with a divided jeved, in which O'odham ancestral homelands are impacted by a border created by war (1846–1848), reasserted by congressional action (1854), then increasingly militarized over more than a century of US border policy, stemming from the Mexican Revolution (1910–1917) to the ongoing War on Terror (2001–present). In response, some in the O'odham community have argued—contrary to much of US immigration policy—that the O'odham himdag obliges O'odham to treat migrants with compassion.[4] After all, O'odham once treated the mimilgahn and the jujkam before them with compassion (hemajimtalig). Such historic acts of O'odham compassion did not go unpunished with respect to their status under American control.

As of the turn of the twenty-first century, O'odham on both sides of the border have endured much yet have retained their sense of peoplehood despite suffering the scars of colonization. Just as I'itoi arose from death four times when the sisivani tried to kill him and returned with Jeved mahkai's people to cleanse the big houses, I'itoi may return yet again to spare his hehemajkam from devastation. Unlike Jesus, though, whose heralded "Second Coming" will usher in the end of days, I'itoi will continue to dwell in the mountains where oral tradition places his kih, his house. Like before, I'itoi will answer hehemajkam entreaties for help from these sacred places when the need is great enough. James Griffith recounts one such time in *Beliefs and Holy Places*, when the jeved was under threat from nehbig, a monstrous creature that lives near "Quito Wa:k [Quitovac]," in "Sonora, between the towns of Caborca and Sonoyta." Nehbig was described as "being like a whale, except that it lay on the ground, inhaling strongly. It sucked things, people, even whole villages, down its throat, simply by breathing in." I'itoi, when summoned, appeared at Quito Wa:k as a strong young man who instructed the people on what to do to help slay this creature. Upon vanquishing nehbig, I'itoi returned to his kih in Baboquivari peak.[5]

As an autochthonous phenomenon, I'itoi is not only the source of oral histories but also an idea, a body of values and teachings, that dwells in the O'odham subconscious, awaiting times when O'odham need to turn to their origins for direction on building a future in the O'odham jeved. I'itoi kih, the man-in-the-maze design that stands as a symbol of the O'odham himdag and that permeates all aspects of contemporary O'odham society, is the clearest example of O'odham resurgence. Another way of explaining this is to say that I'itoi kih is an example of Vh-thaw-hup-ea-ju. In this instance, I'itoi reappeared among the O'odham during a critical time in their history, namely the time of famine. I'itoi kih, Elder brother's house, popularly known as the man in the maze, suddenly began appearing in O'odham baskets everywhere that O'odham women crafted these traditional works.

While the story of I'itoi kih is well known, its presence in the literature going back to the 1880s is scant. In fact, the version that Anna Moore Shaw recounts in *Pima Indian Legends* (1968) is nowhere to be found in Frank Russell's *The Pima Indians*, nor in more recent studies, such as Bahr's 1994 book on the huhugam, *The Short, Swift Time of Gods on Earth*. Given that someone as respected as Shaw regarded the man-in-the-maze story as part of the O'odham oral tradition, one can take its place in O'odham storytelling seriously. In other words, I'itoi kih is as authentically a part of the O'odham himdag as the O'odham baskets bearing its symbol. What this likely means is that both the story and symbol are modern yet indigenous innovations, in which O'odham basket weavers adapted I'itoi, Elder brother, into their lives on the reservation and wove him anew into their baskets. I'itoi kih, in this way, metamorphosed into a symbol of resilience. As such, complementing the I'itoi kih story is a basket-weaving tradition of geometric and maze-like patterns.

In "The Maze, or Se-eh-ha's House," Shaw shares a story about Elder brother's mountainous dwelling, which follows her account of the demise of the big houses, the ge'egdaj kikih, in which Elder brother's "band of warriors" brought the world of the great canal builders to an end. As for "Se-eh-ha's house," Shaw explains that what Elder brother created in South Mountain was something that could confound his enemies—were they ever to pursue him there. Shaw, it is worth noting, does not name I'itoi's enemies, be they Apaches, Yavapai, Yumas, or other O'odham. Maybe all are implied, or the whites (mimilgahn) and the Mexicans as well, not to mention the Spanish that preceded them. In any case, when Elder brother stands at the top of his maze-like home, because he is standing atop a mountain, he can see far. He is always looking eastward, scanning the horizon. It is from the east, after all, that he arrived with Jeved mahkai's people to topple the big houses. Also, it is from the east that o'obga from beyond the Superstition Mountains sometimes attack. And it was from the east that the whites invaded the O'odham jeved. They continue to invade.

One day, as Shaw recounts, a war party of unknown origin appears, causing Elder brother to take cover within his labyrinthine dwelling and await the attack. The unnamed warriors, upon reaching the entrance, hesitate as they gaze into what looks like the mouth of a great beast. Once inside, the enemy warriors soon find themselves groping through the dark as the pathway twists and turns, confusing them. Gasping for air, the enemy warriors perish one after the other; all the while, Elder brother stays safely hidden within. Shaw concludes her story by explaining the prominence of the man-in-the-maze symbol among O'odham. It is an explanation that would be repeated—or has been repeated—for generations:

> It is told by the Old Ones that Se-eh-ha's ki (house) is located in the South Mountains near Phoenix, Arizona. In one of the gorges of these mountains were found an olla and a grinding stone which the Pimas believe are relics of the past and of the maze dwelling of Se-eh-ha. Today the maze pattern is still woven

into the Pima baskets. It is like the pattern of life—with obstacles to dim the way. But happy is the man who rises to the top.[6]

When the author asked his mother about I'itoi's house, she confirmed that it was in South Mountain, then admonished him with "They say if you try to look for it, you'll just get lost."

Shaw complements her account of I'itoi kih with a narrative about basket weaving, the medium through which I'itoi returned to his hehemajkam. Grounded in O'odham and family history, Shaw ventures beyond autobiography and instead created a work of auto-ethnohistory. In a sense, her place-based sense of history is informed by the ooshikbina that formerly preserved O'odham histories. *A Pima Past* recalls Shaw's grandparents' generation, beginning with "Hikwig (Woodpecker) and his brother Komkjed (Turtle), sons of Gray Owl and his wife Red Flowers." *A Pima Past* is unashamedly an idealized portrait of Akimel O'odham life, evoking the himdag of the nineteenth and early twentieth century. This epoch, of course, was also a time of great duress, as hehemajkam at Gila and Salt River reservations endured a horrible water crisis. Yet it was also a time in the O'odham imagination when many elders (kekelimai) held on to their himdag (culture) and their neok (language).

In a chapter titled "The Threshold of Womanhood," Shaw regales her reader with how girls (chechia) were ceremonially prepared for adulthood (wuagida), in particular how they were taught to take care of their homes and families. Dawn, Hikwig's granddaughter, is the center of attention. Among the skills Dawn must learn is basket weaving, which will enable her to keep her home supplied with the utensils of daily life. Apprenticing with her mother's mother (hu'ul), Dawn learns which plants to gather, such as "river willow twigs [ihug] and cattail reeds [udvak]." Dawn "gladly picked the black devil's claws [ban ihugga] at the edges of the irrigated fields, for these weeds would form the striking black designs on her beautiful baskets," namely the "traditional Pima patterns of long ago," which, as Dawn grew into a more accomplished weaver, "marched along the sides [of her baskets] in beautiful symmetry." The symmetrical patterns, however, are not elaborated upon in Shaw's story. Lastly, the skills demanded by basket weaving correspond to the life lessons extrapolated from the man-in-the-maze story, primarily "patience."[7]

In his 2002 book on ancestral O'odham rock art, *Landscape of the Spirits*, Todd Bostwick refers to Shaw's story of I'itoi kih and the mazelike images that appear at different points around Muhadag do'ag (Greasy mountain). Bostwick, however, does not claim to have found I'itoi kih, nor does he state that the images are mazes per se, but only maze-like. As he explains: "Most [of these images] do not present an unobstructed route into the middle of the geometric design, as in a traditional [European?] maze, but are merely meandering, interconnected lines taking complex curvilinear or rectilinear forms or combinations of the two."[8] It is important to note that the reference to mazelike images occurs in a subsection of chapter 9, which is focused on the geometric designs utilized by ancestral rock artists, which Bostwick speculates were "textiles with decorations or pottery designs."[9] As further explained later in the chapter, this predilection for geometric patterns was documented in Russell's 1908 report for the Bureau of American Ethnology (BAE). Bostwick's research juxtaposes Shaw's man-in-the-maze story with Frank Waters' account of the Hopi emergence story, demonstrating that both indigenous traditions regard the maze as a metaphor for life and the cosmos. In a footnote to Waters's *Book of the Hopi*, Waters refers to the "Tápu'at [Mother and Child] symbol," which is also labeled the "Mother Earth symbol" in Figure 1. The caption reads, "Another [Mother Earth symbol] is carved on an inside wall of an upper story of the ruin of Casa Grande near Florence, Arizona," which is an oblique reference to Jesse Walter Fewkes's 1906–1907 BAE report, in which Fewkes cites Juan Nentvig's *Rudo Ensayo* (1764) as documenting the original discovery.[10] What is important to bear in mind is that the maze found at Casa Grande Ruins is not the maze depicted in the well-known I'itoi kih basket pattern. Yet there is an interesting correlation between them that must be acknowledged.

J. F. Breazeale makes an unexpected contribution to O'odham scholarship with his 1923 book *The Pima and His Basket*. In its pages, the man-in-the-maze design appears in a chapter devoted to "Pima Basket Designs." According to Breazeale, the designs are surrounded by an air of mystery: "most of them [are] little understood, even by the [Pima] Indians themselves, as the pictographs that decorate the rocks of the neighboring hills."[11] Given that Indigenous peoples, including O'odham, are reticent about sharing their oral traditions with outsiders—persons that are not recognized as possessing an appropriate kinship tie—it is probable that O'odham weavers were reluctant to share their stories, unlike the baskets that they produced for the arts-and-crafts market. A given basket may be the weaver's property, but stories(a'agha) belong to O'odham collectively. Nevertheless, Breazeale identified ten discrete design categories, namely Grecian fret, squashbloom, turtle-back, whirlwind, star, shield, swastica, coyote tracks, flower-like, and butterfly wings. A tenth category is labeled "modifications," which is where the man-in-the-maze design appears.[12] Breazeale does not regard these innovations as a corruption of the O'odham basketry tradition. On the contrary, O'odham women, as basket weavers, are credited with intelligence, imagination, and the kind of creativity that non-Indian artists possess:

> Thus it is seen that with a comparatively few fundamental or basic designs, the Pima women, in the past ages, have created a large number of distinct and different patterns. . . . The same gradual development is taking place now [1923] as it did in the past ages, and we see the tendency to improve shown in the hundreds of modifications of the already well developed designs. It is in these modifications that the genius of the weaver often asserts itself.[13]

In the case of I'itoi kih as an example of O'odham innovation, Breazeale makes an unexpected observation: "In recent years the design of the labyrinth, or maze, occurs very frequently in basketry, but where it originated and how it came to Pimeria, no one knows."[14]

As noted earlier, Breazeale found it nearly impossible to get any weavers to explain their designs, be it in terms of oral tradition, social custom, or artistic method. He could watch them weave, but the source of the design, as it emerged, was more like watching a natural phenomenon than a set of technical instructions being carried out: "Their conceptions come out slowly; they seem first to make the black center of the basket and then dream over the work until a design stands out before them."[15] Is this how the I'itoi kih design emerged, through this combination of modification and dreaming? Ironically, just as Breazeale is singing the praises of the O'odham artistic mind, his bias as an early twentieth century American appears. Or rather, the biases of his times get in the way, namely the social evolutionary theory of this era that relegated Indigenous peoples to the bottom of humanity, sitting below their more "civilized" counterparts in Europe and North America. Breazeale assumed, therefore, that the designs in question were too complicated to have arisen independently in two different places, specifically ancient Greece and the American Southwest. The European variation, in Breazeale's mind, obviously had to be the original, while the O'odham had to have received this idea through cultural diffusion: "The design, as it appears upon the baskets of the Pimas, is a fairly good reproduction of that found upon prehistoric Grecian coins now being dug up upon the island of Crete."[16] Implied is an assumption that it was unlikely that O'odham could have invented this design on their own. With this prejudiced, not to mention illogical, hypothesis in mind, Breazeale observed: "A few years ago the [maze] design was found scratched upon the adobe wall of one of the inside rooms of the ruins of Casa Grande."[17] The maze in question was the same one documented by Jesse Walter Fewkes in his 1906–1907 BAE report of his excavation at Casa Grande. Fewkes calls the maze-like oval "tcuhuki, or 'the house of Tchuhu,'" but notes in reference to Nentvig's 1764 *Rudo Ensayo*, "The tcuhuki was not a ruin . . . but a game in which the figure mentioned was marked out on the sand."[18] As for the hypothesis that the O'odham maze-like images were of Grecian origin, Harold Sellers Colton published his speculations in an essay titled "Is the House of Tcuhu the Minoan Labyrinth?"

The premise of Colton's essay is Jesse Walter Fewkes's 1907 note for *American Anthropologist*, titled "A Fictitious Ruin in Gila Valley, Arizona," which is an extract from his BAE field report. The reference to a "fictitious ruin" is specifically to the maze-like pattern that was discovered inscribed on one of the wall interiors at the Casa Grande Ruins site. According to Nentvig, and corroborated by Fewkes's Smithsonian report (1912), the symbol was thought be another ancestral O'odham ruin called "House of Tchuhu." As it turned out, according to Nentvig's unnamed O'odham source and Fewkes's informant "Higgins" (Thin Leather's English name), the symbol did not refer to a ruin but a "game."

When Higgins [Thin Leather] was shown the figure and told the contents of [the relevant passage in the *Rudo Ensayo*], he responded, through the interpreter (Ralph Blackwater), that he knew of no ancient house [va'aki] in the region which had a ground-plan like that indicated in the figure. He was familiar, however, with a children's game that employed a similar figure traced in the sand. The Pima, he said, call the figure *Tcuhuki*, "House of Tcuhu," a cultus hero sometimes identified with Moctezuma.[19]

What both Fewkes and Colton ignored was the reference to Tcuhu-ki. As noted elsewhere, I'itoi was regularly equated with Montezuma (Moctezuma). Furthermore, equally important to remember is that in addition to I'itoi and Montezuma, Elder brother is known as Siuuhu or Se:he. What Fewkes could not apprehend is that the maze-like engraving at Casa Grande signified Siuuhu-kih. Why this is so important has to do with how Komal Hok's comments connect the Casa Grande maze symbol with the O'odham origin narrative recounted in *The Pima Indians* and Shaw's *Pima Indian Legends*. But first, a closer look at the *Rudo Ensayo*.

Juan Nentvig was a German-born member of the Society of Jesus who was assigned to the Sonoran parishes in the aftermath of the 1751 Pima rebellion.[20] From his Sonoran travels Nentvig produced ten chapters in which he inventoried the natural resources of the areas that corresponded to the Catholic mission system. Chapters 5 and 6 covered the "Tribes of Sonora." In chapter 2, "On the Rivers and Brooks of Sonora," Nentvig describes his encounter with an enigmatic design carved into a ruin wall. Traveling up the Gila River, Nentvig recalls visiting "Casa Grande, named after Moctezuma," which is an association that has long been held by generations of explorers, settlers, and archaeologists. The O'odham, to the contrary, do not claim that these ruins belonged to the legendary Mexica chief.[21] As Nentvig describes the terrain, including the ruins, which he refers to collectively as "Casas Grandes," he recounts information he obtained from his O'odham guides:

The Pimas tell of another house of odd design and unusual construction that is to be found much farther up the river which, as

> drawn in the sand by the natives, is a kind of labyrinth similar to
> the sketch that follows: [illustration omitted]. This seems more
> like a house of amusement than the residence of a grandee.[22]

Nothing more is said about the ruin or its playful design, let alone if the site was seen firsthand. As evident in Nentvig's narrative, the alleged "labyrinth" was not worth exploring further, since it likely did not promise either riches or converts for either the Church or the Spanish Crown.

When Fewkes referred to the *Rudo Ensayo* in his "Casa Grande, Arizona" report, the Spanish document was spuriously ascribed to "Father Juan Mentuig or Nentoig."[23] Furthermore, Fewkes considered the account of Casa Grande as secondhand, meaning someone other than Nentvig visited the locations named in the narrative, possibly "Father [Ignacio Xavier] Keller."[24] Fewkes then quotes the Eusebio Guiteras translation (1894) of Nentvig's passage, which adds further description:

> [There is yet] another house, more strangely planned and built,
> which is to be found much farther up the river. It is in the style
> of a labyrinth, the plan of which, as it is designed by the [Pima]
> Indians on the sand, is something like the cut on the margin;
> but it is more probable that it served as a house of recreation
> [ballcourt?] than as a residence of a magnate.[25]

The reference to a design drawn in the sand is an implicit reference to Higgins (Komal Hok); while the ballcourt association is to the Mesoamerican-like ballcourts that were slowly being excavated at ancestral O'odham sites.[26] Fewkes then asserts in a footnote: "It is shown elsewhere that this is a misconception. The [Pima] Indians did not intend to suggest a dwelling but the ground plan of a game."[27] As cited earlier, this game diagram appears to correspond to "the house of Tchuhu" which Fewkes documented in the section on "Pictographs."

For some, namely Colton and Breazeale, the evidence at Casa Grande was symptomatic of diffusion theory at work. In fact, the purpose of Colton's essay on Fewkes's reference to the maze-symbol was to postulate a connection with ancient Minoan civilization. As Colton states, unequivocally, "As shown in Fig. 2 [of Colton's essay] this [maze-like] diagram appears on the reverse of a silver coin of Cnossus in Crete of the Greek Period (BC 200–67). In this case the figure represents the Minoan Labyrinth." When juxtaposed with the House of Tcuhu diagram that Fewkes recorded at Casa Grande, there is only once conclusion to make: "A comparison of this Greek coin, with House of Tchuhu when inverted, shows that the two are identical in every respect."[28] As expected, Colton argues for diffusion from the Mediterranean to the Sonoran Desert. The question is how and at what point historically? Clearly, the O'odham oral tradition about I'itoi kih, or Siuuhu-kih, need not be considered as a subject of contemplation.

For Breazeale, influenced by Fewkes and Colton, the origin and meaning of the O'odham maze remained a mystery. This was not, however, for the lack of trying to learn more: "I have talked to many of the old Indians about it [the maze pattern], and I find that they [the O'odham] have a name for the design, 'Si-her-ki' or 'Montezuma's House' and this is all the information that they seem to have."[29] Once again, Siuuhu-kih is invoked without any effect on Breazeale's understanding. Perhaps he was blinded by the common assumption that the "Hohokam" were a mysterious people that simply vanished, so any reference to them, even from O'odham, meant nothing. Nonetheless, Breazeale still managed to say something of true significance about Siuuhu-kih's place in O'odham basketry: "*I have never seen this design upon an old basket*, and as far as I know, it does not occur in any of the pictographs upon the rocks in the neighboring hills. Baskets with this design are usually woven by the younger members of the tribe" (my emphasis).[30]

Alas, Breazeale did not document with whom he inquired about the name and meaning of the maze symbol. These persons may have been among the photos and names of O'odham basket weavers in his book. One of them could have been Emma Newman, who is identified as the artist who made the lone example of a man-in-the-maze basket in Breazeale's set of images.[31] Newman was one of a distinguished generation of young basket weavers that Breazeale highlighted in his admiration for the O'odham basket-making community:

> Talent is born in an individual and it is in childhood that it usually is either developed or crushed. In a few cases, however, talent is

so pronounced that it cannot be crushed and these exceptions are the only basket makers that we now have among the younger generation. They are artists in spite of an education, they learn basketry during the summer, when ordinarily no weaving is done. Katherine Nish, Nellie Preston, Manuella Thomas, Maud Davis and Emma Newman are striking examples of this type.[32]

By being artists despite their education—presumably at institutions like the Phoenix Indian School—Breazeale referred indirectly to the "industrial" education to which Indigenous students were subjected at these so-called Indian schools, which emphasized modern vocational training at the expense of preserving Indigenous knowledge. The purpose, or so the Indian Bureau claimed, was to assimilate Indigenous people into mainstream American society, which they would officially join in 1924 per the provisions of the Indian Citizenship Act.[33]

As for the O'odham basket makers whom Breazeale worked with and featured in his book, if any of these women knew the story that Shaw told in *Pima Indian Legends* (1968), they did not share it with him. At least, not in a way that reached Breazeale. Indeed, Breazeale believed he sensed the basket makers' reluctance: "The talented Indian women are peculiar and they cannot be handled like white people. They are apt to adopt the attitude of the Sphinx and remain that way indefinitely, but they can all be appealed to."[34] Breazeale then makes broad observations, complete with some examples, of the generational differences between young and old. Breazeale clearly prefers talking with the younger weavers, whom he describes as "pliable and anxious to do something to please." Among these is Emma Newman:

> Delicate little Emma Newman, probably at this very moment, is sitting out before her hut in the blistering sun, up in the Mountain Village, weaving a basket for me. There are many coils in that basket and many stitches in each coil, and many long hours will go by before it is finished, but while she now works, Emma is happy in her surroundings, happy in her desert home, she is thinking about gathering mesquite pods that are now hanging yellow in great abundance in the thickets down by

the river, she is thinking about the whirl winds that bear down upon the village, she is thinking about the suhuaro fruit now soft and luscious and tinged with the colors of the sunset that last night lit up the Estrellas [mountains], she is thinking of the tales that her grandmother used to tell her, how the Ho-ho-kum [huhugam] hunted the bighorn among the chollas on the hills across the Gila [River]. Emma is in the right frame of mind as she sits out among the suhuaros and weaves her soul into her matchless baskets, and nothing could be more ideal than her home for her exquisite productions.[35]

Breazeale goes on further with his patronizing remarks, propounding how it is imperative to protect Newman from the material rewards of modern life, lest she become completely spoiled, which would, in Breazeale's opinion, utterly contaminate Newman's otherwise authentic O'odham village life. While it was probable that Newman spoke her O'odham dialect and knew the oral tradition that is characteristic of being a fluent speaker—especially when raised in that language—such a traditional knowledge base did not preempt Newman from engaging with the influences of modern life, complete with its ineluctable connections with the "white man's society." Remember, Newman has an education and is making baskets for the trade market. Furthermore, this is an Indian arts and crafts market that would make the man-in-the-maze basket design into a popular consumer good. As such, Newman is a part of the modern world, just a different part of that world than the one in which Breazeale lives and works. In *A Pima Past*, Shaw remembered the color line that divided the reservation from Phoenix. When Shaw and her husband bought a house in town, she admits that they "wondered if our new neighbors would accept us, a family from 'below the tracks' with copper Pima skins."[36]

Speaking of O'odham storytellers, Komal Hok had much to share about "Ee-toy," Elder brother, including brief but meaningful remarks about his kikih in the mountains. Nonetheless, the story that Shaw tells in her book is not recalled in any of the three major works featuring Thin Leather. I'itoi dominates the origin narrative that Komal Hok relates to Russell, beginning with his birth after Jeved mahkai brought the earth and sky together: "After a time the earth gave birth to one who was afterwards known as Itany [I'itoi] and later as Siuuhû, Elder Brother. He came to Earth Doctor and spoke roughly to him, and Earth Doctor trembled before his power."[37] Vowing to overthrow Jeved mahkai's first people, who were created before Coyote and himself, I'itoi ventured at shaping the O'odham himdag out of the riverine environment along the banks of the Gila and Salt rivers, the akimel and onk akimel. Calamity, as recounted in chapter 3, hits the O'odham jeved twice. First, a great flood wipes out the world that Jeved mahkai created, compelling him to take his followers "to the other side of the earth,"[38] possibly the Pima Bajo region. Second, the I'itoi narrative reaches its climax with the collapse of the big houses (ge'egdaj kikih). After the flood, during the time of the big houses, Thin Leather tells of I'itoi's homes in South Mountain and Baboquivari.

> [After slaying Ho'ok,] Elder Brother continued to live in the cave at Baboquivari for some time. He went about the country from village to village seeking to do mischief. He sang the song of the menstrual period and accompanied it by reviling the [families] of the young girls. At last the people could endure his pranks no longer and drove him away. He went to Mo'hatûk mountain [Greasy mountain], north of the Gila, and the people there gathered to destroy him.
>
> Elder Brother went into his house and the people came and clubbed him to death. They pounded his head until it was flat, then dragged him into the woods and left him there. The news was spread about the country that he was dead, but the next day he reappeared among the people.[39]

Is this the source of Shaw's story in *Pima Indian Legends*? In the absence of either documentation or oral history, one can only speculate. Likely, Komal Hok's reference to Siuuhu-kih in Fewkes's essay on the Casa Grande maze symbol holds the key. Although Russell's BAE report includes an abundance of photographs, including images of baskets and pottery, the man-in-the-maze design, such as the one Emma Newman used in her basket, is nowhere to be seen. That is not to say that Shaw's "Se-eh-ha's

House" story is unique to her work. When Thin Leather identified the Casa Grande maze as Siuuhu-kih, it was a clear indication that this story was an integral part of the Akimel O'odham oral tradition. This means that the story that Shaw tells goes back at least to the turn of the twentieth century, when Komal Hok alluded to this narrative to Fewkes. It was also what the O'odham basket weavers told Breazeale when he asked them about the I'itoi ki pattern's origins. It is also not improbable that this story goes back to the time of Nentvig's *Rudo Ensayo*. What the basket weavers created was an amazing reimagining of that story, which they expressed in the man-in-the-maze symbol. As for the symbol's connection with I'itoi and the story of the big houses, in the story that Komal Hok tells Russell, the zig-zag pattern was created by Gopher (Jewho):

> Elder Brother [after the sisivani killed him four times] sank through the earth and found the people that Earth Doctor had assisted to reach that side in order to escape the flood. Elder Brother told the people there of his ill treatment and asked them to come through and fight with him and to take the land away from the Indians [meaning the sisivani of the big houses]. After four months' preparation they set out upon their journey. . . . Elder Brother told Gopher [Jewho] to bore a hole for the people to come through. Gopher made a hole through the earth like a winding stair.[40]

That "winding stair," or crooked path (jujul wohg), is what the maze pattern symbolizes for I'itoi, which is preserved not only in O'odham oral tradition but also in the ancestral glyphs that inhabit the O'odham jeved in mountains and ruins. The crooked path symbol marks those places that are a part of I'itoi's story when he returned to cleanse the land with an army of Jeved mahkai's hehemajkam. This is what is remembered and renewed in O'odham baskets.

What Russell documents in *The Pima Indians* sheds light on the cultural environment in which the I'itoi kih design emerged: "The cooling ollas in which water was kept about their [the Pimas'] homes are the only vessels that are generally decorated. The potters aver that the designs are copied from the Hohokam [ancestral O'odham] potsherds that bestrew the mesas and that the symbolism is absolutely unknown to them." Similar to Breazeale, Russell encountered a Sphinx-like response to his inquiries. Even Sila Hina, "one of the best potters on the Gila [River reservation]," claimed not to know anything about the symbolism they used on their pots.[41] Also, comparable to basket weavers, Sila Hina and her peers regularly made pottery for the tourist market. In *Pima Indian Legends*, perhaps inspired by Sila Hina, Shaw tells "A Potsherd Speaks," in which the remnants of an ancient olla bemoaned its fate only to be reborn in the work of a young potter: "Long ago, an Indian maiden of [Huhugam] land molded me into an olla and I was so proud to hold water for the braves, the women, and their children. But one day great trouble came . . . and they left their villages in haste," leaving the olla behind in sherds, where it lay buried for centuries. Fortunately, when one day a descendant of the huhugam potter was gathering material for her own pots, she spotted the lonely sherd in the sand: "'A-yah Oh! What a beautiful piece of . . . pottery,' she exclaimed, taking the little sherd in her hand to study the pretty pattern. The maiden took the sherd home and skillfully copied the design on her new olla."[42] Implied in Shaw's story, belying its naiveté, is an implicit understanding on the part of the young potter that she found a piece of ancestral O'odham pottery. What the young potter's elders may have taught her about the huhugam that made the original pot is left to the reader's imagination.

As for the baskets in *The Pima Indians*, Russell begins with an observation about basket making as a common means of income—a consequence of "the poverty of the tribe since the [Gila] river water has been taken from them." Unfortunately, in Russell's estimation, many of the baskets are of poor quality. Because of the tribe's anemic economy and the withering away of O'odham traditions—due to an ineptly managed reservation system—many of the basket makers have not received "the necessary training in girlhood," such as Shaw described in *A Pima Past*, "and without any pride in the finished product, as it is possible to dispose of them at once at a fair price, no matter how wretchedly bad they may be."[43] Nonetheless, Russell went on to record for posterity how basket weaving was practiced at the time of his fieldwork. In a subsection on "Basket Bowls," Russell identifies samples of basketry that he found to be well made. As indicated earlier, despite the adulation, weavers were less than forthcoming with their knowledge about the symbolism: "When questioned as to the meaning of the elements of these patterns, the basket makers invariably replied: 'I don't know; the old women make them in this way. They copied the pattern long ago from the [huhugam] pottery.'"[44] In the end, all that Russell could manage was to summarize the baskets' physical traits as an integral part of O'odham material culture:

> The fret, which the Pimas probably with truth called the oldest motive [sic], leads almost directly into the swastika and suavastika pattern. . . . The flower design based upon the cross is apparently the same as that on the necks of water jars made by the Hohokam [huhugam], and such vessels are similarly decorated to the present day by both Pimas [Akimel O'odham] and Papagos [Tohono O'odham].[45]

Regarding the fret pattern, Russell adds examples in the "Illustrations" portion at the back of his BAE report. Though the featured pottery exhibits an obvious genius for geometric design, I'itoi kih is nonetheless nowhere to be seen.

As for the claim that basket weavers did not know the origin of the arcane patterns they put into their baskets, what may at first look like a case of cultural loss is in fact a cultural divide. What Russell and Breazeale encountered was an ethical boundary that they were not allowed to cross. Basket weavers saying "I don't know" kept them, these mimilgahn, on their side of that line. As basketry was customarily a woman's skill,[46] the basket weavers that Russell and Breazeale spoke with likely thought it was inappropriate to share their knowledge with these men. Furthermore, the assertion that elders "copied" their designs from huhugam may have been the basket weavers' way of saying that these designs have been handed down since the time of the big houses, in which case the knowledge of these designs belong to those huhugam even if weavers learn them from their elders. Feigning ignorance, saying "I don't know" (pi'añi mac), like the O'odham that spoke to the Spaniards that wanted to know who built Casa Grande, is a form of non-aggressive resistance to the intrusion of outsiders. It is part of the O'odham himdag. A tradition that goes back to the time of the Spanish invasion and Velarde's nineteenth-century account. Of course, Akimel O'odham knew their stories about the ge'egdaj kikih (big houses) and Si'al Cehedag (Morning Green), the sivani at Casa Grande. But why do the jujkam and mimilgahn need to know these things, anyway?

Breazeale observed that it was typically young basket makers, such as Emma Newman, who created the man-in-the-maze design, which is comparable to the innovations created by Hopi-Tewa potter Nampeyo. By her own account, Nampeyo was inspired by the Sityaki-style pottery that Jesse Walter Fewkes unearthed during his 1895 excavation, nearly twenty years ahead of his work at Casa Grande.[47] For Nampeyo, ancestral Puebloan pottery was more than a source of old patterns that she could copy; they were lessons from which she derived her own style of Sityaki pottery. Thus, Nampeyo revitalized a once-dormant tradition, making it a part of Hopi-Tewa culture anew. What this suggests is that something similar occurred among Akimel O'odham basket weavers. As argued earlier, huhugam patterns, O'odham baskets, and the teachings of I'itoi were being rendered anew. What is important to acknowledge is that it is Indigenous artists, be they potters or weavers, who are employing their knowledge, skills, and imagination in unexpected but culturally relevant new ways. This is how a people resists the forces, natural and manmade, that strive to erase them from the land. For the mimilgahn that consumed O'odham baskets and pottery, like Breazeale, they could only see themselves and their cultural values in everything around them.

Breazeale firmly believed that the early twentieth-century emergence of the I'itoi kih pattern was due to Fewkes's having rediscovered in 1906 what Nentvig observed in 1764 at Casa Grande Ruins, namely an ovular maze-like pattern. However, whereas Breazeale interpreted Fewkes's excavation as an example of cultural diffusion—from Crete to Hohokam to Pimas—O'odham perceived these ancestral ruins as part of their origin narrative, in which their mazes sprung from the earth, their jeved. Hypothetically, if Breazeale were to ask O'odham if they thought their man-in-the-maze design came from ancient Crete, they would likely say, "I don't know." Then they might refer to their story about when, after the flood, Jeved mahkai sent Bán (Coyote) and I'itoi (Elder brother) to look for the center of the earth, implying that maybe one of them saw "that place" as they searched for *here*.

The basket weavers that Russell and Breazeale knew personally were examples of a community of Indigenous craft makers navigating a world in which their cultural sovereignty was mediated by forces beyond their control. In light of this, the man in the maze, I'itoi kih, is an invention of the O'odham mind, woven by some yet-unknown basket makers. The I'itoi kih narrative that Shaw recounts may have arisen concurrently with the "Well-Baked Man" story, which Richard Erdoes and Alfonso Ortiz included in their monumental 1984 anthology *American Indian Myths and Legends,* in which they note that the story was "based on fragments recorded in the 1880s."[48] Erdoes and Ortiz describe this legend as being about "the creation of the white man," who is portrayed "as one of the Creator's slight mistakes."[49] Like Shaw's man-in-the-maze story, the well-baked man is not recounted in Komal Hok's two versions of the origin narrative. Consequently, the legend's place in O'odham oral tradition is ambiguous except when considered as a modern creation, as a way of explaining or coping with the milgahn invasion and their occupation of the O'odham jeved.[50]

What is apparent at this juncture is the adaptability of the I'itoi narrative tradition, which goes back centuries. More to the point, I'itoi kih enables O'odham to understand their himdag—which is what the maze pattern symbolizes—as still relevant, not to mention empowering. Even during the worst of times, during the long bihugig of the 1870s to 1910s, when scores of O'odham suffered from being cut off from their akimel. As Shaw tells this story, Elder brother prevailed even against such overwhelming odds. He did not even have to overpower his "enemies"; he merely waited for them to defeat themselves. In the end, because he was the one who made that maze in Muhadag do'ag, it was his intellect and his connection to the land that allowed him to endure. So did his descendants, and so shall we.

In conclusion, the O'odham maze of history as told by Komal Hok, his contemporaries, and his descendants narrates the jeved into existence from the first plant, the creosote bush, to the emergence of the s*os*anac/j, the first people, who built the canals and the big houses, to I'itoi's four deaths and rebirths and his return from the land below up a crooked path to cleanse the river valleys. We learned about the hahashañ, the ooshikbina, and the reappearance of I'itoi through O'odham baskets. When I presumed to refer to the book in hand as an O'odham philosophy of history in the introduction, I was conscientious about not raising expectations that the reader would engage in a critique of western theories of history, such as Hegel and Marx, in which an O'odham theory of history would develop. On the contrary, I have forthrightly asserted the validity of the O'odham himdag as the appropriate way to understand our jeved, ourselves as hehemajkam, and our village-based sense of history. The customs characterizing O'odham storytelling—contrary to anthropologists' efforts—are not universalizable into a theory of history that is applicable to other, non-O'odham histories. This is what was meant when it was asserted that O'odham teachings, most importantly the origin narrative, are only for O'odham. Only when the kinship between people and place, O'odham and jeved, is established do the stories' meanings come into clarity.

Moving forward, the discourse on O'odham history and culture ought to begin with the O'odham, not the jujkam, and definitely not the mimilgahn. The discourse within this book began with a modest account of the number of Akimel O'odham that were counted as members of the Society of American Indians. In turn, the manmade time of famine (bihugig), which American settlers and their Indian Office imposed on the hehemajkam, became the desperate circumstances out of which Komal Hok, Thin Leather, emerged to recount the Akimel O'odham origin narrative for Russell and Lloyd and later share his knowledge about ancestral O'odham (huhugam) with Fewkes. A major focus of the previous seven chapters was Komal Hok and the seminal work he did as a "cultural informant" for anthropologists Frank Russell and Jesse Walter Fewkes and writer J. William Lloyd during the early twentieth century. Because of his dedication, three works in which Komal Hok plays a central role appeared in print, consisting of two Bureau of American Ethnology reports, "Casa Grande, Arizona" (1906) and *The Pima Indians* (1908), and a self-published collection of Akimel O'odham oral histories, *Aw-aw-tam Indian Nights* (1911). Subsequent O'odham studies, namely work by Ruth M. Underhill and Donald M. Bahr, are possible only because of what Komal Hok did. The book in hand would not be possible without him, hence the recurring references to his work from one chapter to the next.

Because Komal Hok (born ca. 1825) represented what is likely the last generation to have a storyteller and singer (ne'etham) who knew the origin narrative in its entirety, his legacy in O'odham scholarship is immeasurable. Taken together, Thin Leather's contributions comprise the foundation of O'odham studies, including ethnography, history, archaeology, literature, and philosophy. Not all researchers, of course, have respected O'odham oral tradition in the same way and to the same degree, which is why this book is necessary. There is a profound difference between someone like Donald M. Bahr, author of *The Short Swift Time of Gods on Earth: The Hohokam Chronicles* (1994), and Shepherd Krech III, author of *The Ecological Indian* (1999). Bahr, for his part, learned how to speak O'odham neok, our language, and showed great respect for O'odham knowledge keepers, be they historic ones like Thin Leather or contemporary ones like my maternal grandfather, Simon Lewis. Krech did not speak with any O'odham, limiting his "research" to the archaeological discourse, especially those archaeologists, like Paul Ezell, who did not always have a favorable opinion of O'odham oral history. As expected, Bahr and Krech lead their readers to radically different conclusions about how ancestral O'odham, or "Hohokam," interacted with their homeland. One honors while the other demeans. In light of such controversaries, this book deliberately elevated Komal Hok into the historically important role that he deserves in O'odham intellectual history. Komal Hok is a revered ancestor. His legacy makes him one of the immortals.

As became abundantly clear in the preceding pages, central to the O'odham origin narrative is I'itoi (Elder brother). He is what ethnographers and folklorists call a "cultural hero." I'itoi is the one credited with teaching O'odham their himdag, our way of doing things. Thin Leather's interpretation of the O'odham himdag, in turn, is the basis of the O'odham understanding of history (as recounted in the origin narrative), of the environment (as explained through the O'odham jeved, or homeland), and of community (as explained through kinship). All of these are based on the O'odham neok, our language. In one respect, this book is oriented toward an O'odham reader in the sense that it strove to meet the expectations of the author's community, namely the Gila River Indian Community. With them in mind, what developed in the foregoing chapters is a historical narrative based on two interrelated foundations: first, the O'odham origin narrative (meaning the Thin Leather documents, noted earlier) and, second, O'odham calendar sticks (ooshikbina), village-based ways of recording oral histories. In the end, my objective was twofold: at one level, to compel O'odham and O'odham scholars to rethink how they understand O'odham history; at another level, to influence how historians as a scholarly community think about the O'odham homelands. To put it succinctly, O'odham do not have a word for "world," let alone "world view." We only have jeved, which refers to land, earth, and soil. O'odham were aware of places beyond the O'odham jeved, beyond our mountains and rivers, but those places were given to other peoples by their creators. This jeved-centric perspective on people, events, memories, and stories is an idea, or a philosophy of history, that in the end this O'odham author hopes will inform future reflections on the huhugam and hehemajkam, their akimel and onk akimel, as well as their relatives all over the O'odham jeved. May the crooked path, Gopher's winding stair, always lead back to I'itoi kih.

Acknowledgments

Given that the work in hand is the compilation of previously published and some unpublished papers, my gratitude goes to persons who have been a part of my entire career as a professor of American Indian and Transborder studies. However, as an O'dham, my enduring gratefulness extends to my family and friends, who have been a part of my entire life. There are too many to name and thank in their entirety. Nonetheless, I do want to recognize the key figures who helped make this book possible. First and foremost, my mother, Marilyn Theresa Martinez (1933–2010), who brought me into this world and worked hard at raising me, complete with an awareness of where I am really from, which is Gila Crossing Village, District 6, Gila River Indian Community. Next, my grandfather, the Reverend Simon Lewis (1911–1999), whose little church, the Gila Crossing First Presbyterian Church, was the center of the universe, where it faced—and still does—Komadk do'ag, where Nuwi kih still stands. My grandfather was my role model for comporting myself as an O'odham hemajkam. With respect to my community, I want to thank Ofelia Zepeda, my master's thesis director at the University of Arizona, Angela Garcia-Lewis, cultural preservation compliance supervisor for the Salt River Pima-Maricopa Indian Community, and Robert "Bobby" Stone, former Lt. Governor of the Gila River Indian Community. All three took turns in saving the day when I needed help with our O'odham neok. My work simply would not be the contribution to O'odham studies that it is without them.

Now, I would be remiss in my obligations as a scholar if I did not take a moment to thank the mimilgahn who have supported my work over the years, beginning with Don Bahr (1940–2016), who I got to know because he was visiting my grandfather to pick his brain about Snaketown. Also, I want to thank Keith Kintigh and Frank McManamon, two Arizona State University colleagues who recruited me to participate in the development of the Digital Archives of Huhugam Archaeology (DAHA), which is hosted online by the Digital Archaeological Record (tDAR). Regularly presenting this project at the Four Southern Tribes meetings, in which cultural resources representatives from the four O'odham reservations attended, enabled me to develop my understanding of my O'odham culture and history. In the same regard, I want to thank J. Brett Hill, professor of archaeology at Hendrix College, for inviting me to write an afterword for his excellent book on the history of Hohokam archaeology, in addition to inviting me to co-present with him at the 2020 Southwest Symposium Archaeological Conference. Because of his friendship, two of the chapters published here were written. Speaking of collegial friendships, the last word of thanks goes to Gabe Ricci, professor of philosophy at Elizabethtown College. We only met in person once at an aesthetics conference in Philadelphia many years ago. Yet because of that chance encounter, we have remained colleagues all this time. Equally important, Gabe, as one of my editors, invited contributions from me on different occasions, including a recent publication on the Anthropocene and its relevance to environmental philosophy, which is now a part of this book. Thanks to him, I enjoyed reflecting on the time when Coyote stole Rabbit's heart. Lastly, before I forget, thank you to my two peer reviewers who read my rough draft for the University of New Mexico Press and graciously supported my work. Thank you to Michael Millman, my editor at the press, who energetically shepherded my manuscript into a book, and who wisely assigned my O'odham musings to Anna Pohlod, whose exceptional copyediting skills turned this work into something I can proudly put my name upon.

Glossary

NB: the orthography employed in this text is largely derived from *Tohono O'odham/Pima to English, English to Tohono O'odham/Pima*, second edition, edited by Dean Saxton, Lucille Saxton, and Susie Enos, unless otherwise noted. See endnotes for more information.

akimel. River; refers to the Gila River.

onk. Salty; onk akimel, salty river, written historically as Salt River.

O'odham. People, or speakers of the O'odham language. The term is sometimes used as a synonym of "nation."

Akimel O'odham. River people; all the villages that lived off the Gila River.

Tohono O'odham. Desert people; all the villages below the Akimel O'odham, who lived off the desert.

Hia-Ced O'odham. Sand people, or sand dune people, or people of the sand dunes; "Hia-ced" refers to the kind of sand that is endemic to the sand dunes near the Gulf of California.

Sobaipuri (unknown origin). The name refers to another branch of Akimel O'odham whose villages historically were along the San Pedro River and whose current lands are located in the San Xavier del Bac district of Tohono O'odham Nation.

Pima Bajo, or Lower Pima. Historical name for O'odham villages in Sonora and Chihuahua, Mexico, namely Óob O'odham, Ó O'odham, and Taramil O'odham.

huhugam. Ancestral O'odham who inhabited the "big houses," ruins of which are preserved at Casa Grande Ruins National Monument and Pueblo Grande (now called S'edav Va'aki Museum). "Huhugam" is synonymous with "shohshon," ancestor(s); however, "huhugam" refers to the O'odham that are recounted in the origin narrative, meaning the first people created by Jeved mahkai and I'itoi as well as the big house dwellers, the people in Elder brother's army, and the people who resettled the land after the big houses fell.

Hohokam. An archaeological concept, articulated by Adolph Bandelier, Jesse Walter Fewkes, Frank Russell, Emil Haury, Paul Ezell, and other archaeologists and anthropologists focusing on the ruins, artifacts, and human remains excavated at hundreds of locations between Phoenix and Tucson, Arizona.

jeved. Earth, land, soil. May also mean homeland, as this term is only used in reference to places that O'odham recognize as part of the world that Jeved mahkai (Earth medicine maker), created from the muhadag (grease) from their chest, as recounted in the origin narrative.

mahkai, mamahkai. Medicine person, medicine people. Someone learned in the ways of healing, in which songs, chants, smoke, crystals, rattles, and basket drums, among other paraphernalia, are used to extract the gewkdag (power) causing someone to feel ill.

hemajkam, hehemajkam. Person, persons. Refers to ordinary men and women in their everyday roles as relatives and as members of their villages.

sivani, sisivani. Chief priest, chief priests. Refers to the leaders of the various huhugam big houses recounted in the origin narrative, a title not typically used for leaders of O'odham villages after the Elder brother swept through the jeved with his army.

I'itoi. Elder brother (also called Siuuhu). Of unknown origin. Komal Hok says that I'itoi was "later called Siuuhuu" in the story he shared with Frank Russell in *The Pima Indians*. Others claim that "I'itoi" is customary among Tohono O'odham and "Siuuhuu" is customary among Akimel O'odham. The different terms may possibly refer to how Elder brother was known among huhugam and what he was called when he returned with his army.

do'ag, dodoag. Mountain, mountains. Typically used when referring to mountain peaks that define the sacred geography of the various O'odham, as O'odham did not have a word for "boundary" or "territory" or "border" as is commonplace among contemporary nation-states.

Notes

Introduction

1. For Deloria's legendary takedown of the anthropological profession, see Deloria, *Custer Died for Your Sins*, 78–100. For more on Eastman's critique of turn-of-the-century ethnography, see Eastman, *The Soul of the Indian*. For my analysis of Deloria's work, in particular his critique of the social sciences, see Martínez, *Life of the Indigenous Mind*, 175–209.
2. Martínez, "The Soul of the Indian," 79.
3. For more on this history, see DeJong, *Stealing the Gila*. For my review of DeJong's book, see Martínez, "Stealing the Gila."
4. Russell, *The Pima Indians*, 229.
5. On a personal note, I began thinking about nonanalytical discourses as philosophy when I wrote my doctoral dissertation for the Department of Philosophy at SUNY at Stony Brook, which is titled "The Epic of Peace: Poetry as the Foundation of Philosophical Reflection" (1997). The major focus of this work was *El arco y la lira* (The Bow and the Lyre) by Octavio Paz, which was a phenomenology of the poetic experience.
6. See Bahr, "Who Were the Hohokam?," 245–66; and Bech, "De la tradición oral a la escritura," 131–65.
7. The Piipaash, or Maricopa (as they are called in the historical record), have long been a distinct yet integral part of the Akimel O'odham community. For more, see Harwell and Kelly, "Maricopa," 71–85.
8. For more on the economic impact of the Bureau of Plant Industry during the "Time of Famine" in the Akimel O'odham communities, see Bess, *Where the Red-Winged Blackbirds Sing*.
9. For an overview of the impact of the US-Mexico border on the O'odham, see Leza, *Divided Peoples* and Amaya-Schaeffer, *Unsettled Borders*, 55–80.
10. Webb, *A Pima Remembers*.

Chapter One

1. Parker, ed., "List of Active Members," 247–49. It should be noted that the membership list only notes names and place of residency, but not tribal affiliation. Therefore it was not possible to determine the tribal identity of anyone listing, say, a boarding school address.

2. Montezuma, "Light on the Indian Situation," 50. In a footnote to this article, it states this was "an address delivered at the [SAI's] Second Conference, at Ohio State University, Joint Session, Oct. 5, 1912." Montezuma wrote of this seminal event: "In one of these midnight raids made by the Pimas in 1871 many Apaches were slaughtered, and I was captured. That dark memorable night with all its awful horrors of massacre is indelibly impressed upon my mind." Noteworthy is the fact that although Montezuma went on to become known as "the fiery Apache," he was actually a Yavapai, who are "Apaches" only because of a misnomer applied by white settlers.

3. See "Executive Order—Pima and Maricopa Indian Reserve," The American Presidency Project, accessed December 26, 2024, https://www.presidency. ucsb.edu/documents/executive-order-pima-and-maricopa-indian-reserve.

4. Bess, *Where the Red-Winged Blackbirds Sing*, 8.

5. Lloyd, *Aw-aw-tam Indian Nights*, 6.

6. Bahr, *The Short Swift Time of Gods on Earth*, 291. See also Lloyd, *Aw-aw-tam Indian Nights* and Fewkes, "Casa Grande, Arizona."

7. What does exist are sound recordings of Komal Hok. See "Comalk-Hawk-Kih songs of Akimel O'odham (Pima) stories" Smithsonian Institution, National Museum of the American Indian, accessed December 27, 2024, https://sova.si.edu/record/nmai.ac.435.

8. For an overview of the historical significance of the Native American literature that coincided with the Red Power Era (1964–1974), see Lincoln, *Native American Renaissance*.

9. Certainly in the western intellectual tradition it is not unusual for an important thinker to not have authored their own texts. Socrates and Aristotle immediately come to mind.

10. Martínez, "Neither Chief Nor Medicine Man," 30.

11. This is not meant to imply that American Indians did not appreciate when their young people had the opportunity to attend institutions of

higher learning. See, for example, Roe Cloud, "Education of the American Indian," 192–97.

12. For more about Alice Paul's life and career, see "Dr. Alice Paul," University of Arizona, Women's Plaza of Honor, accessed May 31, 2024, https://plaza.sbs.arizona.edu/honoree/2591.

13. Lloyd, *Aw-aw-tam Indian Nights*, 1.

14. Technically one cannot call Komal Hok an American, at least as of when he collaborated with Russell, Fewkes, and Lloyd. The Indian Citizenship Act was not passed by Congress until 1924, which might have accorded such a legal status to Thin Leather (I have not found when Thin Leather died). Also, there is nothing to indicate that Komal Hok possessed an allotment under the provisions of the 1887 General Allotment Act, which provided an albeit difficult path to citizenship.

15. Russell, *The Pima Indians*, 18na. Originally published as the *Twenty-Sixth Annual Report of the Bureau of American Ethnology, 1904–1905*.

16. Ezell, "History of the Pima," 157, fig. 8.

17. Russell, *The Pima Indians*, 54. See also Bourke, *On the Border with Crook*, 191–200.

18. Shaw, *A Pima Past*, 87. Shaw names Owl Ear as a revered storyteller in "The Rattlesnake Receives His Fangs." See Shaw, *Pima Indian Legends*, 17–19.

19. Russell, *The Pima Indians*, 200–206.

20. Parker, ed., "What Indian Students Say About Education," 296.

21. For more, see "Sells District History," Sells District, accessed May 21, 2024, https://www.sellsdistrict.com/history.

22. Smith, "Education and Progress for the Indian," 292–94.

23. For an overview of American Indian intellectual history prior to the Indian protest movement, which is more commonly called Red Power, see Martínez, *The American Indian Intellectual Tradition*.

24. Russell, *The Pima Indians*, 347–52.

25. Russell, *The Pima Indians*, 352.

26. Oskison, "Acquiring a Standard of Value," 47–48. A footnote states that this article was first "An Address delivered before the Third Annual Conference of the Society of American Indians at Denver, Colorado."

27. See "Oskison, John Milton (1874–1947)," Oklahoma Historical Society, The Encyclopedia of Oklahoma History and Culture, accessed June 1, 2024, https://www.okhistory.org/publications/enc/entry?entry=OS008.

28. Parker, ed., "Shall the Pimas Be Robbed of Water?" For more on the San Carlos Project and its impact on the Gila River Indian Community, see DeJong, *Damming the Gila*.

29. Russell, *The Pima Indians*, 54. Russell noted regarding Salt River: "By Executive order of June 14, 1879, the land occupied by the Pimas on Salt River was set apart as the Salt River reservation. It embraces about three townships on the north side of the river about 30 miles north of the original Pima villages. There are several large ruins and at least one large canal upon the reservation that were built by the Hohokam. By an arrangement with the canal companies the Pimas have insured for themselves a constant supply of water, and the Salt River community is regarded as the most prosperous among the Pimas," *The Pima Indians*, 54na.

30. Russell, *The Pima Indians*, 65, 65na.

31. *Salt and Gila Rivers—Reservations and Reclamation Service: Hearings Before a Subcommittee of the Committee on Expenditures in the Interior Department of the House of Representatives Under H Res 103*, April 23, 1912, 467. The author was unable to find any record of Jones's education, either in the Carlisle Indian School Digital Resource Center or the Research Database Center for the National Native American Boarding School Healing Coalition (NABS).

32. Hensley, Walter Lewis, Mondell, Frank Wheeler, Burke, Charles Henry, *Report in the Matter of the Investigation of the Salt and Gila Rivers—Reservations and Reclamation Service*, H.R. Rep. No. 1506-62 (1913), 465.

33. "Earl Whitman Student File," Carlisle Indian School Digital Resource Center, accessed June 12, 2024, https://carlisleindian.dickinson.edu/index.php/student_files/earl-whitman-student-file.

34. Russell, "A Pima Constitution," 222.

35. Russell, "A Pima Constitution," 222.

36. Russell, "A Pima Constitution," 222.

37. Russell, "A Pima Constitution," 222.

38. Office of Indian Affairs, Report of the Commissioner of Indian Affairs, for the year 1901 (Washington, DC: Government Printing Office, 1901), 183.

39. Russell, "A Pima Constitution," 226.

40. Also spelled as Siwañ Wa'a Ki.

41. Jesse Walter Fewkes, "Casa Grande, Arizona," Twenty-Eighth Annual Report of the Bureau of American Ethnology, 1906–1907 (Washington,

DC: Government Printing Office, 1912), 115. See also Russell, "A Pima Constitution," 225, specifically, the section titled "Labor on Ditch or Dam."

42. Different historians will mark the beginning of the American Era of the Southwest differently, depending on the narrative they want to establish. Most often the dates 1848 (Treaty of Guadalupe Hidalgo), 1850 (New Mexico Territory), 1854 (Gadsden Purchase), and 1863 (Arizona Territory) are common for Arizona histories. My preference for 1850, however, has nothing to do with New Mexico Territory. 1850 marks when "Pimo villages" are mentioned for the first time by Office of Indian Affairs.

43. Russell, *The Pima Indians*, 46. Given the reference to the Piipaash, or "Maricopas," in this anecdote, this is likely a reference to the 1857 Battle of Pima Butte. Akimel O'odham does not distinguish between Apache, Yavapai, Cocopah, or Quechan—they are all o'obga (enemies). Therefore the reference in the above quote to "Apaches" may be misleading. Although the US was at war with virtually every band of Apaches between Arizona and New Mexico, from the O'odham point of view enemy tribes included the adversaries to their Piipaash friends in Maricopa Village.

44. Ezell, "History of the Pima," 157.

45. Ezell, "History of the Pimas," 157–58.

46. Ezell, "History of the Pimas," 158.

47. Ezell, "History of the Pimas," 158–59. See also Russell, *The Pima Indians*, 156–66.

48. "Carlisle Indian Industrial School Tribal Enrollment Tally," Carlisle Indian Industrial School (1879-1918), http://home.epix.net/~landis/tally.html.

49. "Hampton Normal & Agricultural Institute," Jon L. Brudvig, http://www.twofrog.com/hampton2.txt

50. Russell, *The Pima Indians*, 237na.

51. Society of American Indians, "Platform of the Second Conference," 72.

52. Montezuma, "Let My People Go," 208. It is worth noting that there were Akimel O'odham who were greatly influenced by Montezuma's campaign against the Indian Bureau, even subscribing to his self-published newsletter *Wassaja*. For more on Montezuma and the Akimel O'odham, see David Martínez, *My Heart Is Bound Up with Them: How Carlos Montezuma Became the Voice of a Generation* (Tucson: The University of Arizona Press, 2023): 137–63.

53. Russell, "A Pima Constitution," 227.

54. Russell, "A Pima Constitution," 228.

55. Russell, "A Pima Constitution," 228. For a comprehensive analysis of the relationship between Progressive Era social science and federal Indian policy, see Hoxie, *A Final Promise*.

56. Nabakov and Easton, *Native American Architecture*, 340. See photo caption.

57. Russell, *The Pima Indians*, 153.

58. Russell, *The Pima Indians*, 153.

59. Webb, *A Pima Remembers*, 16.

60. *Hearings before the Committee on Indian Affairs, The Condition of Various Tribes of Indians, "History of Irrigation on the Gila River,"* 66th Cong. 1st sess. (June 30, 1919), 138.

61. Haury, *The Hohokam*, 9.

62. See Amadeo M. Rea, *Folk Mammology of the Northern Pimas* (Tucson: The University of Arizona Press, 1998): 142–45.

63. Russell, *The Pima Indians*, 215.

64. Russell, *The Pima Indians*, 17na.

65. Russell, *The Pima Indians*, 17.

66. The likely source of Russell's phonetic notations was John Wesley Powell's *Introduction to the Study of Indian Languages, with Words, Phrases, and Sentences to Be Collected* (US Government Printing Office, 1880), archived February 25, 2010, https://archive.org/details/introductiontost00powe/page/22/mode/2up.

67. Russell, *The Pima Indians*, 17–18na.

68. Russell, *The Pima Indians*, 17. An alternate orthography for Thin Leather is Comalk Hawk-Kih (Komalk Hok), which is sometimes translated as Thin Buckskin and is the name used in J. William Lloyd's book, *Aw-aw-tam Indian Nights*. According to Jesse Walter Fewkes, Thin Leather (which he spells "Kamalkcak" in O'odham) was "popularly called Higgins" in addition to being "a member of the Eagle clan." See Fewkes, "A Fictitious Ruin in Gila Valley, Arizona," 511n1.

69. Lloyd, *Aw-aw-tam Indian Nights*, 6–7.

70. Russell, *The Pima Indians*, 18na.

71. Cook and Whittemore, *Among the Pimas*, 32. Alexander was likely Major A. J. Alexander, who was at one time dispatched to Fort Union, New

Mexico. See "Chapter Ten. Fitness and Discipline: Health Care and Military Justice," Fort Union Historic Resource Study, accessed May 24, 2024, http://npshistory.com/publications/foun/hrs/chap10.htm.

72. Shaw, *A Pima Past*, 64.

73. Russell, *The Pima Indians*, 18. For more on Brennan's work and legacy, see Fontana and Brennan, "Jose Lewis Brennan's Account,'" 226–37; and Jose Lewis Brennan, Bernard L. Fontana, and Hazel M. Fontana, "Gold Placer of Quijotoa, Ariz," *Journal of the Southwest* 33, no. 4 (Winter, 1991): 459–74. See also "MS 1744 Papago material obtained from Jose Lewis Brennan," Smithsonian, National Museum of Natural History, accessed December 28, 2024, https://www.si.edu/object/archives/sova-naa-ms1744.

74. Bahr, *Pima and Papago Ritual Oratory*, 8. With respect to Brennan's work, see Fontana and Brennan, "Jose Lewis Brennan's Account,'" 226–37.

75. Bahr, *Pima and Papago Ritual Oratory*, 9.

76. See Bech, "De la tradición oral a la escritura," 131–65.

77. Bahr, *Pima and Papago Ritual Oratory*, 9.

78. Zepeda, *When It Rains*, 78.

79. Fontana and Brennan, "Jose Lewis Brennan's Account of Papago 'Customs and Other References,'" 226.

80. Russell, *The Pima Indians*, plate XLIV.

81. Russell, *The Pima Indians*, 196.

82. Russell, *The Pima Indians*, 106.

83. Russell, *The Pima Indians*, 148.

84. Russell, *The Pima Indians*, 148.

85. Russell, *The Pima Indians*, 148. Russell includes a description of the process in a footnote to his text written by Lieutenant Emory in 1846; see *The Pima Indians*, 148–49na.

86. See Roffler, "Frank Russell at Gila River," 373–95.

87. Russell, *The Pima Indians*, 36.

88. Russell, *The Pima Indians*, 36. The "Gisap" is identified as a verdin, a small songbird with a gray body and a yellowish head. See Rea, *Wings in the Desert*, 216–18.

89. Russell, *The Pima Indians*, 20.

90. Russell, *The Pima Indians*, 22.

91. Russell, *The Pima Indians*, 22.

92. Russell, *The Pima Indians*, 20. Paul H. Ezell notes: "When the written records of the Pimas begins, they occupied at least seven rancherias separated from each other by distances of from seven to nearly 40 miles. One of these, Santa Catarina, was on the Santa Cruz River west of Picacho Peak; five were on the south side of the Gila between Casa Grande Ruins and a few miles above Gila Bend; and one was on the north bank of the Gila above the junction of the Salt River." See Ezell, "History of the Pimas," 150–51.

93. Russell, *The Pima Indians*, 206na. Russell also notes that smoke talk is "from tcu-utc, smoke, and nyiâk, talk. This myth is also called Hâ-âk Akita, 'Hâ-âk Telling.'" In Webb's *A Pima Remembers*, he states that telling of traditional stories is called *"ha'ichu'aga,"* which means "Something Told," 91.

94. Lloyd, *Aw-aw-tam Indian Nights*, 36.

95. Russell, *The Pima Indians*, 225na. Russell notes that "Antonio [Azul] thinks it [Elder brother's home] is in Baboquivari mountain." Baboquivari is the prominent mountain near Sells, on the Tohono O'odham reservation, south of Sacaton.

96. Russell, *The Pima Indians*, 225.

97. Russell, *The Pima Indians*, 225. The location is likely just north of the Estrella Mountains and south of West Lower Buckeye Road.

98. Russell, *The Pima Indians*, 265.

99. Russell, *The Pima Indians*, 265–66.

100. Russell, *The Pima Indians*, 272. In a footnote Bahr elaborates on the translation of Jeved mahkai, stating: "Sometimes translated as 'Earth Shaman' or 'Earth Medicine Man.' The word jeved, 'earth, also means 'land' or 'ground' as opposed to sky or water. At its lowest level of contrast, the word also means 'soil' or 'dirt' as opposed to sand or rock." See Bahr, *The Short Swift Time of Gods on Earth*, 45.

101. Russell, *The Pima Indians*, 206.

102. Jeved mahkai's gender is ambiguous. Arbitrary selection of the masculine possessive, when it occurs, is merely in keeping with the existing literature on O'odham religion. It is more accurate to say that gender is a human limitation that can only be tenuously ascribed to sacred beings.

103. Russell, *The Pima Indians*, 206.

104. Russell, *The Pima Indians*, 206–7.

105. Russell, *The Pima Indians*, 331–32.

106. Russell, *The Pima Indians*, 347na.

107. Russell, *The Pima Indians*, 347.

108. Russell, *The Pima Indians*, 347.

109. Russell, *The Pima Indians*, 347–49.

110. Russell, *The Pima Indians*, 348.

111. Russell, *The Pima Indians*, 349.

112. Russell, *The Pima Indians*, 350.

113. Russell, *The Pima Indians*, 351–52.

114. Russell, *The Pima Indians*, 334.

115. Russell, *The Pima Indians*, 210–11.

116. Webb, *A Pima Remembers*, 116.

117. Shaw, *A Pima Past*, 231.

Chapter Two

1. Kino, *Las Misiones de Sonora y Arizona*, 28.

2. Kino, *Kino's Historical Memoir of Pimería Alta*, 127.

3. For more on the history of Hohokam archaeology, see Hill, *From Huhugam to Hohokam*.

4. Fewkes, "Casa Grande, Arizona" 153.

5. Fewkes, "Casa Grande, Arizona," 45. See Teggart, *The Anza Expedition of 1775–1776, Diary of Pedro Font*, 18, 20, 22. Teggart provides his reader an English translation on the facing pages, specifically 19, 21, and 23. With respect to the reliability of Komal Hok's storytelling, Donald Bahr compared the two primary texts, namely *The Pima Indians* and *Aw-aw-tum Indian Nights*. See Bahr, *How Mockingbirds Are*, 23–24.

6. Fewkes, "Casa Grande, Arizona," 45–47.

7. Fewkes, "Casa Grande, Arizona," 34n1.

8. Fewkes, "Casa Grande, Arizona," 34.

9. See Holt, "A Cultural Resource Management Dilemma," 594–99.

10. Russell, *The Pima Indians*, 17na.

11. Fewkes, "Casa Grande, Arizona," 140n1.

12. Lloyd, *Aw-aw-tam Indian Nights*, 1–2. The fact that Komal Hok would tell stories during the summer is a clear indication that he may have felt just as urgently about preserving the Pima oral tradition as Lloyd, not to mention Russell before him. O'odham, like other indigenous people, normally did not tell stories, least of all the origin narrative, during the summer months It was commonly restricted it to the dead of winter.

13. Lloyd, *Aw-aw-tam Indian Nights*, 217n.

14. Lloyd, *Aw-aw-tam Indian Nights*, 1.

15. Amadeo M Rea, *Wings in the Desert: A Folk Ornithology of the Northern Pimans* (Tucson: The University of Arizona Press, 2007): 25. As noted in the introduction, Webb observed in *A Pima Remembers* that few Akimel O'odham are knowledgeable about O'odham oral tradition. In addition to language declination, learning the corpus of O'odham narratives is a formidable undertaking. "The whole story of White Clay Eater takes four nights to tell so I did not attempt to tell it all, only a short part" (np).

16. All are available on the Internet Archive as of June 6, 2024.

17. "Auto-biographical essay by J Wm Lloyd," archived June 22, 2005, https://web.archive.org/web/20081122005828/http://www.zetetics.com/mac/blog/00000933.html. See also Lloyd, *Songs of the Desert*.

18. Lloyd, *Aw-aw-tam Indian Nights*, 90–94.

19. Lloyd, *Aw-aw-tam Indian Nights*, 105.

20. Lloyd, *Aw-aw-tam Indian Nights*, 164–65. See also Kroeber and Fontana, *Massacre on the Gila*.

21. Emory, "Notes of a Military Reconnoissance."

22. Lloyd, *Aw-Aw-Tam Indian Nights*, 234. It is unclear, however, from which of Emory's writings Lloyd is quoting. Lloyd's scholarship leaves much to be desired.

23. Lloyd, *Aw-aw-tam Indian Nights*, 234.

24. Lloyd, *Aw-aw-tam Indian Nights*, 233.

25. Russell, *The Pima Indians*, 240. Inasa is nearly anonymous because there is no information about this person anywhere in Russell's text. S/he did not warrant recognition in Russell's list of informants, which included Thin Leather, Sala Hina, and Owl Ear. As of this writing, no information about Inasa has been located elsewhere. As for Russell's documentation of "Children of Cloud," Russell observes the parallels between the Akimel

O'odham narrative and the "Mohaves" and "Navahos," citing, respectively, Bourke, "Notes on the Cosmogony," 169–89; and Matthews, "A part of the Navajo's mythology," 1–18. With respect to Inasa's story, Russell notes at the end that William H. Emory recorded yet another version from "Chief Juan Antonio Llunas," in which the woman gives birth to a son, similar to the Piipaash story, "who was the founder of a new race which built all these houses." When Emory asked Llunas if he believed this story, he reportedly said, "No; but most of the Pimos do. We know, in truth, nothing of their origin. It is all enveloped in mystery." See Russell, *The Pima Indians*, 240na, in which is cited W. H. Emory, "Notes of a Military Reconnoissance," [sic] S. Ex. Doc. No. 41, S3 30th Cong., first sess. (1848).

26. For an overview of the a'ud, or agave, tradition among the Akimel O'odham, see Rea, *At the Desert's Green Edge*, 250–53.

27. For more on McCarthy, see H. David Brumble, *American Indian Autobiography* (University of Nebraska Press, 2008), 241–42.

28. Fantasia Painter, Onk Akimel, enrolled in the Salt River Pima-Maricopa Community, is the only one not cited in the present work. Currently Painter is an assistant professor of global and international studies in the School of Social Sciences at the University of California, Irvine. She is the author of "'Our Constitution Makes Provisions for All These Things:' Changing Tohono O'odham Protocols and Powers in the 1930s."

29. Russell, *The Pima Indians*, 33.

30. For more on this historically damaging process, see McCool, *Native Waters*.

31. See Winters v. United States, 207 U.S. 564 (1908), accessed June 7, 2024, https://supreme.justia.com/cases/federal/us/207/564/.

32. For more, see "Ephraim George Squier," Smithsonian Institution Archives, accessed January 17, 2025, https://siarchives.si.edu/history/featured-topics/latin-american-research/ephraim-george-squier.

33. For more, see Donna J. Seifert, "Charles C. Di Peso, 1920–1982," *Historical Archaeology* 17, no. 2 (1983): 106–11.

34. For a critical analysis of major works in Hohokam archaeology, see Hill, *From Huhugam to Hohokam*, 201–13.

35. See Odham Elder Barnaby V. Lewis's explanation in Archaeology Southwest, "Hohokam or Huhugam?," https://www.archaeologysouthwest.org/exhibit/online-exhibits/pieces-puzzle/piece-1/.

36. In addition to Hill's *From Huhugam to Hohokam*, see Fish and Fish, *The Hohokam Millennium*.
37. Ezell, "Is There a Hohokam-Pima Culture Continuum?," 61.
38. Nentvig, *Rudo Ensayo*, 57.
39. Ezell, "Is There a Hohokam-Pima Culture Continuum?," 65.
40. Ezell, "Is There a Hohokam-Pima Culture Continuum?," 64.
41. Loendorf and Lewis, "Ancestral O'odham, 125.
42. Paul Martin, "Africa and Pleistocene Overkill," *Nature* 212, 339–42 (1966), https://doi.org/10.1038/212339a0
43. For an Indigenous critique of Paul Martin's "Pleistocene Overkill" thesis, see Deloria, *Red Earth, White Lies*, 93–112. For Krech's retort, see *The Ecological Indian*, 42–43.
44. Krech, *The Ecological Indian*, 66–67.
45. Krech, *The Ecological Indian*, 252n33.
46. Krech, *The Ecological Indian*, 68.
47. Krech, *The Ecological Indian*, 70–71.
48. Shaw, *A Pima Past*, 4.
49. Russell, *The Pima Indians*, 19.
50. Russell, *The Pima Indians*, 19–20.
51. Russell, *The Pima Indians*, 19.
52. Kino wrote ambiguously about Casa Grande, *"It is said that the ancestors of Montezuma* deserted and depopulated it, and, beset by the neighboring Apaches, left for the east or Casas Grandes, and that from there they turned towards the south and southwest" (my emphasis). See Kino, *Kino's Historical Memoir of Pimería Alta*, 128. For the original Spanish text, see Kino, *Las misiones de Sonora y Arizona*, 29.
53. Russell, *The Pima Indians*, 23–24.
54. Font, *The Anza Expedition of 1775–1776*, 18.
55. Font, *The Anza Expedition of 1775–1776*, 19.
56. See Bandelier, "Appendix." See also Bandelier, *The Southwestern Journals*, 385n233, 389n275, 390n277.
57. Bandelier, *The Southwestern Journals*, 130–31.
58. Bandelier, *The Southwestern Journals*, 138. In an endnote, the editors added information about the current (1970) status of Hohokam archaeological research, most likely referring to Haury: "On present evidence, it would seem that the Pima Indians are Hohokam descendants" (392n311).

59. Russell, *The Pima Indians*, 58–59. Russell cites Bandelier multiple times. See, *The Pima Indians*, 25ne, 67na, 144na, 221na. The reference to drunkenness in this citation should not be taken lightly. It symbolizes the social affliction of alcohol abuse that was besotting the community as a consequence of the oppressive conditions in the reservation, including the likelihood of tragic deaths. In turn, the reference to the railroad symbolizes the economic changes wrought by American colonization, which transformed southern Arizona as a throughway for transnational commerce and migration.

60. Ezell, "Is There a Hohokam-Pima Culture Continuum?," 65. Ezell cites himself on this point, see Ezell, "The Hispanic Acculturation of the Gila River Pimas."

61. See Odham Elder Barnaby V. Lewis's explanation in "Hohokam or Huhugam?," Archaeology Southwest, accessed June 9, 2024, https://www.archaeologysouthwest.org/exhibit/online-exhibits/pieces-puzzle/piece-1/.

62. Webb, *A Pima Remembers*, 53.

63. Webb, *A Pima Remembers*, 94. Interestingly, Webb claims that Blue Hawk was the sivani at Blackwater Village as opposed to Morning Green, which is what Komal Hok tells in all three of his versions, which are cited throughout this discourse.

64. Webb, *A Pima Remembers*, 71. Edward S. Curtis, in *The North American Indian* (1908), divides the Coyote and Vulture moieties further into five clans: "The Pima have five tribal divisions, known as wúmakult [wehmkal], which may be designated phratries, as they are aggregations of gentes with totemic names. Children belong to the father, whom they call by the phratral name. The five totemic names, all synonymous with the word 'father' and bearing obscure meanings, are Ápap, Apk, Mam, Vâh, and Ókali. Ápap and Apk are associated with the coyote, and Mam and Vâh with the buzzard. The people of the first four are numerous, but of the Ókali only a few representatives survive. This division, according to the genesis myth, was broken in its inception, only a few succeeding in reaching the upper world" (9).

65. Webb, *A Pima Remembers*, 92.

66. Odham Elder Barnaby V. Lewis in "Hohokam or Huhugam?," Archaeology Southwest, accessed June 9, 2024, https://www.archaeologysouthwest.org/exhibit/online-exhibits/pieces-puzzle/piece-1/.

67. Shaw, *A Pima Past*, 2. For Haury's corroborating remarks, see Haury, "The Excavations of Los Muertos."
68. Shaw, *A Pima Past*, 2. How much Shaw knew about archaeological concepts like "Salado" is impossible to say. Shaw's reference is brief, suggesting that she took Haury's broad references to the Salado in his work on Hohokam archaeology at face value. There is nothing in O'odham oral traditions that corresponds to the Salado. For more on this archaeological epoch, see Lekson, "Salado Archaeology of the Upper Gila, New Mexico"; and the Digital Archaeological Record (tDAR), "New Perspectives on Salado."
69. Shaw, *Pima Indian Legends*, 8. Shaw, it should be noted, also made reference to Sivan vahki and Casa Grande Ruins in *The Pima Past*, using the alternate spelling "Siwani Walakih," 4.
70. In a footnote, Russell cites an explanation that Bandelier learned from an Akimel O'odham he met during his 1883 journey to Casa Grande Ruins: "I asked particularly why they did not again build houses with solid walls like those of their ancestors. The reply was that they were too weak in numbers to attempt it, and had accustomed themselves to their present mode of living," *The Pima Indians*, 25ne.

Chapter Three

1. See Hobbes, *Leviathan*, 74–100; Locke, *Two Treatises of Government*, 106–11; and Rousseau, *The Social Contract and Discourses*, 182–84.
2. For more about George's economic theories, see Henry George, *Progress and Poverty* (Oxford University, 1886), accessed January 1, 2025, https://www.google.com/books/edition/Progress_and_poverty/ lnVbAAAAQAAJ?hl=en&gbpv=1.
3. American Indian Religious Freedom Act Report: P.L. 95–341. United States: Task Force, 1979, 14.
4. Doyel, "Irrigation, Production, and Power in Phoenix Basin Hohokam Society," 83, 87.
5. Boas, "The Method of Ethnology," 316.
6. Hegel, *The Philosophy of History*, 79–102.

7. For more on what Marx did write about colonialism, see Karl Marx, *Karl Marx on Colonialism and Modernization: His Despatches [sic] and Other Writings on China, India, Mexico, the Middle East and North Africa*, ed. Schlomo Avineri (New York: Doubleday, 1968).

8. Emerson, *The Annotated Emerson*, 93–99; Thoreau, *Extracts Relating to the Indians*.

9. For an example of this kind research, see Left Handed, *Left Handed, Son of Old Man Hat: A Navajo Autobiography*, recorded by Walter Dyk (University of Nebraska Press, 2018).

10. In the philosophical anthropological tradition, one of the most important themes was the relationship between totem and totemism, in which the concept of taboo arises as a controlling mechanism in a "primitive" world defined by fear and magic. The French tradition, from Lévy-Bruhl to Lévi-Strauss, has been especially intrigued by this supposed connection. Fortunately, the racist assumptions intrinsic to Freud's psychoanalytical approach have been curtailed over the years, leading to greater respect for non-Western modes of thinking as effective adaptations to a given environment, as opposed to a primitive fear of the natural world. Alfred L. Kroeber, known for his work with California Indigenous peoples and whose most famous subject was Ishi, was a major critic of Freud's theory.

11. See Hrdlička, *Physical Anthropology of the Lenape*.

12. With respect to the Akimel O'odham intellectual tradition in terms of published writings, it has largely been limited to collaborating with anthropologists on their field research. Noteworthy among these is Thin Leather, whose contributions to Russell's BAE report and J. William Lloyd's *Aw-aw-tam Indian Nights* are discussed in chapter 1. Subsequent contributions to the Akimel O'odham literary tradition include George Webb's *A Pima Remembers* (1959) and Anna Moore Shaw's *A Pima Past* (1974). For more on Akimel O'odham intellectual history, see Martínez, "Pulling Down the Clouds."

13. Exceptions to this rule, which are beyond the scope of the present volume, are the "codices" created by Nahua- and Mayan-speaking peoples throughout Mesoamerica. Mexican anthropologist Miguel Léon-Portilla has done the most to elevate these writings into global literature. See "Miguel León-Portilla to Receive Living Legend Award at Celebration of

Mexico, Dec. 12," Library of Congress, accessed January 2, 2025, https://www.loc.gov/item/prn-13-206/.

14. For an assortment of the sources available on the Akimel O'odham, including their cousins in the Tohono O'odham community, see Fontana, "Pima and Papago," 135–36.

15. Historically, the American Indian encounters with European and American missionaries and politicians has often produced rather robust debates over values and ideas regarding the land, religion, and government. In the case of American Indian relationships with Christian churches and missionaries, a great deal of research and historical documentation has been amassed that demonstrate the vibrant, not to mention violent, encounters between institutional Christianity and a diverse number of American Indian nations, their leaders, holy people, and scholars, from Seneca leader Red Jacket to Standing Rock Sioux activist-intellectual Vine Deloria Jr. While the scholarship and archival material is too vast to summarize here, one helpful resource for someone new to the topic is The Pluralism Project of Harvard University, which maintains the page "First Encounters: Native Americans and Christians," http://pluralism.org/encounter/historical-perspectives/first-encounters-native-americans-and-christians/.

16. President James E. Polk signed and proclaimed the treaty, titled "Treaty of Peace and Friendship, Limits, and Settlement with the Republic of Mexico," the law of the land on July 4, 1848. See Unnumbered Executive Orders, Directives, and Proclamations, Stat. 9; pp 922–43. However, the area of Arizona that existed between the Gila River and the international boundary—which included the Akimel O'odham homeland—was not added until the 1854 Gadsden Purchase. See "Gadsden Purchase, 1853–1854," Office of the Historian, accessed July 10, 2017, https://history.state.gov/milestones/1830–1860/gadsden-purchase.

17. For a history of the Akimel O'odham during the American period that began in 1853, see Ezell, "History of the Pima," 156–60.

18. For insight into Azul's legacy as an Akimel O'odham headman during the time of famine, including his successful effort at expanding the reservation boundaries, see Bess, *Where the Red-Winged Blackbirds Sing*, 93–122.

19. For more on the role of Adamsville in Akimel O'odham history, see DeJong, *Stealing the Gila*, 57–70.

20. Edward Abbey famously brought the water crisis in the American Southwest to a national audience in 1968 when he published his influential memoir *Desert Solitaire*.

21. The decades of struggle that the Gila River Indian Community endured in pursuit of its water rights is recounted in DeJong, *Stealing the Gila*.

22. When Russell provided an account of each one of the Akimel O'odham informants who assisted him with his field research for *The Pima Indians*, he said of Thin Leather: "an old man, is said to be the most popular of the few remaining narrators of myths and speeches, or 'speakers.' He is an intimate friend of the head chief, Antonio Azul, and has always occupied a prominent place in the councils of the tribe. In his prime he exceeded 6 feet in stature and was strong and sturdy of frame. Indeed, his hand grasp is yet vigorous enough to make his silent and friendly greeting somewhat formidable. Intelligent, patient, dignified, his influence must have been helpful to those youths who formerly came to him for of material pertaining to the Pimas" (17na). For a historical analysis of Thin Leather's contribution to the Akimel O'odham intellectual tradition, see Martínez, "Pulling Down the Clouds."

23. Whereas for archaeologists, such as Harold S. Gladwin, Emil W. Haury, and Paul H. Ezell, there was a question about what they called "the Hohokam-Pima continuum." For the Akimel O'odham, as recounted in their origin narrative, there is no question that the huhugam that built the canal system were their ancestors. For more, see Ezell, "Is There a Hohokam-Pima Culture Continuum?," 61–66; and Hayden, "Of Hohokam Origins and Other Matters," 87–93.

24. It was commonplace for missionaries and Indian agents to refer to American Indian medicine people, regardless of tribe, as "jugglers," which was meant to imply that these individuals were little more than charlatans, conning people with sleight-of-hand tricks.

25. Descartes, *The Philosophical Writings of Descartes*, 9.

26. For the US Supreme Court's decision, see Johnson & Graham's Lessee v. McIntosh, 21 U.S. 543 (1823), accessed August 13, 2024, https://supreme.justia.com/cases/federal/us/21/543/.

27. Russell, *The Pima Indians*, 206.

28. Lloyd, *Aw-Aw-Tam Indian Nights*, 27.

29. For more on the cultural value of the creosote bush, see Rea, *At the Desert's Green Edge*, 139–42.

30. Russell, *The Pima Indians*, 206–8. The black insects that Komal Hok claims were the first creatures that Jeved mahkai made were likely *Tachardiella larreae*, a scale insect that is found on the branches of the creosote bush. Thank you to Sharon Suzuki-Martinez, author of *The Way of All Flux* and insectophile, for helping me identify this. With respect to Komal Hok's recounting of how the earth was made, see also Lloyd, *Aw-aw-tam Indian Nights*, 27–35.

31. Russell, *The Pima Indians*, 207–8.

32. Russell, *The Pima Indians*, 208. Thank you to Mizuki Miyashita, professor of linguistics at the University of Montana, for assisting me with deciphering Russell's arcane O'odham orthography, which resulted in the use of "S*os*anac/j." Also, thank you to Ofelia Zepeda (Tohono O'odham), professor of linguistics and American Indian studies at the University of Arizona, for providing me a meaningful translation of S*os*anac/j. For the narrative on how Elder brother created the S*os*anac/j, see Russell, *The Pima Indians*, 213–15. See also Lloyd, *Aw-aw-tam Indian Nights*, 47–50; and Shaw, *Pima Indian Legends*, 4–7.

33. *The Pima Indians*, 209.

34. Elder brother's names are clouded in mystery, which may be the result of a number of factors. The names quoted in this text may be of such ancient origin that their definitions in contemporary O'odham is impossible. Or it may be the case that O'odham who served as resources for anthropologists such as Russell who were researching O'odham oral traditions may have been reluctant to divulge any except the vaguest of knowledge about this sacred being's name. For an ethnohistorical summary of Elder brother's names, see Bahr, *The Short, Swift Time of Gods on Earth*, 298–99.

35. Russell, *The Pima Indians*, 209. For more on the cultural meaning of the white brittlebush, see Rea, *At the Desert's Green Edge*, 131–32.

36. Russell, *The Pima Indians*, 209.

37. Bahr identified this material as "creosote bush gum," in *The Short Swift Time of Gods on Earth*, 303n5. Rea corroborates this analysis in *At the Desert's Green Edge*, 140. Interestingly, Frances Densmore records another version of this episode of the O'odham flood narrative in *Papago Music*, 17.

38. Russell, The Pima Indians, 209.

39. Russell, *The Pima Indians*, 209–10. See also Lloyd, *Aw-aw-tam Indian Nights*, 38–61. For contemporary interpretation of the flood narrative, see Webb, *A Pima Remembers*, 69–70; and Shaw, *Pima Indian Legends*, 1–3.

40. Russell, *The Pima Indians*, 210.

41. Russell, *The Pima Indians*, 211. For more on the cultural meaning of the hummingbird, see Rea, *Wings in the Desert*, 192–95.

42. Donald M. Bahr uses Russell's translation, rendering it with an updated orthography as "Towa Kuadam Oks, 'White Eater Old-woman.'" According to Bahr, Jesse Walters Fewkes sees a connection between this O'odham female sacred being and the Navajo references to "White Shell Woman." Bahr questions Fewkes's interpretation and instead proposes an influence from the Yuman communities. For more, see Bahr, *The Short Swift Time of Gods on Earth*, 310–11n6. Lloyd's translation, "The Wampum Eater," is a completely erroneous translation. Nonetheless the reference to wampum is suggestive of how the name was explained to him by his O'odham collaborators. As wampum is a type of seashell, the name Wampum Eater implies that this sacred woman was identified with white sea shells, which in turn may be a reference to the Gulf of California, a place of great cultural significance in O'odham mythology and religion. In light of which, Towa Kuadam Oks likely possessed Ocean power, as evidenced in her ability to control the river's strong current in her work at assisting the O'odham with their canal. For more on the O'odham regard for the ocean, see Underhill, *Rainhouse and Ocean* and Underhill, *Singing for Power* (1993).

43. For more on the lives of O'odham women, see Underhill, *Papago Woman*; and Neff, *Desert Indian Woman*.

44. Russell, *The Pima Indians*, 215.

45. Lloyd, *Aw-aw-tam Indian Nights*, 120–24.

46. Russell, *The Pima Indians*, 215.

47. For another version of how snake got its fangs, see Shaw, *Pima Indian Legends*, 17–19.

48. Russell, *The Pima Indians*, 216–17.

49. Russell, *The Pima Indians*, 218–21. For a longer version of the eagle-man story, see Lloyd, *Aw-aw-tam Indian Nights*, 72–95. See also Webb, *A Pima Remembers*, 99–103; and Shaw, *Pima Indian Legends*, 20–26.

50. Russell, *The Pima Indians*, 221.

51. Russell, *The Pima Indians*, 221–23. For a longer version of the Ho'ok story, see Lloyd, *Aw-aw-tam Indian Nights*, 106–19. See also Webb, *A Pima Remembers*, 95–98.

52. *Aw-aw-tam Indian Nights*, 125. Bahr indicates that the name "Moehahdheck" is the same as "Muhadag," (Greasy). However, the story's reference to Salt River Mountain points away from the landmark now called South Mountain. See Bahr, *The Short Swift Time of Gods on Earth*, 190nd.

53. Russell, *Aw-aw-tam Indian Nights*, 128–29. With respect to the enigmatic reference to the sun's gun, Bahr interprets the O'odham term that Thin Leather uses in this way: "Wainom Ga:t, 'Iron [or perhaps any metal except gold] Gun.' *Ga:t* means either 'bow' or 'gun' (=lethal shooting device)." See Bahr, *The Short Swift Time of Gods on Earth*, 194nf.

54. Lloyd, *Aw-aw-tam Indian Nights*, 129–30.

55. Lloyd, *Aw-aw-tam Indian Nights*, 133–44, 147–48.

56. For an overview of the Pima Bajo, see Thomas, "Indian Languages of Mexico and Central America," 4.

57. Shaw states in her version of I'itoi's conquest narrative, "Se-he-ha in a quivering voice shouted, 'Those of you who are on the other side, do not weep. You will not be forgotten. As long as the sun rises and sets, a bond of *pe-cul-tha-lick* [love] will bind you to your people, though the distance divides you,'" *A Pima Past*, 12.

58. Webb, *A Pima Remembers*, 92–94.

59. Shaw, *A Pima Past*, 8.

60. Lloyd, *Aw-aw-tam Indian Nights*, 149–53, 154–65. *The Pima Indians*, 228–29.

61. Shaw, *A Pima Past*, 13.

62. For examples of the Indigenous critique of the scientific and religious assault on Indigenous ways of knowing, see Cajete, *Native Science: Natural Laws of Interdependence*; and Deloria, *Evolution, Creationism, And Other Modern Myths*.

63. For a less than favorable appraisal of Huhugam, or Hohokam, history, see Krech, *The Ecological Indian*, 45–72.

64. For more, see Ravesloot, "Changing Views of Snaketown in a Larger Landscape," 91–97; and Clark, "A San Pedro Valley Perspective," 99–107.

65. For more on the post-Huhugam adaptation to the Gila and Salt river environment, see Hackenberg, "Pima and Papago Ecological Adaptations," 161–77.

66. For a comprehensive account of the epochs of colonization in the American Southwest, including its impact on the Akimel O'odham, see Spicer, *Cycles of Conquest*.

Chapter Four

1. Nentvig, *Rudo Ensayo*, 36. *Gente de razón* is a term that developed in New Spain "to distinguish the Christianized tribal Mexicans from the non-Christian ones." For more, see Gloria E. Miranda, "Racial and Cultural Dimensions of 'Gente de Razón' Status in Spanish and Mexican California," *Southern California Quarterly* 70, no. 3 (1988): 265–78, https://doi.org/10.2307/41171310.

2. Nentvig, *Rudo Ensayo*, 37. For more about the genetic diversity of the saguaro, or *Carnegiae gigantea*, see Michael J. Sanderson, Alberto Búrquez, Dario Copetti, Michelle M. McMahon, Yichao Zeng, Martin F. Wojciechowski, "Origin and Diversification of the Saguaro Cactus (*Carnegiea gigantea*): A Within-Species Phylogenomic Analysis," *Systematic Biology* 71, no. 5, (September 2022): 1178–94, https://doi.org/10.1093/sysbio/syac017.

3. See "Plant Fact Sheet: Saguaro Cactus," Arizona-Sonora Desert Museum, accessed June 17, 2024, https://www.desertmuseum.org/kids/oz/long-fact-sheets/Saguaro%20Cactus.php.

4. Rea, *At the Desert's Green Edge*, 253.

5. Russell, *The Pima Indians*, 244–45.

6. Russell, *The Pima Indians*, 247.

7. Bahr, *O'odham Creation & Related Events*, 88.

8. Bahr, *O'odham Creation & Related Events*, 89. "Carrying Basket Mountain" refers to Giwho do'ag, also known as Quijotoa. See Barnes, *Arizona Place Names*, 253.

9. Since July 9, 1832, it was federal Indian policy to prohibit the sale, trade, or giving of alcohol to Indians (see 4 Stat. 564, Sec. 4, 1832), a policy still

in effect as the Office of Indian Affairs assumed control of the reservation system in Arizona. However, the drive to rid Indian Country of alcohol intensified as the Prohibition movement, which culminated in the Eighteenth Amendment, hit O'odham communities with a concentrated effort at suppressing the wiigida.

10. Underhill, *Singing for Power: The Song Magic of the Papago Indians of Southern Arizona* (1993): 21, 22.

11. Private message to the author, dated October 29, 2020. Included was an attached announcement from Austin Nunez, San Xavier District representative for Tohono O'odham Nation. Nunez referred to the pilgrimage to Magdalena in Sonora, Mexico, which passes through Quitobaquito. For more on this pilgrimage, see Schermerhorn, *Walking to Magdalena*.

12. Rea, *At the Desert's Green Edge*, 254.

13. Underhill, "A Papago Calendar," 7.

14. Russell, *The Pima Indians*, 35.

15. Russell, *The Pima Indians*, 53.

16. Russell, *The Pima Indians*, 64.

17. Russell, *The Pima Indians*, 64, 65, 59.

18. Steenbergh and Lowe, "Ecology of the Saguaro," 74.

19. Steenbergh and Lowe, "Ecology of the Saguaro," 142. The authors cited Tatom, "A Chronology of Papago and Pima History Taken from Calendar Sticks," 41–51.

20. "A Disappearing Icon," Desert Botanical Garden, accessed June 18, 2024, https://dbg.org/a-disappearing-icon/.

21. Tyson Hudson, "Ancient Tohono O'odham Custom of Saguaro Fruit Harvesting Kept Alive," *Arizona Daily Star*, July 13, 2019, accessed June 18, 2024, https://tucson.com/news/local/ancient-tohono-o-odham-custom-of-saguaro-fruit-harvesting-kept-alive/article_c49da205-8b1a-5404-bbe3-20776652c30c.html.

22. With respect to wiigida occurring in the modern era, specifically the late twentieth century, see Galinier et al., "From Montezuma to San Francisco," 486–538.

23. See Galinier et al., "From Montezuma to San Francisco," 486–538.

24. Curtis, *The North American Indian*, 11.

25. Russell, *The Pima Indians*, 170.

26. Russell, *The Pima Indians*, 170–71.

27. Giff, "Pima Blue Swallow Songs of Gratitude," 127.

28. Underhill, *Social Organization of the Papago Indians*, 161.

29. See Saxton, et al., *Tohono O'odham/Pima to English, English to Tohono O'odham/Pima Dictionary*, 122. The O'odham neok for the salt pilgrimage is difficult to find. None of the major studies, including Underhill's *Singing for Power*, records the ancestral term. In fact, when the author inquired with O'odham neok specialists, no answer was forthcoming. The author did consider that either the word had been forgotten, perhaps due to the term being archaic, or that the word may not be appropriate to share. Fortunately, the author was aided by Robert Stone, a longtime community leader in the Gila River Indian Community, as well as a valued cultural resource. For more, see "Bobby Stone, Vice Chair," Native Seed Search, accessed January 11, 2025, https://www.nativeseeds.org/pages/bobby-stone-board-member. When the author shared his findings with O'odham linguist Ofelia Zepeda, she stated, "Onmed [sic?] does make sense. Literally meaning going for salt" (email, dated January 13, 2025).

30. Underhill, *Papago Indian Religion*, 212.

31. Underhill, *Singing for Power* (1993), 8.

Chapter Five

1. See Buber, *I and Thou*.

2. See Levinas, *Totality and Infinity: An Essay on Exteriority*, 194–219.

3. See Wasley and Doyel, "Classic Period Hohokam," 337–52.

4. See "Casa Grande Ruins National Monument," National Park Service, accessed May 15, 2023, https://www.nps.gov/cagr/index.htm.

5. For more, see Wolf, *Europe and the People Without History*.

6. The O'odham jeved is divided into four discrete groups, namely Akimel O'odham, Tohono O'odham, Sobaipuri O'odham, and Hia-Ced O'odham. Each historically occupied a different area of the Sonoran Desert. See "O'odham Jewed," Native Land Digital, accessed May 8, 2023, https://native-land.ca/maps/territories/tohono-oodham/. For Pima Bajo territory,

see "O'ob (Lower Pima)," Native Land Digital, accessed January 10, 2025, https://native-land.ca/maps/territories/pima-tohono-oodham.

7. Russell, *The Pima Indians*, 27. See also Shaw, *A Pima Past*, 4, for an account of Kino's mass.

8. Fewkes, "Casa Grande, Arizona," 54. See Juan Mateo Mange, *Luz de Tierra incógnita en la América Septentrional y diario de las exploraciones en Sonora* (Talleres graficos de la Nacion, 1928).

9. Over the generations, because "Pima" became the historical name of the groups occupying the Gila and Salt River valleys, the story of Kino's confusion became a part of Akimel O'odham oral history. See Bolton, *Rim of Christendom*, 284–87; Kino, *Kino's Historical Memoir of Pimería Alta*, 127–29. See also, Ronald L. Ives, "Father Kino's 1697 Entrada to the Casa Grande Ruin in Arizona: A Reconstruction," *Arizona and the West* 15, no. 4 (Winter, 1973): 345–70.

10. Kino, *Pimería Alta*, 269–70.

11. See Spicer, *Cycles of Conquest*, 146–51.

12. An unfortunate consequence of the American colonization of the O'odham mind is the way in which jujkam became a racialized pejorative; see the entry for "Juhkam" in Saxton, et al., *Tohono O'odham/Pima to English, English to Tohono O'odham/Pima Dictionary*, 28. With respect to how O'odham may have understood the place of jujkam in the role of creation, meaning the jeved that Jeved mahkai made, an indirect but enlightening example appears in Richard Erdoes and Alfonso Ortiz's seminal anthology *American Indian Myths and Legends*. In the section dedicated to "Tales of Human Creation," a Pima legend is identified as "The Well-Baked Man," which is allegedly based on "fragments recorded in the 1880s," which is a possible reference to Bandelier. In essence, the story recounts when "Magician" (Jeved mahkai) determined to make people that were "shaped like himself." Coyote (Bán) was around, as usual, causing mischief. When Magician attempted to bake the two clay figures in his specially made oven, or "horno," Bán wanted to help and said suddenly, "They're done now." However, when Magician examined the results, he found them to be "underdone" and way too light skinned. Magician stated firmly, "They don't belong here—they belong across the water someplace." Attempting again to bake a pair of figurines, Coyote

interfered again, causing Magician to leave his people in the oven much longer than before. When he examined these figures, once again he was disappointed. "These are overdone. They're burned too dark." These people too were destined for someplace "across the water." Naturally, the story concludes with Magician baking the third pair to the desired complexion. "These are just right." Curiously, the story ends with the claim, "So, that's why we have the Pueblo Indians" (46–47). Likely, the unexpected reference to Pueblo Indians was a misunderstanding of the reference to the ancestral O'odham that built the big houses. The jujkam have an absent presence in the story. Undoubtedly, by the time this story was recorded in the 1880s, the Akimel O'odham were long-acquainted with Mexicans, many of whom are "well baked," if you will. With this in mind, the fact that the story did not claim that the jujkam "did not belong here," as it did for the milgahn (underdone) and the s-cuckcu (overdone), implies that they do belong here. However, because jujkam are not O'odham, they were accepted without comment.

13. Since the environmental movement began in the early 1970s, Indigenous peoples have had to respond to racially biased evolutionary theories that asserted that ancestral Indigenous peoples, i.e. "Paleo-Indians," were harmful to their environments, and that their "oneness with nature" is a modern myth. See Gill, *Mother Earth*; Krech, *The Ecological Indian*. For criticism, see Deloria, *Red Earth, White Lies*.

14. See Watt-Cloutier, *The Right to Be Cold*.

15. See Ferro, *Colonization*.

16. Among archaeologists, the relation between "Hohokam" who built Casa Grande and the "Pimas" who now inhabit the area became known as the "Hohokam-O'odham Continuum," in which the Hohokam were presumed to be an extinct tribe. This persisted in the archaeological literature despite O'odham assertions that the huhugam were ancestral O'odham. See Loendorf, *The Hohokam-Akimel O'odham Continuum*; Hill, *From Huhugam to Hohokam*.

17. The ancestral ruins and artifacts of the huhugam, or ancestral O'odham, have been found across southern Arizona and Sonora, Mexico. See the Digital Archive of Huhugam Archaeology at https://daha.tdar.org/.

18. Russell, *The Pima Indians*, 23–24.

19. Russell, *The Pima Indians*, 24n*b*. For Barrett's full report, see Bartlett, *Personal Narrative of Explorations and Incidents*, vol. 1.
20. See Ezell, "Is There a Hohokam-Pima Culture Continuum?" 61–66.
21. See Martínez, "Pulling Down the Clouds."
22. I am deliberately citing Russell and Lloyd not only to provide my reader resources that s/he can consult but also to recognize Komal Hok as a historically important O'odham philosopher.
23. See Haury, *The Hohokam*, 5.
24. See Shaw, *Pima Indian Legends*, 15–16.
25. Deni J. Seymour is the leading authority on Sobaipuri O'odham historical culture. According to her, the Sobaipuri are a "subgroup" of Akimel O'odham, implying a relation with Muhadag do'ag. See Seymour, "Unveiling Tucson's Namesake," 115–52. However, this author is skeptical of the categorization of subgroup. The Hia-Ced O'odham have, by comparison, been categorized as a subgroup of Tohono O'odham, which is misleading. Insofar as Seymour describes the Sobaipuri as a discrete community, it stands to reason that they believed that I'itoi kih could be found in a mountain, a do'ag, that was unique to their jeved, or homeland.
26. Thin Leather, in Russell's *The Pima Indians* (1908): "For a time they increased and over spread the earth until it became so populous that food became scarce and there was not sufficient water to supply their needs. . . . Hungering, they began to kill one another and to eat human flesh. Earth Doctor pitied them in their extremity, but could devise no plan for relieving their distress, except to destroy all" (208).
27. Since mahkai, healer or medicine maker, is a gender-neutral term, I have chosen to refer to Jeved mahkai (Earth medicine maker) as "they," as opposed to simply she/he.
28. The author wishes to thank linguistic anthropologist Mizuki Miyashita at the University of Montana for her assistance with deciphering Frank Russell's orthography. Email to author, dated July 3, 2017. Miyashita originally assisted with this perplexing question for my paper "Earth Medicine Man Makes This Place: A Prolegomenon to an Akimel O'odham Environmental Ethics."

29. See Rea, *Folk Mammalogy of the Northern Pimans*, 193–99.
30. In Komal Hok's narrative for Lloyd, according to Edward H. Wood, who assisted with the translation, he referred to the s*os*anac as "new people." Moreover, in a differing account of the demise of original O'odham: "And now for a time the people increased till they filled the earth. For the first parents were perfect, and there was no sickness and no death. But when the earth was full, then there was nothing to eat, so they killed and ate each other," *Aw-aw-tam Indian Nights*, 29, 30.
31. Komal Hok makes it clear for Lloyd that Jeved mahkai created multiple worlds and first peoples prior to the flood, after which Siuuhu made the huhugam. See Lloyd, *Aw-aw-tam Indian Nights*, 27–35.
32. In the narrative for Lloyd, Komal Hok said: "And to this man whom he had made, Seeurhuh (whose other name was Ee-ee-toy) gave a bow & arrows, and guarded his arm against the bow string by a piece of wild-cat skin, and pierced his ears & made ear-rings for him, like turquoises to look at, from the leaves of the weed called quah-wool. And this man was the most beautiful man yet made," *Aw-aw-tam Indians Nights*, 36. For more about kuávul (wolfberry), see Rea, *At the Desert's Green Edge*, 142–45.
33. According to Thin Leather, when Jeved mahkai created another people after destroying the first for cannibalism, they too exhibited unusual traits: "And [Jeved mahkai], being now on the top of this fallen sky, again made a man and a woman, in the same way as before. But this man and woman became grey when old, and their children became grey still younger, and their children became grey younger still, and so on till the babies were gray in their cradles," *Aw-aw-tam Indian Nights*, 31.
34. Russell, *The Pima Indians*, 209.
35. The olla mentioned is a nawaitakud ha'a, the ceremonial vessel used to prepare the wine (nawait) for the wiigida, the harvest ceremony. See Bahr, *How Mockingbirds Are*, 57–67.
36. Russell, *The Pima Indians*, 210.
37. Common reed or carrizo that once grew in abundance along the banks of the Gila River, is called "wahpk" (also vaapk). See Rea, *At the Desert's Green Edge*, 102–4. See also Webb, *A Pima Remembers*, 76–77.

38. Russell, *The Pima Indians*, 213. Given the Gila River flows west, from New Mexico to the Colorado River, Jeved mahkai's eastern destination remains clouded in earth's history.

39. In *O'odham Creation and Related Events: As Told to Ruth Benedict in 1927*, Donald Bahr (editor) quotes an O'odham speech that makes a passing reference to a boy on the warpath against the Apache, who states, "I will go to the south, to Driftwood Shaman" (University of Arizona Press, 2001), 140.

40. Russell, *The Pima Indians*, 213.

41. See Burckhalter and Mirocha, "Hia-Ced O'odham Places," 515–19.

42. Russell, *The Pima Indians*, 214. What Siuuhu spread were the powers or strengths (gegewkdag) that inhabit all beings. When something's himdag is violated, that being will throw its gewkdag into the violator. Komal Hok adds: "And he [I'itoi] washed himself in a pool or pond and the impurities remaining in the water are the source of the malarias and all the diseases of dampness," in Lloyd, *Aw-aw-tam Indian Nights*, 49. See also Bahr, *Piman Shamanism and Staying Sickness*, 23–48.

43. Russell, *The Pima Indians*, 215. Thin Leather also describes the original tribes as playing together when trouble arose: "And they all took to playing together, and in their play they kicked each other as the Maricopas do in sport to this day; but the Apaches got angry and said: 'We will leave you and go into the mountains and eat what we can get, but we will dream good dreams and be just as happy as you with all your good things to eat.' And some of the people took up their residence on the Gila, and some went west to the Rio Colorado. And those who builded [sic] vahahkkees," in *Aw-aw-tam Indian Nights*, 49–50.

44. Russell, *The Pima Indians*, 215. Komal Hok adds to Elder brother's tales of mischief: "[I'itoi] lived in the Salt River Mountain, which is called by the [O'odham] [Muhadagi], or the Brown Mountain, and whenever the girls had ceremonial dances because of their arrival at womanhood he would come and sing the appropriate songs. And it often happened that he would tempt these young girls away to his mountain, to be his wives, but after keeping them awhile he would grow tired of them and send them back." Moreover, "[I'itoi] would often shoot his hot arrows thru the [crop] fields, and wither up the growing things; and tho the people did not see him do this, they knew he was guilty, and they

wanted to kill him, but they did not know how to do it," *Aw-aw-tam Indian Nights*, 125.

45. Russell, *The Pima Indians*, 217. Thin Leather calls Coyote "Toehahvs," or Tohavs, referring to the White Brittlebush, Bán's birthplace, *Aw-aw-tam Indians Nights*, 103–5. However, he does not tell the story of Rabbit's death. See also, Shaw, *Pima Indian Legends*, 17–19. Similar to Komal Hok, Shaw omits Rabbit's death and cremation.

46. The name Väntre remains an enigma in O'odham scholarship. Bahr states, "Perhaps not a Pima name, because the word has no known meaning in the Pima language. See Bahr, *O'odham Creation and Related Events*, 64n18. Adding to the mystery is the absence of an O'odham word for "gambler" in either of the dictionaries referenced in the present discourse, namely Saxton, et al. (1983) or Zepeda (1983).

47. Russell, *The Pima Indians*, 221. In *Aw-aw-tam Indian Nights*, the gambler's name is rendered "Vaindah," for which no translation is provided. See Lloyd, *Aw-aw-tam Indians Nights*, 72–95. See also, Bahr, *The Short Swift Time of the Gods on Earth*, 157–77.

48. See Webb, *A Pima Remembers*, 43–44.

49. If native to the O'odham jeved, the lizard may be either a western banded gecko or a whiptail. See "Western Banded Gecko (*Coleonyx variegatus*)," Arizona-Sonora Desert Museum, accessed May 24, 2023, https://www.desertmuseum.org/books/nhsd_cloeonyx.php.

50. The "green stone" may refer to turquoise. "Chethagi" means blue-green.

51. Parrots are also chehthagi. See Rea, *Wings in the Desert*, 168–69.

52. This indicates the introduction of a nonindigenous species, likely military macaw (*Ara militaris*). See Crown and Teague, *Hohokam Archaeology Along the Salt-Gila Aqueduct*. See also "Ara militaris, military macaw," University of Michigan, Museum of Zoology, accessed May 25, 2023, https://animaldiversity.org/accounts/Ara_militaris/.

53. Russell, *The Pima Indians*, 222. Thin Leather tells an alternate version of Ho'ok's story in *Aw-aw-tam Indian Nights*, 99–102. See also Bahr, *The Short Swift Time of the Gods on Earth*, 141–50.

54. The name Ho'ok is meant to evoke the creature's long claw-like fingernails (huc, singular; huhuc; plural).

55. Russell, *The Pima Indians*, 224.

56. Russell, *The Pima Indians*, 224.

57. Russell, *The Pima Indians*, 225. Komal Hok tells an alternate version in *Aw-aw-tam Indian Nights*, 125–32. See also Bahr, *The Short Swift Time of the Gods on Earth*, 181–201; Rea, *Wings in the Desert*, 94–101.

58. Russell, *The Pima Indians*, 226.

59. See "District 4: Santan," Gila River Indian Community, accessed May 25, 2023, https://www.gilariver.org/index.php/districts/district-4-santan.

60. See "District 4: Santan," Gila River Indian Community, accessed May 25, 2023, https://www.gilariver.org/index.php/districts/district-5-casa-blanca. Sweet Water Village is one of the six historic villages that comprise this district.

61. See "District 5: Casa Blanca," Gila River Indian Community, accessed May 25, 2023, https://www.gilariver.org/index.php/districts/district-5-casa-blanca.

62. Russell, *The Pima Indians*, 227.

63. While not corroborated in Russell, I'itoi, who is often identified with Montezuma, is believed to have left the O'odham jeved, promising to return someday with a new era of peace and prosperity. See Griffith, *Beliefs and Holy Places*, 15–17. See also Hoy, "Organ Pipe Cactus National Monument," 136.

64. Russell, *The Pima Indians*, 229. See also, Bahr, *O'odham Creation & Related Events*, 134–35.

65. George Webb observes: "Adobe houses were supposed to be more civilized than the old arrow-reed shelters. But the Pimas did not want to change. So the agency issued a wagon to any Pima family who would build and live in an adobe house," *A Pima Remembers*, 50.

66. See Russell, *The Pima Indians*, 347–52. See also Underhill, *Singing for Power* (2021); Underhill, *Rainhouse and Ocean*.

67. See "Gila River Climate profile," Gila River Indian Community Department of Environmental Quality, accessed May 30, 2023, https://www.gricdeq.org/climate-change.

68. President James Buchanan, Exec. order, February 28, 1859 (11 Stat. 401).

69. See Fritz, *The Movement for Indian Assimilation*.

70. See DeJong, *Stealing the Gila*.

71. Cook and Whittemore, *Among the Pimas*, 31.

72. Cook and Whittemore, *Among the Pimas*, 63.

73. Cook and Whittemore, *Among the Pima*, 93.

74. Under the provisions of the 1934 Indian Reorganization Act (48 Stat. 984; 25 U.S.C. 461 et seq), members of federally acknowledged tribes may organize into constitutional governments, which are empowered to manage the internal affairs of the community covered by its respective constitution.

75. See Ezell, "The History of the Pima," 156–60.

76. Doyle, *Presbyterian Home Missions*, 86–87.

77. See "Our Mission," Presbyterian Church, USA, Presbyterian Mission, accessed May 13, 2023, https://www.presbyterianmission.org/who-we-are/our-mission/.

78. Both Cook and Kino have been accorded this sobriquet. See Cook, *Apostle to the Pima Indians* and Bolton, *The Padre on Horseback*.

Chapter Six

1. Hackenberg, "Pima and Papago Ecological Adaptations," 171.

2. Shaw, *A Pima Past*, 92.

3. James, *The Varieties of Religious Experience*, 177.

4. James, *The Varieties of Religious Experience*, 192.

5. See Salmón, "A Marginal Man: Luis of Saric and the Pima Revolt of 1751," 61–77; and Rentería-Valencia, "Colonial Tensions in the Governance of Indigenous Authorities," 345–64.

6. For a historical analysis of O'odham self-determination during the time of famine, see Bess, *Where the Red-Winged Blackbirds Sing*.

7. Spicer, *Cycles of Conquest*, 118.

8. Bancroft, *The History of Mexico: Vol III 1600–1803*, 14.

9. Nentvig, *Rudo Ensayo*, 71.

10. Shaw, *A Pima Past*, 4.

11. Kessell, *Mission of Sorrows*, 37.

12. See "History," San Xavier del Bac Mission, accessed June 20, 2024, https://sanxaviermission.org/history.

13. Thaddeus P. Jost, *Missionary-discoverer: Father Eusebio Kino* (Lisboa, Portugal: Junta de Investigações Científicas do Ultramar, 1978): 10.

14. Yetman, *Conflict in Colonial Sonora*.

15. Russell, *The Pima Indians*, 28.
16. Erickson, *Sharing the Desert*, 24.
17. Erickson, *Sharing the Desert*, 24–25.
18. Russell, *The Pima Indians*, 29na. Russell stated he did his own translation from the Spanish original. Teggart, *The Anza Expedition of 1775–1776* states for November 1, 1775:

> Salimos de la Laguna à las nueve y media de la mañana , y à la una de la tarde llegamos al Pueblo de San Juan Capistrano de Vturituc, haviendo caminado quatro leguas, con el rumdo de oesnoroeste. Nos recibieron los Yndios que regule como mil almas, puestos en dos filas, los hombres de un lado y las mugeres del otro, y haviendonos apeado, vinieron todos por su turno à saludarnos y darnos la mano, primero los hombres y luego las mugeres, manifestando mucho contento de vernos; y nos hosperdaron en una gran ramada que hicieron para esse fin, delante la qual plantaron una cruz grande aunque gentiles, y luego traxeron agua al real para la gente (22).

For more of the original Spanish text, see "Diario of Father Pedro Font," Web de Anza, accessed January 10, 2025, https://webdeanza.org/sp_f76diary_pg1.html.
19. Russell, *The Pima Indians*, 29na. See also Bolton, *Font's Complete Diary of the Second Anza Expedition*, 42. For Elliott Coues's translation of this passage, see *On the Trail of the Spanish Pioneer: The Diary and Itinerary of Francisco Garcés* (Francis P. Harper, 1900): 102–6.
20. Russell, *The Pima Indians*, 28–29, 29na.
21. See Bahr, *The Short Swift Time of Gods on Earth*, 46–53. The text quoted was taken from the unpublished manuscript of Bahr's book, which Bahr shared with the author and other members of the Gila River Indian Community prior to book's release in 1994. The author quoted Juan Smith in his master's thesis for the Department of American Indian Studies at the University of Arizona. For the thesis, see Martínez, "The Epiphany of the Earth," 29.
22. Bahr, "Pima-Papago Christianity," 142.
23. See Griffith, *Beliefs and Holy Places*, 67–99.

24. Fontana, "History of the Papago," 138.

25. Russell, *The Pima Indians*, 188.

26. Spicer, *Cycles of Conquest*, 147.

27. Grossman, "The Pima Indians of Arizona," 413.

28. Grossman, "The Pima Indians of Arizona," 414.

29. For an overview of this exceptional time in Akimel O'odham history, see Bess, *Where the Red-Winged Blackbirds Sing*, 65–91.

30. Spicer, *Cycles of Conquest*, 148.

31. Ezell, "History of the Pima," 158.

32. Zepeda, "Still Singing Down the Clouds," vii.

33. Russell, *The Pima Indians*, 39.

34. Southworth, "A Pima Calendar Stick."

35. Underhill, "A Papago Calendar Record."

36. Underhill, *Papago Indian Religion*, 135. It should be noted that Underhill misunderstood the Tohono O'odham reference to the wiigida as taking place at "harvest time," which she likely thought of in terms of the western agricultural tradition as signified by the "harvest moon," meaning October. Her O'odham informants were referring to the saguaro cactus fruit harvest that customarily takes place sometime in late June to July. Also, Underhill exhibits a tendency in this text to try to fit her observations of the Tohono O'odham into the concepts and customs established by students of the Puebloan communities such as Zuñi and Hopi.

37. For a full account of the alleged extinction of the Hia-Ced O'odham, see David Martínez, "Sand People and Yellow Fever: O'odham Himdag, Arizona Territory, Calendar Sticks, and Resistance, 1851–1860," *Journal of Arizona History* 64, no. 2 (Summer 2023): 139–72.

38. Underhill, "A Papago Calendar Stick," 26, 28, 29.

39. Underhill, "A Papago Calendar Stick," 43.

40. Long before the current era of the cartels, white Americans perceived Arizona and New Mexico territories as chronically dangerous areas. During the nineteenth century, white immigrants and soldiers were mostly worried about Apache attacks. However, Mexican settlements were also seen as lawless. For more on the demonization of the southern border, see Hernández, *Coloniality of the US/Mexico Border*.

41. Cook and Whittemore, *Among the Pimas*, 31.

42. Cook and Whittemore, *Among the Pimas*, 63.

43. Cook and Whittemore, *Among the Pimas*, 64.

44. F. E. Grossman, letter to Lt. Col. George L. Andrews, superintendent, Indian Affairs Arizona Territory, September 1, 1870, *Second Annual Report of the Board of Indian Commissioners to the Secretary of the Interior, for Submission to the President: For the Year 1870*, 589.

45. Russell, The Pima Indians, 60.

46. Russell, *The Pima Indians*, 53–63. *Tizwin*, or *tiswin*, is a Mexican Spanish neologism signifying any fermented drink made from indigenous contents. In the historical record, the word came to signify alcoholism and the scourge of alcohol in the minds of Indian agents and missionaries. O'odham does not have a word for *tizwin*. However, there is a word for beer, sil-wihsa, and a word for ceremonial wine, nawait.

47. Cook and Whittemore, *Among the Pimas*, 93.

48. Cook and Whittemore, *Among the Pimas*, 93.

49. Cook and Whittemore, *Among the Pimas*, 93–94.

50. Spicer, *Cycles of Conquest*, 149.

51. Giff Pablo, "Contemporary Pima," 213.

52. Webb, *A Pima Remembers*, 84.

53. Edward H. Spicer, "The Book and Its Author," in Webb, *A Pima Remembers*.

54. Webb, *A Pima Remembers*, 87.

55. Shaw, *A Pima Past*, 228.

56. Shaw, *A Pima Past*, 228.

57. Shaw, *A Pima Past*, 209.

58. Shaw, *A Pima Past*, 231.

59. An example of how O'odham thought about Vh-Thaw-Hup-EaJu philosophically is found in a 1967 report sponsored by the US Bureau of Indian Affairs, titled "In-Service Education Series and Consultant Services." In a subsection titled "Future of the Area," meaning the Gila River Pima-Maricopa reservation, the report states: "The Gila River Indian Community has initiated an 'action' plan known as 'VH-THAW-HUP-EA-JU.' In English, this would mean 'It Must Happen' or 'It Will Happen.' The Gila River Indian Community feels that now is the time that it must move forward. Although this initial plan focuses primarily on short-range objectives, it will form a basis for long-range development.

The Community is ready for an imaginative, action-oriented attack on the causes of persistent poverty" (14). See Demeke, "In-Service Education Series and Consultant Services."

60. Shaw, *A Pima Past*, 219.

61. Russell, *The Pima Indians*, 206.

Chapter Seven

1. Hernández, *Coloniality of the US/Mexico Border*, 44.

2. See Schaeffer, *Unsettled Borders*.

3. Leza, *Divided Peoples*, 135. In regard to derogatory language, an unfortunate development in the O'odham neok is the inflection in juhkam. While most translators will render this as "Spanish speaker," colloquially, when spoken with anger or derision, it can mean "wetback," or s-wadag juhkam.

4. See Michael Steven Wilson and José Antonio Lucero, *What Side Are You On? A Tohono O'odham Life across Borders* (University of North Carolina Press, 2024).

5. Griffith, *Beliefs and Holy Places*, 17.

6. Shaw, *Pima Indian Legends*, 16.

7. Shaw, *A Pima Past*, 49–50.

8. Bostwick, *Landscape of the Spirits*, 169.

9. Bostwick, *Landscape of the Spirits*, 168.

10. See Fewkes, "Casa Grande, Arizona," 56–57.

11. Breazeale, *The Pima and His Basket*, 52.

12. Breazeale, *The Pima and His Basket*, 56–83.

13. Breazeale, *The Pima and His Basket*, 73.

14. Breazeale, *The Pima and His Basket*, 79.

15. Breazeale, *The Pima and His Basket*, 74.

16. Breazeale, *The Pima and His Basket*, 79. As noted earlier, in reference to Franz Boas, the notion of diffusion was gaining currency among social scientists, who were of the opinion that ideas, customs, and innovations traveled synchronously between peoples, who adapted the imports into their culture and environment. Diffusion did not presume a racial hierarchy but did stipulate that given developments were likely to arise as unique

events in human history, as opposed to concurrent innovations among disparate peoples. Unfortunately, this did not preclude assumptions about whose people or nation was the likely originator of the invention in question.

17. Breazeale, *The Pima and His Basket*, 79–80.

18. Fewkes, "Casa Grande, Arizona," 149n1.

19. Fewkes, "A Fictitious Ruin in Gila Valley, Arizona," 511. See also, Colton, "Is the House of Tcuhu the Minoan Labyrinth?," 667–68.

20. See Salmón, "A Marginal Man," 61–77; Rentería-Valencia, "Colonial Tensions in the Governance of Indigenous Authorities," 345–64; and Ruiz Medrano, "Rebelión y patrones de resistencia indígena," 200–237.

21. Since the Spanish colonial era, there has been a recurring claim that it was O'odham who informed jujkam that the big houses, such as Casa Grande, were the domain of Montezuma (Moctezuma). This error continued into the American period, which began in the 1850s. John Russell Bartlett, who led the United States and Mexico Boundary Commission, brought the Montezuma tradition into O'odham studies, specifically in the American historical field. Similar to others, he asserted that his reference to "the houses of Montezuma" was due to what "our Indian friends called them." See Bartlett, *Personal Narrative of Explorations and Incidents*, vol. 2, 242. Adolph Bandelier, in turn, is credited with perpetuating the misnomer in the field of archaeology. See Lange and Riley, *The Southwest Journals of Adolph F. Bandelier, 1883–1884*, 130–31. In Frank Russell's *The Pima Indians* (1908), he cites Bartlett's *Personal Narrative* as authoritative. See Russell, *The Pima Indians*, 24nb. In all likelihood, just as the Spanish corrupted the name Akimel O'odham into "pimas" because they misapprehended the O'odham phrase for expressing uncertainty—"pi 'añi matc," meaning "I don't know"—so too did they probably misapprehend the names of the chief priests who led the big houses. The chief priest at Casa Grande was called "Morning Green Chief great-house," or Si'al Cehedag Sivani Vahki. If the Spaniards, through their guides and interpreters—likely Tohono O'odham from around the Altar River, Sonora—were able to understand "Morning Green," it may have been translated literally as "Mañana Verde," which became "Montezuma."

22. Nentvig, *Rudo Ensayo*, 14. Because Nentvig was a German missionizing on behalf of Spain for a latinized church, the spelling of Nentvig's

name, like the names of other Jesuits and Franciscans, went through various articulations. See Alberto Pradeau and Robert R. Rasmussen, "Biographical Sketch," *Rudo Ensayo: A Description of Sonora and Arizona in 1764* (University of Arizona Press, 2022): xix-xxi.

23. Fewkes, "Casa Grande, Arizona," 56.

24. Fewkes, "Casa Grande, Arizona," 56. For an overview of Keller's work and legacy, see "Ignacio Xavier Keller," National Park Service, Tumacácori National Historical Park, accessed July 7, 2024, https://www.nps.gov/tuma/learn/historyculture/ignacio-xavier-keller.htm.

25. Fewkes, "Casa Grande, Arizona," 57.

26. See, for example, Wilcox, "The Mesoamerican Ballgame in the American Southwest," 101–25.

27. Fewkes, "Casa Grande, Arizona," 57n2.

28. Colton, "Is the House of Tcuhu the Minoan Labyrinth?," 667.

29. Breazeale, *The Pima and His Basket*, 80.

30. Breazeale, *The Pima and His Basket*, 80–81.

31. See figure 67, "The Labyrinth by Emma Newman," in *The Pima and His Basket*, 80.

32. Breazeale, *The Pima and His Basket*, 137.

33. For an overview of the historical significance of the 1924 statute, see "Indian Citizenship Act," Library of Congress, Today In History—June 2, accessed July 7, 2024, https://www.loc.gov/item/today-in-history/june-02/.

34. Breazeale, *The Pima and His Basket*, 131.

35. Breazeale, *The Pima and His Basket*, 131–32.

36. Shaw, *A Pima Past*, 180.

37. Russell, *The Pima Indians*, 209.

38. Russell, *The Pima Indians*, 210.

39. Russell, *The Pima Indians*, 224.

40. Russell, *The Pima Indians*, 226.

41. Russell, *The Pima Indians*, 124.

42. Shaw, *Pima Indian Legends*, 29–31.

43. Russell, *The Pima Indians*, 131.

44. Russell, *The Pima Indians*, 135–36.

45. Russell, *The Pima Indians*, 136.

46. Although the literature and studies of O'odham basketry predominantly features female weavers, in the current era it is not unheard of see males learning the basketry art. Some, like the late Terrol Dew Johnson (1973–2024), distinguished themselves as major artists in the field. For more about Johnson's work and legacy, see "Terrol Dew Johnson: A Legacy of Artistry and Culture Keeping," Native Arts & Cultures Foundation, accessed July 8, 2024, https://www.nativeartsandcultures.org/terrol-dew-johnson.

47. Fewkes, *Archeological Expedition to Arizona in 1895*.

48. See Spicer, *Cycles of Conquest*.

49. See Erdoes and Ortiz, *American Indian Myths and Legends*, 46–47. Unfortunately, Erdoes and Ortiz did not think to document from where they derived these "fragments." The bibliography located in the back pages (522–25) is inadequate. Is Bandelier once again the source?

50. Oral tradition explaining the origin of white people is not uncommon among Indigenous peoples. A widely-read example appeared in Sarah Winnemucca Hopkins's *Life Among the Piutes*, 6–7.

Bibliography

Secondary Sources

Amaya-Schaeffer, Felicity. *Unsettled Borders: The Militarized Science of Surveillance on Sacred Indigenous Lands*. Duke University Press, 2022. https://doi.org/10.1215/9781478022565.

Bahr, Donald M. *How Mockingbirds Are: O'odham Ritual Orations*. State University of New York Press, 2011.

Bahr, Donald M. *Pima and Papago Ritual Oratory: A Study of Three Texts*. Indian Historian Press, 1975.

Bahr, Donald M. "Pima-Papago Christianity." *Journal of the Southwest* 30, no. 2 (Summer, 1988): 133–167.

Bahr, Donald M., ed. *O'odham Creation and Related Events: As Told to Ruth Benedict in 1927*. University of Arizona Press, 2001.

Bahr, Donald M. *The Short Swift Time of Gods on Earth: The Hohokam Chronicles*. University of California Press, 1994.

Bahr, Donald M. *The Short, Swift Time of Gods on Earth: The Hohokam Chronicles*. University of California Press, 1994.

Bahr, Donald M. "Who Were the Hohokam? The Evidence from Pima-Papago Myths." *Ethnohistory* 18, no. 3 (Summer 1971): 245–66. https://doi.org/10.2307/481534.

Bahr, Donald M., Juan Gregorio, David I. Lopez , Albert Alvarez, and Bernard L. Fontana (Preface). *Piman Shamanism and Staying Sickness (Ká:cim Múmkidag)*. University of Arizona Press, 1974.

Bancroft, Hubert Howe. *The History of Mexico: Vol III 1600–1803*. Bancroft & Company, Publishers, 1883.

Bandelier, Adolph F. *The Southwestern Journals of Adolph F. Bandelier, 1883–1884*, edited by Charles H. Lange and Carroll L. Riley. The University of New Mexico Press, 1970.

Barnes, Will Croft. *Arizona Place Names*. University of Arizona Press, 2016.

Bartlett, Russell. *Personal Narrative of Explorations and Incidents in Texas, New Mexico, California, Sonora, and Chihuahua*, vol. 1. D. Appleton & Company, 1854.

Bartlett, Russell. *Personal Narrative of Explorations and Incidents in Texas, New Mexico, California, Sonora, and Chihuahua*, vol. 2. D. Appleton & Company, 1854.

Bech, Julio Amador. "De la tradición oral a la escritura: Mitos de origen de los O'odham: Formas de transmission y transcripción." *Anales de antropología* 39, no. 1 (2005): 131–65.

Bess, Jennifer. *Where the Red-Winged Blackbirds Sing: The Akimel O'odham and Cycles of Agricultural Transformation in the Phoenix Basin*. University Press of Colorado, 2021.

Boas, Franz. "The Method of Ethnology." *American Anthropologist* 22, no. 4 (October-December, 1920): 311–21.

Bolton, Herbert Eugene, ed., *Font's Complete Diary of the Second Anza Expedition*. Berkeley: University of California Press, 1930.

Bolton, Herbert Eugene. *Rim of Christendom: A Biography of Eusebio Francisco Kino, Pacific Coast Pioneer*. Russell & Russell, 1960.

Bolton, Herbert Eugene. *The Padre on Horseback: A Sketch of Eusebio Francisco Kino, SJ, Apostle to the Pimas*. Loyola University Press, 1986.

Bostwick, Todd W. *Landscape of the Spirits: Hohokam Rock Art at South Mountain Park*. University of Arizona Press, 2016.

Bourke, John Gregory. "Notes on the Cosmogony and Theogony of the Mojave Indians of the Rio Colorado, Arizona." *The Journal of American Folklore* 2, no 6. (July-September, 1889): 169–89.

Bourke, John Gregory. *On the Border with Crook*. C. Scribners' Sons, 1891.

Breazeale, J. F. *The Pima and His Basket*. Arizona Archaeological and Historical Society, 1923.

Buber, Martin. *I and Thou*. Translated by Ronald Gregor Smith. Scribner's Sons, 1958.

Burckhalter, David, and Paul Mirocha. "Hia-Ced O'odham Places," *Journal of the Southwest* 59, nos. 3–4 (Autumn-Winter, 2017): 515–19.

Cajete, Gregory. *Native Science: Natural Laws of Interdependence*. Clear Light Publishers, 1999.

Clark, Jeffrey J. "A San Pedro Valley Perspective on Ancestral Pueblo Migration in the Hohokam World." In *The Hohokam Millennium*, edited by Suzanne K. Fish and Paul R. Fish. School for Advanced Research Press, 2007: 99–107.

Coe, Javier Urcid, and Rex Koontz. *Mexico: From the Olmecs to the Aztecs*. 8th ed. Thames & Hudson, 2019.

Colton, Harold Sellers. "Is the House of Tcuhu the Minoan Labyrinth?" *Science* 45, no. 1174, Friday, June 29, 1917, 667–68.

Cook, Charles H., and Isaac T. Whittemore, *Among the Pimas, or The Mission to the Pima and Maricopa Indians*. Printed for the Ladies' Union Mission School Association, 1893.

Cook, Minnie A. *Apostle to the Pima Indians: The Story of Charles H. Cook, the First Missionary to the Pimas*. Omega Books, 1976.

Curtis, Edward S. *The North American Indian: The Pima. The Papago. The Qahatika. The Mohave. The Yuma. The Maricopa. The Walapai. The Havasupai. The Apache-Mohave, or Yavapai*. Johnson Reprint Corporation, 1908.

DeJong, David H. *Damming the Gila: The Gila River Indian Community and the San Carlos Irrigation Project, 1900–1942*. University of Arizona Press, 2024.

DeJong, David H. *Stealing the Gila: The Pima Agricultural Economy and Water Deprivation, 1848–1921*. University of Arizona Press, 2009.

Deloria, Vine, Jr., *Custer Died for Your Sins: An Indian Manifesto*. University of Oklahoma Press, 1988.

Deloria, Vine, Jr., *Evolution, Creationism, And Other Modern Myths*. Fulcrum Publishing, 2002.

Deloria, Vine, Jr., *Red Earth, White Lies: Native Americans and the Myth of Scientific Fact*. Fulcrum Publishing, 1997.

Derrida, Jacques. *Of Grammatology*. Johns Hopkins University Press, 1976.

Descartes, René. *The Philosophical Writings of Descartes*, vol. 1. Edited and translated by Dugald Murdoch, John Cottingham, and Robert Stoothoff. Cambridge University Press, 1984.

Doyel, David E. "Irrigation, Production, and Power in Phoenix Basin Hohokam Society." In *The Hohokam Millennium*, edited by Suzanne K. Fish and Paul R. Fish, 83–89. School for Advanced Research Press, 2007.

Doyle, Sherman H. *Presbyterian Home Missions*. Presbyterian Board of Publication and Sabbath-School Work, 1902.

Eastman, Charles A. (Ohiyesa). *The Soul of the Indian: An Interpretation*. Houghton Mifflin Company, 1911.

Emerson, Ralph Waldo. *The Annotated Emerson*. Edited by David Mikics. Harvard University Press, 2012.

Erdoes, Richard, and Alfonso Ortiz, eds. *American Indian Myths and Legends*. Knopf Doubleday Publishing, 1984.

Erickson, Winston P. *Sharing the Desert: The Tohono O'odham in History*. University of Arizona Press, 1994.

Ezell, Paul H. "The Hispanic Acculturation of the Gila River Pimas." *Memoirs of the American Anthropological Association*, no. 90 (1961).

Ezell, Paul H. "History of the Pima." In *Handbook of North American Indians*, vol. 10: *Southwest*, edited by William C. Sturtevant (general editor) and Alfonso Ortiz (volume editor). Smithsonian Institution, 1983: 149–60.

Ezell, Paul H. "Is There a Hohokam-Pima Culture Continuum?" *American Antiquity* 29, no. 1 (July, 1963): 61–66.

Ferro, Marc. *Colonization: A Global History*. Taylor & Francis, 2005.

Fewkes, Jesse Walter. "A Fictitious Ruin in Gila Valley, Arizona," *American Anthropologist*, New Series, vol. 9, no. 3 (July–September, 1907): 510–12.

Fewkes, Jesse Walter. *Archeological Expedition to Arizona in 1895*. Government Printing Office, 1899. https://www.loc.gov/item/rc01000258/.

Fish, Suzanne, and Paul R. Fish. *The Hohokam Millennium*. School of Advanced Research Press, 2007.

Fontana, Bernard L. "History of the Papago." In *Handbook of North American Indians*, vol. 10: *Southwest*, edited by William C. Sturtevant (general editor) and Alfonso Ortiz (volume editor). Smithsonian Institution, 1983.

Fontana, Bernard L. "Pima and Papago: An Introduction." In *Handbook of North American Indians*, vol. 10: *Southwest*, edited by William C. Sturtevant (general editor) and Alfonso Ortiz (volume editor). The Smithsonian Institution, 1983.

Fontana, Bernard L., and Jose Lewis Brennan. "Jose Lewis Brennan's Account of Papago 'Customs and Other References.'" *Ethnohistory* 6, no. 3 (Summer, 1959): 226–37.

Fritz, Henry E. *The Movement for Indian Assimilation, 1860–1890*. University of Pennsylvania Press, 2017.

Galinier, Jacques, Adelaide Bahr, and Donald Bahr, "From Montezuma to San Francisco: The Wi:gita Ritual in Papago (Tohono O'odham) Religion." *Journal of the Southwest* 33, no. 4 (Winter, 1991): 486–538.

Gill, Sam D. *Mother Earth: An American Story*. University of Chicago Press, 1991.

Giff Pablo, Sally. "Contemporary Pima." In *Handbook of North American Indians*, vol. 10: *Southwest*, edited by William C. Sturtevant (general editor) and Alfonso Ortiz (volume editor). Smithsonian Institution, 1979.

Griffith, James S. *Beliefs and Holy Places: A Spiritual Geography of the Pimería Alta*. University of Arizona Press, 1992.

Hackenberg, Robert A. "Pima and Papago Ecological Adaptations." In *Handbook of North American Indians*, vol. 10: *Southwest*, edited by William C. Sturtevant (general editor) and Alfonso Ortiz (volume editor). Smithsonian Institution, 1983: 161–77.

Harwell, Henry O. and Marsha C. S. Kelly. "Maricopa." In *Handbook of North American Indians*, vol. 10: *Southwest*, edited by William C. Sturtevant (general editor) and Alfonso Ortiz (volume editor). Smithsonian Institution, 1983: 71–85.

Haury, Emil W. *The Hohokam: Desert Farmers and Craftsmen, Excavations at Snaketown, 1964–1965*. University of Arizona Press, 1976.

Hayden, Julian D. "Of Hohokam Origins and Other Matters." *American Antiquity* 35, no. 1 (January, 1970): 87–93.

Hegel, Georg Wilhelm Friedrich. *The Philosophy of History*. Translated by J. Sibree Dover Publications, Inc., 1956.

Hernández, Roberto D. *Coloniality of the US/Mexico Border: Power, Violence, and the Decolonial Imperative*. University of Arizona Press, 2018.

Hill, J. Brett. *From Huhugam to Hohokam: Heritage and Archaeology in the American Southwest*. Lexington Books, 2019.

Hobbes, Thomas. *Leviathan*. Hackett Publishing Company, Inc., 1994.

Holt, H. Barry. "A Cultural Resource Management Dilemma: Anasazi Ruins and the Navajos," *American Antiquity* 48, no. 3 (July, 1983): 594–99.

Hoxie, Frederick E. *A Final Promise: The Campaign to Assimilate the Indians, 1880–1920*. University of Nebraska Press, 2001.

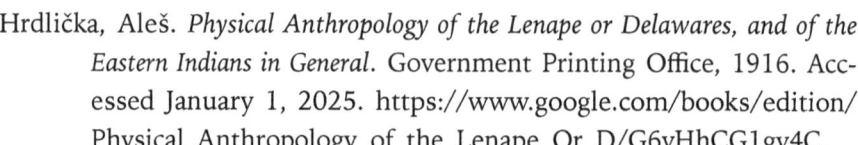

Hrdlička, Aleš. *Physical Anthropology of the Lenape or Delawares, and of the Eastern Indians in General.* Government Printing Office, 1916. Accessed January 1, 2025. https://www.google.com/books/edition/Physical_Anthropology_of_the_Lenape_Or_D/G6vHhCG1gv4C.

James, William. *The Varieties of Religious Experience.* Vintage Books / The Library of America, 1990.

Kessell, John L. *Mission of Sorrows: Jesuit Guevavi and the Pimas, 1691–1767.* University of Arizona Press, 1970.

Kino, Eusebio Francisco. *Kino's Historical Memoir of Pimería Alta.* Edited by Herbert Eugene Bolton. Arthur H. Clark Company, 1919.

Kino, Eusebio Francisco. *Las misiones de Sonora y Arizona. Comprendiendo: la crónica titulada: "Favores celestials" y la "Relación diaria de la entrada al norueste."* Edited by Francisco Fernández del Castillo. Editorial "Cultura," 1922.

Krech, Shepherd, III. *The Ecological Indian: Myth and History.* W. W. Norton & Company, 1999.

Kroeber, Clifton B. and Bernard L. Fontana. *Massacre on the Gila: An Account of the Last Major Battle Between American Indians, with Reflections on the Origin of War.* University of Arizona Press, 1986.

Lange, Charles H., and Carroll L. Riley, eds. *The Southwest Journals of Adolph F. Bandelier, 1883–1884.* University of New Mexico Press, 1970.

Lévi-Strauss, Claude. *The Savage Mind.* University of Chicago Press, 1962.

Levinas, Emmanuel. *Totality and Infinity: An Essay on Exteriority.* Translated by Alfonso Lingis Martinus Nijhoff Publishers, 1979.

Lévy-Bruhl, Lucien. *The "Soul" of the Primitive.* Translated by Lilian A Clare. The Macmillan Company, 1928.

Leza, Christina. *Divided Peoples: Policy, Activism, and Indigenous Identities on the US-Mexico Border.* University of Arizona Press, 2019.

Lincoln, Kenneth. *Native American Renaissance.* University of California Press, 1985.

Lloyd, J. William. *Aw-aw-tam Indian Nights: Being the Myths and Legends of the Pimas of Arizona: As Received by J. William Lloyd From Comalk-Hawk-Kin (Thin Buckskin) Thru the Interpretation of Edward Hubert Wood.* The Lloyd Group, 1911.

Lloyd, J. William. *Songs of the Desert.* Berryhill Co., 1911.

Locke, John. *Two Treatises of Government*. Printed for Thomas Tegg, 1823.

Loendorf, Chris. *The Hohokam–Akimel O'odham Continuum: Sociocultural Dynamics and Projectile Point Design in the Phoenix Basin, Arizona*. University of Arizona Press, 2013.

Loendorf, Chris, and Barnaby V. Lewis. "Ancestral O'odham: Akimel O'odham Cultural Traditions and the Archaeological Record." *American Antiquity* 82, no. 1 (2017), 123–39.

Manuel, Frances, and Deborah Neff. *Desert Indian Woman: Stories and Dreams*. University of Arizona Press, 2001.

Martínez, David, ed. *The American Indian Intellectual Tradition: An Anthology of Writings from 1772 to 1972*. Cornell University Press, 2011.

Martínez, David. *Dakota Philosopher: Charles Eastman and American Indian Thought*. Minnesota Historical Society Press, 2009.

Martínez, David. "Earth Medicine Man Makes This Place: A Prolegomenon to an Akimel O'odham Environmental Ethics." In *Natural Communions, Religion and Public Life*, vol. 40, edited by Gabriel Ricci, 33–57. Routledge, 2019.

Martínez, David. "The Epiphany of the Earth: An O'odham Environmental Ethic." Master's thesis, University of Arizona, 1993. https://www.academia.edu/17624050/The_Epiphany_of_the_Earth_An_Oodham_Environmental_Ethic.

Martínez, David. *Life of the Indigenous Mind: Vine Deloria Jr and the Birth of the Red Power Movement*. University of Nebraska Press, 2019.

Martínez, David. "Neither Chief Nor Medicine Man: The Historical Role of the 'Intellectual' in the American Indian Community." *Studies in American Indian Literatures* 26, no. 1 (Spring 2014): 29–53.

Martínez, David. "Pulling Down the Clouds: The O'odham Intellectual Tradition During the 'Time of Famine,'" *American Indian Quarterly* 34, no. 1 (Winter, 2010): 1–32.

Martínez, David. *Review of Stealing the Gila: The Pima Agricultural Economy and Water Deprivation, 1848–1921*. *The American Indian Quarterly* 35, no. 1 (Winter 2011): 143–45.

Martínez, David. "Sand People and Yellow Fever: O'odham Himdag, Arizona Territory, Calendar Sticks, and Resistance, 1851–1860," *Journal of Arizona History* 64, no. 2 (Summer 2023):

Martínez, David. "The Soul of the Indian: Lakota Philosophy and the Vision Quest," *Wicazo Sa Review* 19, no. 2, Colonization/Decolonization special issue (Autumn, 2004): 79–104.

Matthews, Washington. "A part of the Navajo's mythology." *American Antiquarian* (April, 1883): 1–18.

Mauss, Marcel. *The Gift: Forms and Functions of Exchange in Archaic Societies.* Cohen & West, 1954.

McCool, Daniel. *Native Waters: Contemporary Indian Water Settlements and the Second Treaty Era.* University of Arizona Press, 2006.

Montezuma, Carlos. "Let My People Go." In *The American Indian Intellectual Tradition: An Anthology of Writings from 1772 to 1972*, edited by David Martínez, 203–12. Cornell University Press, 2011.

Montezuma, Carlos. "Light on the Indian Situation." *The Quarterly Journal of the Society of American Indians* 1, no. 1 (April 15, 1913): 50.

Nabakov, Peter, and Robert Easton. *Native American Architecture.* Oxford University Press, 1989.

Nentvig, Juan. *Rudo Ensayo: A Description of Sonora and Arizona in 1764.* Edited by Alberto Francisco Pradeau and Robert R. Rasmussen. University of Arizona Press, 2022.

Oskison, John M. "Acquiring a Standard of Value." *The Quarterly Journal of the Society of American Indians* 2, no. 1 (January-March, 1914): 47–48.

Painter, Fantasia. "'Our Constitution Makes Provisions for All These Things:' Changing Tohono O'odham Protocols and Powers in the 1930s." *Journal of Arizona History* 65, no. 2 (Summer, 2023): 203–26.

Parker, Arthur C., ed. "List of Active Members." *The Quarterly Journal of the Society of American Indians* 1, no. 2 (April-June, 1913): 247–49.

Parker, Arthur C., ed. "Shall the Pimas Be Robbed of Water?" *The Quarterly Journal of the Society of American Indians* 2, no. 2 (April-June, 1914): 159.

Parker, Arthur C., ed. "What Indian Students Say About Education." *The Quarterly Journal of the Society of American Indians* 1, no. 3 (July-September, 1913): 295–99.

Peyer, Bernd, ed. *American Indian Nonfiction: An Anthology of Writings, 1760s–1930s.* University of Oklahoma Press, 2005.

Radin, Paul. *Primitive Man as Philosopher.* D. Appleton and Company, 1927.

Radin, Paul. *The Trickster: A Study in American Indian Mythology.* Philosophical Library, 1956.

Ravesloot, John C. "Changing Views of Snaketown in a Larger Landscape." In *The Hohokam Millennium,* edited by Suzanne K. Fish and Paul R. Fish, 91–97. School for Advanced Research Press, 2007.

Rea, Amadeo M. *At the Desert's Green Edge: An Ethnobotany of the Gila River Pima.* University of Arizona Press, 1997.

Rea, Amadeo M. *Folk Mammalogy of the Northern Pimans.* University of Arizona Press, 1998.

Rea, Amadeo M. *Wings in the Desert: A Folk Ornithology of the Northern Pimans,* with Culver Cassa, linguistic consultant. University of Arizona Press, 2007.

Rentería-Valencia, Rodrigo F. "Colonial Tensions in the Governance of Indigenous Authorities and the Pima Uprising of 1751." *Journal of the Southwest* 56, no. 2, O'odham and the Pimería Alta special issue (Summer 2014): 345–64.

Roe Cloud, Henry. "Education of the American Indian." In *The American Indian Intellectual Tradition: An Anthology of Writings from 1772 to 1972,* edited by David Martínez, 192–97. Cornell University Press, 2011.

Roffler, Joshua. "Frank Russell at Gila River: Constructing an Ethnographic Description," *Kiva* 71, no. 4 (Summer, 2006): 373–95.

Rousseau, Jean-Jacques. *The Social Contract and Discourses.* Everyman's Library, 1973.

Ruiz, Medrano, and Carlos Rubén. "Rebelión y patrones de resistencia indígena en las Fronteras de San Luis Colotlán, Nueva España, siglos xvi-xviii." *Mexican Studies/Estudios Mexicanos* 29, no. 1 (Winter 2013): 200–37.

Russell, Frank, ed. "A Pima Constitution." *The Journal of American Folklore* 16, no. 63 (October–December, 1903): 222–28.

Russell, Frank. *The Pima Indians,* re-edition with Introduction, Citation Sources, and Bibliography by Bernard L. Fontana. University of Arizona Press, 1975. Originally published in 1908 by the Government Printing Office.

Salmón, Roberto Mario. "A Marginal Man: Luis of Saric and the Pima Revolt of 1751." *The Americas* 45, no. 1 (July, 1988): 61–77. https://doi.org/10.2307/1007327.

Saxton, Dean, Lucille Saxton, and Susie Enos. *Tohono O'odham/Pima to English, English to Tohono O'odham/Pima Dictionary*. University of Arizona Press, 1983.

Schermerhorn, Seth. *Walking to Magdalena: Personhood and Place in Tohono O'odham Songs, Sticks, and Stories*. University of Nebraska Press, 2019.

Seymour, Deni J. "Unveiling Tucson's Namesake: The Sobaipuri O'odham Village of San Cosme del Tucsón." *Journal of Arizona History* 63, no. 2 (Summer, 2022): 115–52.

Shaw, Anna Moore. *A Pima Past*. University of Arizona Press, 1974.

Shaw, Anna Moore. *Pima Indian Legends*. University of Arizona Press, 1968.

Shaw, Ross. "Training an Indian Boy," *The Native American* 17, no. 12 (June 10, 1916): 208.

Smith, James. "Education and Progress for the Indian." *The Quarterly Journal of the Society of American Indians* 1, no. 3 (July-September, 1913): 292–94.

Spicer, Edward H. *Cycles of Conquest: The Impact of Spain, Mexico, and the United States on the Indians of the Southwest, 1533–1960*. University of Arizona Press, 1962.

Society of American Indians. "Platform of the Second Conference." *The Quarterly Journal of the Society of American Indians* 1, no. 1 (January-April, 1913).

Southworth, C. H. "A Pima Calendar Stick," *Arizona Historical Review* (June, 1931).

Teggart, Frederick J., ed. *The Anza Expedition of 1775–1776, Diary of Pedro Font*. University of California, 1913.

Thoreau, Henry David. *Extracts Relating to the Indians: Notebook 1*. Upstart Crow Publishing, 2008.

Tinker, George. *American Indian Liberation: A Theology of Sovereignty*. Orbis Books, 2008.

Treglia, Gabriella. "The Consistency and Inconsistency of Cultural Oppression: American Indian Dance Bans, 1900–1933," *Western Historical Quarterly* 44, no. 2 (Summer 2013): 145–65.

Underhill, Ruth, Donald M. Bahr, Baptisto Lopez, Jose Pancho. *Rainhouse and Ocean: Speeches for the Papago Year*. University of Arizona Press, 1997.

Underhill, Ruth M. "A Papago Calendar Record," *The University of New Mexico Bulletin*, Anthropological Series 2, no. 5 (March 1, 1938): 7.

Underhill, Ruth. *Papago Indian Religion*. AMS Press, 1946.

Underhill, Ruth. *Papago Woman*. Waveland Press, Inc., 1979.

Underhill, Ruth. *Singing for Power: The Song Magic of the Papago Indians of Southern Arizona*. University of Arizona Press, 1993.

Underhill, Ruth. *Singing for Power: The Song Magic of the Papago Indians of Southern Arizona*. University of California Press, 2021.

Underhill, Ruth M. *Social Organization of the Papago Indians*. AMS Press, 1939.

Wasley, William W., and David E. Doyel, "Classic Period Hohokam," *Kiva* 45, no. 4 (Summer, 1980): 337–52.

Watt-Cloutier, Sheila. *The Right to Be Cold: One Woman's Fight to Protect the Arctic and Save the Planet from Climate Change*. University of Minnesota Press, 2018.

Webb, George. *A Pima Remembers*. University of Arizona Press, 1959.

Wilcox, David R. "The Mesoamerican Ballgame in the American Southwest." In *The Mesoamerican Ballgame*, edited by Vernon L. Scarborough and David R. Wilcox, 101–25. University of Arizona Press, 1991.

Winnemucca Hopkins, Sarah. *Life Among the Piutes*. GP Putnam's Sons, 1883.

Wolf, Eric R. *Europe and the People Without History*. 2nd edition. University of California Press, 2010.

Wyllys, R. K. ed. "Padre Luis Velarde's Relación of Pimería Alta, 1716," *New Mexico Historical Review* 4, no. 2 (April, 1931): 111–57.

Yetman, David. *Conflict in Colonial Sonora: Indians, Priests, and Settlers*. University of New Mexico Press, 2020.

Zepeda, Ofelia. "Still Singing Down the Clouds." In *Singing For Power: The Song Magic of the Papago Indians of Southern Arizona*. University of Arizona Press, 1993.

Zepeda, Ofelia, ed. *When It Rains: Tohono O'odham and Pima Poetry*. University of Arizona Press, 2019.

Government Documents and Archives

American Indian Religious Freedom Act Report: P.L. 95–341. United States: Task Force, 1979.

Bandelier, Adolph F. "Appendix: Reports by AF Bandelier on his Investigations in New Mexico during the Years 1883–1884." In *Fifth Annual Report of the Archaeological Institute of America*, 55–87. John Wilson and Son, 1884.

Demeke, Howard J., compiler. "In-Service Education Series and Consultant Services. Final Report." Arizona State University, Tempe. Bureau of Educational Research and Services. Bureau of Indian Affairs, Department of the Interior, Sacaton, Arizona, Pima Indian Agency. 1967.

Densmore, Frances. *Papago Music.* Bureau of American Ethnology, Bulletin 19, Smithsonian Institution. Government Printing Office, 1929.

Emory, William H. "Notes of a Military Reconnoissance," [sic] S. Ex. Doc No. 41, S3 30th Congress, 1st session, 1848.

Fewkes, Jesse Walter. "Casa Grande, Arizona." In *Twenty-Eighth Annual Report of the Bureau of American Ethnology, 1906–1907.* Government Printing Office, 1912.

Giff, Joseph. "Pima Blue Swallow Songs of Gratitude." Translated by Donald M. Bahr. In *Speaking, Singing and Teaching: A Multidisciplinary Approach to Language Variation—Proceedings of the Eighth Annual Southwestern Areal Language and Linguistics Workshop,* edited by Florence Barkin and Elizabeth Brandt. Arizona State University Anthropological Research Papers, no. 20, 1980.

Grossman, F.E. Letter to Lt. Col. George L. Andrews, superintendent, Indian Affairs Arizona Territory, September 1, 1870, Second Annual Report of the Board of Indian Commissioners to the Secretary of the Interior, for Submission to the President: For the Year 1870, 589.

Grossman, F. E. "The Pima Indians of Arizona." In *Annual Report of the Board of Regents, Smithsonian Institution,* 407–20. Government Printing Office, 1873.

Haury, Emil W. "The Excavations of Los Muertos and Neighboring Ruins in the Salt River Valley, Southern Arizona." *Papers of the Peabody Museum of American Archaeology and Ethnology, Harvard University* 24, no. 1 (1941).

Hensley, Walter Lewis, Frank Wheeler Mondell, and Charles Henry Burke. *Report in the Matter of the Investigation of the Salt and Gila Rivers—Reservations and Reclamation Service.* US Government Printing Office, 1913.

Hoy, Wilton E. "Organ Pipe Cactus National Monument. Historical Research." 3 volumes: "Administrative, Early Period, and Frontier Period." Organ Pipe Cactus National Monument, 1976.

Lekson, Stephen H. "Salado Archaeology of the Upper Gila, New Mexico." Anthropological Papers of the University of Arizona. University of Arizona Press, 2002.

Office of Indian Affairs. Report of the Commissioner of Indian Affairs, for the year 1901. Government Printing Office, 1901.

Polk, James E. "Treaty of Peace and Friendship, Limits, and Settlement with the Republic of Mexico." Unnumbered Executive Orders, Directives, and Proclamations, Stat. 9 (July 4, 1848), 922–43.

Salt and Gila Rivers—Reservations and Reclamation Service: Hearings Before a Subcommittee of the Committee on Expenditures in the Interior Department of the House of Representatives Under H. Res 103. April 23, 1912. U.S. Government Printing Office, 1912.

Steenbergh, Warren F., and Charles H. Lowe. "Ecology of the Saguaro." U.S. Department of the Interior, National Park Service. 1983.

Tatom, W. M., ed. "A Chronology of Papago and Pima History Taken from Calendar Sticks." The Papago Tribe of Arizona, Bureau of Indian Affairs Papago Agency, U.S. Public Health Service, Sells, Arizona, 1975.

Teague, Lynn S., and Crown, Patricia L. Hohokam, eds. *Archaeology Along the Salt-Gila Aqueduct, Central Arizona Project: Habitation Sites on the Gila River.* The Division, 1982.

Thomas, Cyrus. "Indian Languages of Mexico and Central America." Bureau of American Ethnology, Smithsonian Institution, Bulletin 44. Government Printing Office, 1911.

U.S. Congress, House of Representatives. *Hearings before the Committee on Indian Affairs, The Condition of Various Tribes of Indians, "History of Irrigation on the Gila River,"* 66th Congress, 1st session, June 30, 1919.

Wilson, John P., ed. "Peoples of the Middle Gila: A Documentary History of the Pimas and Maricopas, 1500's–1945." Researched and Written for the Gila River Indian Community, Sacaton, Arizona, 1998 (revised July 1999). Report no. 77, 92.

Index

www.ingramcontent.com/pod-product-compliance
Lightning Source LLC
Chambersburg PA
CBHW021354260326
41887CB00002B/82